Measuring Museum Impact and Performance

Measuring Museum Impact and Performance

Theory and Practice

John W. Jacobsen

ROWMAN & LITTLEFIELD
Lanham • Boulder • New York • London

Access to MIIP 1.0 and the Museum Theory of Action

MIIP 1.0 was developed under the author's management by the White Oak Institute, a nonprofit museum research initiative. MIIP 1.0 and the Museum Theory of Action diagram are available to all for free, independent of this book publication. To access copies, go to http://www.whiteoakassoc.com/library.html.

Alternatively, search the Internet for "MIIP" or "Museum Indicators of Impact and Performance." The MIIP database is read-only, so that the original version remains intact online; however, you can rename and save the file with your initials and go to work adapting it to your needs offline.

While access to MIIP 1.0 is free, you do not get any rights to the indicators, especially not commercial rights. You may need to obtain rights to use some of the indicators if you want to publish any source's collection of indicators. You should contact the sources directly.

Reprint acknowledgments.

The Logic Model, shown in table 1.1, is from the W. K. Kellogg Foundation, Logic Model Development Guide, 2004 and is used with their permission. The listing of types of museums (table A.2) is used with the permission of the American Alliance of Museums. The Museum Theory of Action, the Categories of Potential Museum Impacts, the Audience and Supporter Map, and other tables developed by the White Oak Institute are used with their permission, although they are free for all to use. The extensive quotes in chapter 1 from Carol Scott are used with her permission, and Wendy Luke has authorized the key quotes from her late husband, Stephen E. Weil.

Published by Rowman & Littlefield
A wholly owned subsidiary of The Rowman & Littlefield Publishing Group, Inc.
4501 Forbes Boulevard, Suite 200, Lanham, Maryland 20706
www.rowman.com

Unit A, Whitacre Mews, 26-34 Stannary Street, London SE11 4AB

British Library Cataloguing in Publication Information Available

Library of Congress Cataloging-in-Publication Data Available

978-1-4422-6329-1 (cloth)
978-1-4422-6330-7 (paper)
978-1-4422-6331-4 (ebook)

♾™ The paper used in this publication meets the minimum requirements of American National Standard for Information Sciences—Permanence of Paper for Printed Library Materials, ANSI/NISO Z39.48-1992.

Printed in the United States of America

This book is dedicated to Jeanie Stahl:
Without her extensive experience with indicators, this book would be groundless;
Without her contributions and support, this book would be much less;
And, without her partnership and collaboration, this author would be lost.

Contents

PART I: THEORY: HOW AND WHY DO MUSEUMS DO WHAT THEY DO?

PART 2: PRACTICE: HOW DO YOU MEASURE YOUR MUSEUM'S IMPACT AND PERFORMANCE?

List of Tables and Worksheets

TABLES

WORKSHEETS

Foreword

Over the course of my eight years as president of the American Alliance of Museums, I had the privilege of being able to visit 463 museums spread across forty-six states. And I learned something very important from those visits: that museums in our country fill diverse roles and take on diverse challenges in the communities that they serve. I know from my experience at AAM that museums A to Z, art museums to zoos, are essential community institutions, serving as our society's primary providers of access to the arts and culture, but also as research institutions and, above all, as providers of innovative and imaginative educational experiences in the realms of art, history, science, conservation biology, and early learning. The fact that attendance at our country's museums far exceeds that at all major league games, for all four sports, underscores both the popularity and the importance of museum institutions. And museums, along with libraries, remain the most trusted institutions in the United States, a trust that has been earned over more than two centuries of service to the American public.

I came away from virtually every museum visit with a good story to tell about something that the museum was doing for its community, and all of us who work, or have worked, in the museum field have our own stories to tell about innovative community outreach, about life-changing experiences, about our institutions "being there" for their communities, day in and day out, year after year. Museums are at the heart of successful communities.

But today, we need more than good stories if we are going to compete for a continuously shrinking pool of dollars that is available to support the work of museums. Government funding for museums, at all levels, is shrinking, and, as John Jacobsen points out in this excellent new book, *Measuring Museum Impact and Performance: Theory and Practice*, "the recent trend in private funding is toward partnership initiatives where the donor and a nonprofit work closely together to address significant social issues, *especially those where the results can be measured*" (emphasis added).

Jacobsen asks important questions in this book: How can museums more effectively communicate their societal importance today? How can museums better quantify their social value? And, above all, how can museums make better use of metrics to help funders and elected officials understand that our institutions are not amenities, for the benefit of a few, but community resources that benefit everyone. Attendance figures, sophisticated exhibits, and collection size may be impressive, but, in the final analysis, they don't speak to impact.

As Jacobsen notes in his introduction, "the field still lacks an accepted way to measure impact," and in the subsequent chapters he goes on to provide an important overview of museum research and evaluation, and then lays out a framework for museum professionals, one that will enable them to effectively measure impact and performance using key performance indicators that are readily available to the institution. This book is a toolkit that can help museums move from the subjective to the objective in communicating the value that they bring to communities.

During my time as president of AAM, I had the opportunity to speak with foundation executives, individual donors, and elected officials about museums and their role in society today. In almost all cases, they conveyed their personal love of museums, but too many times they went on to say something about the importance of other priorities—hunger, illiteracy, joblessness, community health and wellness—as if museums were irrelevant to those concerns. A governor who had recently eliminated all state funding for museums offered his rationale for the cuts, saying to me, "We just have so many needs in our state," revealing his belief that museums could not contribute to building a stronger, more competitive state, when in fact museums are uniquely positioned to do just that.

By helping museums measure the value of the work that they do, this groundbreaking book will enable them to effectively communicate their impact to key stakeholders, allowing museums to have the support that they need to serve their communities in new and creative ways, for the benefit of all.

Ford W. Bell, DVM
Wayzata, Minnesota

Acknowledgments

The museum field is far better for Ford Bell's leadership of the American Alliance of Museums (AAM), and I am honored by his foreword. During his busy tenure at AAM I was fortunate to collaborate with him on founding PIC-Green and on the Museum Operating Data Standards (MODS) initiative, which was the spark of this book. Thank you, Ford, for your vision, support, and leadership.

This book reflects my desire to recognize the many colleagues who have inspired me with their research, innovations, leadership, and love of museums. Their names fill the text and citations. I am also grateful to the museum field that nurtured me professionally and provided me and the White Oak team with a livelihood for over four decades.

I owe a huge debt to my friends and colleagues who spent time reading drafts and commenting on them so thoughtfully. Whatever good qualities this book has, I credit to the edits and suggestions from Al DeSena, Bob Janes, Carol Scott, David Ellis, Duane Kocik, Ford Bell, George Hein, Jeanie Stahl, Jeanne Vergeront, Pelle Persson, and Richard Rabinowitz. Thank you all—your guidance and insight were very helpful. Thanks also to Charles Harmon, Robert Hayunga, and Elaine McGarraugh at Rowman & Littlefield for their editorial and publication support.

Measuring Museum Impact and Performance: Theory and Practice is intellectually indebted to the colleagues who have collaborated on developing aspects of its ideas and evaluation framework. I start with my partner, Jeanie Stahl, who has pioneered the use of KPIs for museum analysis over decades. The MIIP 1.0 database evolved from work and collaboration with others interested in measuring museum impact and value, including museum professionals Beth Tuttle, Beverly Sheppard, Dennis Schatz, Larry Suter, Martin Storksdieck, Mary Ellen Munley, Minda Borun, and Phil Katz. I was especially pleased to collaborate closely with Christine Reich, Clara Cahill, and Ryan Auster at my alma mater as a museum manager, the Museum of Science, Boston.

The museum field has passionate and articulate writers and thinkers who have influenced my thinking and have informed White Oak's museum analysis and planning. I am indebted to all who write and speak out thoughtfully about museum purposes and values, and I am particularly grateful to those who have personally commented on my evolving thinking, including Alf Hatton, Elizabeth Merritt, Elaine Gurian, John Fraser, John Falk, Laura Roberts, Lynn Dierking, Marilyn Hoyt, Marsha Semmel, Nina Simon, Peter Linett, and Sheila Grinell.

White Oak's team members and clients have shaped this framework over decades and over a hundred museum analysis and planning projects. One of the many joys of this work is to collaborate with great minds and museum leaders, including all those mentioned above plus Al Klyberg, Anne D. Emerson, Bill Peters, Christine Ruffo, Chuck Howarth, Eric Siegel, George Smith, Ian McLennan, Jeanie Stahl, Jim Richerson, Joseph Wisne, Kate Bennett, Kate Schureman, Mark B. Peterson, Mary Sellers, Robert (Mac) West, and Victor Becker.

I caught my love for museums from four museum mentors who may be gone, but certainly not forgotten: Roger Nichols, the director of the Museum of Science and my boss during one of the museum's most vibrant and successful eras; Roy Shafer, the museum director who went on to coach museums to develop their "conceptual frameworks"; Alan Friedman, the committed museum educator who led by the example of his principled character and brilliance; and Stephen Weil, whose writings underlie all contemporary assumptions about museums and their value and whose thinking weaves throughout this book.

Special acknowledgments go to Rebecca Robison of the White Oak Institute for her excellent and patient research and editing, to Karen Hefler of White Oak Associates for her painstaking dedication to producing the manuscript and its tables and worksheets, and to my partner in everything, Jeanie Stahl, for her guidance and support.

INTRODUCTION

How are we doing? Are we achieving our desired impacts? Are we performing effectively and efficiently?

I have long been interested in why and how museums do what they do. Museums have not had convincing and actionable answers to these fundamental questions. Without ways to measure our impacts, museums will remain unaccountable in a new world that demands accountable results. Museums risk being sidelined, while we ardently believe we are central.

Of course museums have value and impact, but how do we, as museum professionals, measure the impacts and other benefits that museums provide their communities? Museums are valued for a wealth of beneficial results beyond their focused missions, and I believe that studying the alignment between a museum's intentions and its results will improve a museum's impact and performance. I assume throughout that you, dear reader, are also a museum professional, and that you share both my love of museums and my desire to see our professional field mature into an accountable, effective, and highly valued force "building a better and more democratic society" (Hein 2006).

More recently I have become worried about the possible decline of public support for museums. After two and a half decades of the museum boom in the United States (roughly the early 1980s to the Great Recession of 2008), money, time, effort, and public support may now move on to other nonprofits and NGOs. The American Alliance of Museums (AAM) reports a steady decline over the last four decades in the share of museum operating budgets covered by government (Merritt and Katz 2009). While growth in private support has covered the balance so far, the recent trend in private funding is toward partnership initiatives where the donor and a nonprofit work closely together to address significant social issues, especially those where the results can be measured (Raymond 2010). Bill Gates says, "I have been struck again and again by how important measurement is to improving the human condition. You can achieve amazing progress if you set a clear goal and find a measure that will drive progress toward that goal in a feedback loop" (Gates 2013). Museums now have to compete for support against organizations that can measure their impacts and demonstrate their social good.

The museum field, still shaking off its legacy of inwardly focused, autonomous privilege, faces critically important questions: What are museums contributing that is important? How are we solving critical social problems? Why have we not been able to account for the value of our contributions? How do museums break through the obstacles to use carefully selected metrics to convince skeptics and help us increase our value?

Museums need measurements to prove and advocate our value, but more fundamentally, we need the right metrics to drive progress toward our goals so that we can improve the human condition, and conserve the trust and value the public has placed on museums. We need measurements to make museums better.

Museums are vitally diverse. Our field already had many categories—art, nature, military, history, technology, children, zoos, aquaria, historic sites, planetariums, botanic gardens, and more—before the explosion of new forms during the museum boom—Experience Music Project (EMP—Seattle), the Newseum (D.C.), Tate Modern (London), the District Six Museum (Cape Town), Inhotim (Brumadinho, Brazil), and Science Gallery Dublin are just a few examples of innovations in form that have one foot in museum tradition while another steps in a different direction. We are also diverse in size, from tiny historical sites like the two-room Maritime Museum run by volunteers in Marblehead's old town hall, to the vast Smithsonian system in the United States. We are diverse in business models, with the Getty Museum covered by its substantial endowment, the Minnesota History Center covered primarily by public funds, the Pacific Science Center (Seattle) covered mostly by earned revenues, and the Yale University Art Gallery covered by Yale. We are an inclusive field: We include both the Morgan Library and Museum (New York City) and the NASCAR Hall of Fame (Charlotte); both the Louvre (Paris) and the Lucy Desi Center for Comedy (Jamestown, New York); and both the Denver Museum of Nature & Science and the Creation Museum (Petersburg, Kentucky).

In the 1990s, the Institute of Museums and Library Services (IMLS) estimated 17,500 museums in the United States alone. The number of U.S. museums[1] has clearly grown during the museum boom, perhaps to around 22,000 to 25,000 museums, most of them small, some of them very large. Globally, museums continue growing, most dramatically in China and the Middle East.

In the United States, however, the boom is over. Who survived? Who may not continue to survive? It is fun to build a museum, but challenging to sustain its operation. How many museums can our economic, educational, and cultural ecosystems support? Sustainability will depend on delivering important benefits, measuring impact and performance, and constantly tuning the museum's mix of community services to respond to changing community needs.

These factors and my concern for the health of the museum field drove the research and publication of this book. In response to a long-expressed need for metrics that museum managers and evaluators can use to evaluate museums, the first part of this book builds a Theory of Action to frame museum research and evaluation, and identifies fourteen categories of potential impact. The second part offers steps to quantify changes in a museum's annual impact and performance, historically within a museum, and concurrently among peer museums.

THE NEED TO MEASURE IMPACT AND PERFORMANCE

All nonprofits are facing pressure to account for their impact, as outlined in a 2010 Harvard Business School working paper on the limits of nonprofits:

> The world of nonprofit organizations, philanthropy, and social enterprise has been preoccupied with two powerful mantras in recent years. Since the early 1990s, the refrain of "accountability" has been ascendant, with demands from funders, taxpayers, and concerned citizens and clients for nonprofits to be more transparent about their fundraising and spending, how they are governed, and what they have achieved with the resources entrusted to them.[2] A more recent manifestation of this discourse has centered on the mantra of "impact" or demonstrating results in addressing complex social problems such as poverty and inequality.[3] (Ebrahim and Rangan 2010)

The philanthropic sector now demands metrics through donor-funded initiatives like DataArts and the Charity Navigator's rating system. Charity Navigator's system focuses on "the two most important questions ever to face the sector: how to define the value of all the work we are doing, and how to measure that value . . . [in pursuit] of how to identify high-performing nonprofits and how to better direct donors' contributions to them" (Berger, Penna, and Goldberg 2010). In addition to their ratings based on fiscal metrics, Charity Navigator is working on approaches based on measuring impact.

Museums and their stakeholders have been using key performance indicators (KPIs) to monitor progress for years (Legget 2009; Persson 2011). KPIs in common use include a wide range of measures such as energy costs per square foot of building, the ratio of adult to child admissions, the percentage of the collection on display, and the number of visits per membership. These familiar calculations use operating, resource, and market data to help management monitor trends and pursue objectives, but they are seldom linked systematically to measure impact and performance. A careful selection of KPIs can be like the many gauges in an airplane cockpit that pilots need to fly safely to their destination. In order to fly where it wants to go, a museum needs to integrate and prioritize its KPIs to understand what they say collectively about where the museum is going and how that relates to where they intend to go.

Museums already use data *operationally*. Staff annual objectives, attendance forecasts, and the number of grant proposals are examples of common tactical uses of data, and museum managers have dashboards of indicators and metrics that matter to them so that they can make operational adjustments. The next step is to use data *strategically* in forward planning to prove and improve value.

The DataArts 2013 analysis by Sarah Lee and Peter Linett of the use of data in the cultural sector, which includes museums, performing arts, and other cultural nonprofits, found that:

> We face an abundance of data about the cultural sphere. But it is not yet clear that the cultural sector is making effective and strategic use of all of this data. The field seems to be approaching an inflection point, where the long-term health, sustainability, and effectiveness of cultural organizations depend critically on investment in and collective action around enhancing the field's capacity for using data strategically and thoughtfully to inform decision-making. (Lee and Linett 2013)

Lee and Linett also found that the cultural sector needs to address "the lack of a strong organizational vision for how data can be used to inform internal planning and decision making, as well as the lack of examples of such vision from the field" (Lee and Linett 2013, 1–2).[4]

Museums are not alone, just behind. Museum leader and former interim director of the IMLS Marsha Semmel says, "Much more needs to be done to provide a fully textured analysis of—and case for—the public value of museums in the United States" (Semmel 2009).

There is no lack of data—there are decades of evaluation studies, museum operating data, financial reports, museum sector surveys, and government forms. The DataArts report also found issues with non-standardization of data definitions, which means all these data cannot be aggregated easily. However, the DataArts existing online survey is setting the standard for the top level of data collection as it focuses on audited financial records using accounting definitions.[5] Ideally, this standardization will continue to grow as the DataArts data fields get beyond a museum's finances and further into its engagement counts and outcomes.

The late museum sage Stephen E. Weil recognized that in the wide variety of potential outcomes available to a museum lies complexity:

> What this complexity suggests is that, over time, the museum field will need to develop a vast arsenal of richer and more persuasive ways to document and/or demonstrate the myriad and beneficial outcomes that may occur for their individual visitors and have impact on the community beyond. Some of these ways may be quantitative but, to the horror of some social scientists, a great

many may be anecdotal or qualitative. What is critical is that these evaluation techniques fit the real complexity of what museums actually do. (Weil 2003, 53)

To address this complexity, we need to adopt a framework for thinking about and monitoring the museum field's complex mixture of outcomes, audiences, and supporters, necessarily aligned with how the rest of the world thinks about value, and ideally aligned with museum counting and accounting systems and with shared data definitions.

Because we have so many impacts, audiences, and supporters, because every museum is unique, and because each museum pursues its different missions differently, the global field of museums has no easy metric to measure impact and performance. Our richness and complexity challenge any simplistic assessment of a museum's value and impact, such as attendance or collection size.

THE RESEARCH METHODOLOGY

Fortunately, the recent pressure on museums to prove and improve their value has produced much thought, data, and literature with many diverse suggestions for how to measure value. As reviewed in chapters 1 and 2, museum leaders, researchers, and evaluators have proposed many ways to talk about and measure what a museum offers, and this book looks at the patterns that emerge. This prior work (see Appendix B, Source Documents, and chapter citations) provided a robust, global research sample that my colleagues at the White Oak Institute and I could explore in search of a sensible framework that addresses the complexity of the museum field. I analyzed eleven evaluation frameworks and an aggregation of 1,025 Museum Indicators of Impact and Performance (MIIP 1.0) suggested in fifty-one sources by scholars, museum associations, and selected museum managers. Each indicator has a number traceable to its author and source in Appendix B.

I selected the sources for MIIP 1.0 the way many survey respondents are chosen: using a random, but sufficiently large selection of available and representative sources. I looked for international perspectives, for different disciplines (art, history, science, etc.), and from different domains (evaluators, survey instruments, articles, etc.). MIIP 1.0 most likely contains both widely used and untested indicators, though all are from experts; MIIP 1.0 makes no claim to be comprehensive, but the database of 1,025 indicators is deep and representative enough to see the broad range of museum impacts and benefits and to explore for common ground in how museums go about achieving their impacts and benefits.

As used in this book, *impact* and *benefit* are both words for the outcomes of a museum's activities. They may describe the same outcome, but from different perspectives: Impacts are what the museum wants to accomplish; benefits are what the community, audiences, and supporters want from the museum. The opportunity to experience the intrinsic beauty of the Vermeers and other great masterpieces is a benefit to visitors to the Frick Collection (New York), and the art museum desires that exact impact. Benefits and impacts do not always align so neatly. People engage with museums in return for all sorts of perceived benefits, not all of which are desired impacts on the part of the museum. Museums can also pursue impacts that no one, including donors, finds beneficial—but not for long. Museums can decide which benefits they desire to address, and any benefit can potentially become a desired impact by some museum. Because this book is written to help museum professionals improve *impact*, that word is used in preference, but *benefit* could also have been used from the audience and supporter perspective (see also Appendix A, "Definitions and Assumptions").

The research also involved a second literature search of relevant evaluation theories as described in chapter 1 that structured the exploration of the MIIP database for patterns and range, using various tags described in chapter 2. This research and analysis led to this book's evaluation framework and set of terms for proving and improving a museum's public, private, personal, and institutional impacts, which is introduced in chapter 3. The second part of this book applies these findings to help each museum set up metrics right for its unique context, resources, and intentional purposes.

THE SUMMARY ANALYSIS

The research expands the public value discussion outlined in chapter 1 to include private and personal values on an equal conceptual footing, leaving to others the debate about whether one kind of value or impact is more worthy than another. *Public impacts* benefit society as a whole; *private impacts* benefit businesses, donors, and private foundations, which are often pursuing public impacts; and *personal impacts* benefit individuals, families, and households. The book also recognizes internal *institutional impacts*, as some museum outcomes are beneficial to the museum itself.

The findings reveal an underlying Museum Theory of Action with seven steps that link intentional purposes to fourteen areas of potential museum impacts—the how and why of museums, respectively.

In chapter 1 a review of established nonprofit and museum evaluation frameworks finds that they overlap. Analysis of the overlap informs the development of what I call the Museum Theory of Action, with seven steps, which are: (1) intentional purposes, (2) guiding principles, (3) resources, (4) activities, (5) operating and evaluation data, (6) key performance indicators, and (7) perceived benefits. The narrative version of this numbered sequence is: The museum, in service to its community, decides on its intentional purposes and desired impacts. Then, guided by its principles, the museum uses its resources to operate activities for its community and its audiences and supporters that result in valued impacts and benefits. Engagements with these activities generate operating and evaluation data that can be incorporated into KPIs that monitor the museum's effectiveness and efficiency. This Theory of Action is diagrammed in tables 3.1 and 9.1 as a two-way loop, and in tables 0.1 and 1.3 as a logic model.

Chapter 2 applies this theory to the MIIP 1.0 database, and finds fourteen Categories of Potential Museum Impacts. These categories of potential museum contributions and benefits fall under four impact sectors and include seven categories of public impacts (broadening participation, preserving heritage, strengthening social capital, enhancing public knowledge, serving education, advancing social change, and communicating public identity and image); two private impacts (contributing to the economy and delivering corporate community services); three personal impacts (enabling personal growth, offering personal respite, and welcoming personal leisure); and two institutional impacts (helping museum operations and building museum capital).

In summary, this book provides comprehensive and useful framework adaptable by any museum, offers a database of indicators and a family of terms for evaluating and enhancing the impact and

Table 0.1. The Museum Theory of Action: Logic Model Version.

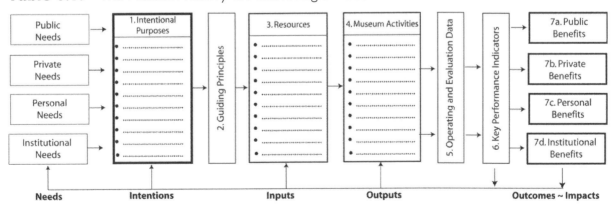

Source: The White Oak Institute

Table 0.2. Categories of Potential Museum Impacts.

		# of MIIP indicators
Public Impacts		
A	Broadening participation	85
B	Preserving heritage	47
C	Strengthening social capital	76
D	Enhancing public knowledge	43
E	Serving education	56
F	Advancing social change	40
G	Communicating public identity & image	27
Private Impacts		
H	Contributing to the economy	85
I	Delivering corporate community services	9
Personal Impacts		
J	Enabling personal growth	147
K	Offering personal respite	4
L	Welcoming personal leisure	11
Institutional Impacts		
M	Helping museum operations	308
N	Building museum capital	87
Total indicators in the MIIP 1.0 database		1,025

Source: The White Oak Institute

performance of museums, and outlines practical steps for selecting and using the right impact and performance measures for your museum.

Several themes that underlie all these chapters warrant an introduction: the idea of museum value; museums as servants of many masters; integrating big and small data to inform decisions; and the need to standardize and report operating data.

THE IDEA OF VALUE

Free choice gets to the essential business difference between free-choice learning organizations such as museums, libraries, and public television, and formal schooling. *Informal learning institutions*—a label pasted onto museums—says only what we are not (we are not formal schools), while implying that we are somehow looser in our standards. While both may be true, the alternative of *free-choice learning institutions* emphasizes that everyone has to choose to come to or support a museum. Unlike schools with their truancy laws, our audiences and supporters have to want to engage with a museum. In an increasingly noisy and competitive world, museums must compete for their time, effort, and money. This means we have to offer them value in return.

If you follow's Weil's approach, as I do, that a museum's value lies in what impacts it delivers, then one way to evaluate a museum on its impacts is to look at how others value those impacts through their exchanges of time, effort, and money. While we cannot measure total impact and hence total value, we can seek indicators of changes in that value by looking at changes in these exchanges, as described in part 2.

MUSEUMS ARE SERVANTS OF MANY MASTERS

Embedded into their community's cultural, educational, and economic ecosystems, today's museums compete in the marketplace to survive, perchance to grow. Museums pursue multiple purposes for multiple audiences and supporters (Jacobsen 2014). For example, museums can have both learning and tourism impacts, for both school and tourist audiences, supported by paying visitors, government agencies, private foundations, and corporate sponsors.

Traditional museum writing focuses on internal leadership's intentionality to change their audiences in some specified way. Weil says, "How has somebody's life been made a little better?" (Weil 2000, 10), and museums do see themselves as "changing lives" (Museums Association 2013). Museum evaluator Randi Korn writes, "Mission statements should clarify what the museum values, reflecting what staff members feel their museum embodies and describing how they want to affect their public and community" (Korn 2007). This is an internal focus on why museums do what they do. I am suggesting we balance attention between our internal desires and the external desires of the audiences and supporters we serve. What are they asking us for? How do they want to make us better? Why do they do what they do? Of course, both internal and external perspectives are needed to evolve to the best fit between the "whys."

Becoming intentional about providing our audiences and supporters the benefits that meet their needs may improve impact and performance in those areas, and it may give the museum greater opportunities to further its intentions. Counting all of a museum's impacts and benefits totals a more complete picture of the museum's contributions, without taking sides about the relative worthiness of any category of potential museum impact. We need equally rational ways to measure learning outcomes as well as societal and economic impacts, even though some may feel that one is more worthy than the others. To conserve the prestige and value long enjoyed by museums, but now facing stiff competition, we need to deliver value to our audiences and supporters and count every benefit we provide.

INTEGRATING BIG AND SMALL DATA TO INFORM DECISIONS

In a 2009 address to CARE (the AAM's professional interest Committee on Audience Research and Evaluation), and later published by *Curator*, I challenged our field:

> We need to integrate audience research with [operating] research, and we need to do it conceptually, personally, and sustainably. . . . We need to get rid of the prejudice that marketing and money are somehow separate from learning and mission. . . . To achieve this vision, we will need to merge audience and [operating] research . . . build upon the prior work of our peers . . . standardize research definitions . . . [and] expand professional and organizational skills. (Jacobsen 2010)

This book balances operating data analysis with evaluation studies to shed light on what museums accomplish and how they do it. Both cultures within the museum field have advanced their professional knowledge: Program evaluation and visitor research have robust survey instruments and share professional networks (the Visitor Studies Association and CARE); and marketing, development, and finance have sophisticated means of attracting audiences and funding, and of keeping track of operations. However, these two camps have not yet developed an integrated framework to evaluate museums as institutions: How much good are we doing?

Perhaps we can take a hint about how to bridge these two camps from two Facebook and Google data scientists: "Big data in the form of behaviors and small data in the form of surveys complement each other and produce insights rather than simple metrics" (Peysakhovich and Stephens-Davidowitz 2015). Therein lies the integrating link: Museum annual operating data offers an increasingly reliable and accurate picture of behavior (what people and organizations actually do in real time), and evaluation studies help us understand why they do it and what they get from it. We may believe that big data is telling us something—for instance, that rising grant renewal rates mean rising grant impacts—but we need to test such assumptions periodically using evaluation studies (small data) to see if changes in the big data correlate with changes in the impact. This distills to a mantra for museum evaluation: *Measure constantly; validate periodically.*

KPIs can include both operating data and quantitative evaluation study findings. Evaluation studies are strong in qualitative findings, but there are methodologies such as Likert scales and contingent valuation that can help translate survey results into numbers. Larger surveys allow for cross-tabulations and respondent percentages. Using both evaluation study findings and operating data may shed light on how many visitors learned something, or the relationship between degrees of gallery crowdedness and satisfaction.

Another bridge between evaluation studies and operating data comes when we respect the expertise of our audiences and supporters as reflected in their collective choices (behavior). For instance, changes in the yearly cumulative number of volunteer shifts or the average shift length (operating data), especially by repeating volunteers, may be a good indicator of changes in the perceived quality of the program in the eyes of its volunteers. This indicator might align with the museum's intentional purpose to "strengthen civic engagement." However, periodically, qualitative evaluators should actually ask a representative sample of volunteers about the quality they perceive and other matters (opinion data). Pairing "big" operating data and "small" evaluation study data will thus test and improve the meaningfulness of a metric, and inform decisions to increase the volunteer program's impact and performance.

THE NEED TO STANDARDIZE MUSEUM OPERATING DATA AND REPORTING

DataArts (formerly the Cultural Data Project) established rigorous standards and reporting mechanisms for collecting, aggregating, and reporting on financial data from grant-seeking, cultural nonprofits, and they are adding programmatic data fields. The Center for Advancement of Informal Science Education (CAISE) has developed a searchable database of evidence of science learning, many in science museum contexts. Evaluation reports are summarized in museum professional journals, such as *Visitor Studies*. The American Association for State and Local History (AASLH) has standardized comparison and assessment resources in their *Visitors Count!* survey and Standards and Excellence Program (StEPs). The Museum of Science (Boston) established a national Collaboration for Ongoing Visitor Experience Studies (COVES) to develop shared metrics, and the Association of Children's Museums (ACM) established its Online ACM Benchmark Calculator. My organization, the White Oak Institute, partnered with the Museum of Science's evaluation department to develop the Museum Indicators of Impact and Performance (MIIP) evaluation model, and I am an adviser on COVES.

These initiatives seek to strengthen, standardize, and document operating and evaluation data. This book shares those goals. However, these initiatives are recent, and their long-term impacts and benefits are largely aspirational at this writing. Earlier efforts to standardize data, such as an IMLS call in the 1990s and the Museum Operating Data Standards (MODS) initiative of 2007–2011,[6] have not had any real impact. Further, participation in online data reporting portals run by the associations appears to be declining since the days of printed surveys. Why the resistance to data sharing and standardization, when most agree it is a worthy goal?

The museum field has not aligned data definitions and collection because alignment is difficult: (1) Someone has to establish the field-wide standards, and no association was willing to take on the job, as each already has its definitions; (2) each association and museum needs to compare its current definitions to the new standards and decide whether the effort and disruption is worth the effort and (3) every museum must see worthwhile benefits from shifting to shared data standards and from taking the effort to report their data.

In response to these resistance points, this book establishes definitions and shared assumptions in part 1 and Appendix A, and provides a process for selecting metrics for the benefit of individual museums in part 2. Good shared data helps museums evidence and improve their impact; hence, in this time of need, museums need good data.

DEFINITIONS AND LANGUAGE

This book does not take sides. I develop a neutral framework that is independent of specific "whys" and "purposes." I do assume some common bonds and assumptions in my definition of *museum* (see Appendix A, #1), which stipulates a nonprofit permanent institution committed to some external public, private, and/or personal benefit—striving to build George Hein's "better and more democratic society" in some way.

I use terms and definitions based on familiar museum practice, but applied more broadly. An important example: The umbrella term *museum engagements* collects attendance at all the museum's activities—gallery attendance, lecture series attendance, volunteer shifts, board meetings, interactions with partners, outreach participations, etc.—into one number. A physical museum engagement is defined as one person-trip to a museum site or to a museum-sponsored program off site by a person not employed or contracted by the museum to be there. The person-trip is a measure of effort spent by the person (time and often money are also spent). Virtual museum engagements involve much less effort, but still require time.

The family of terms and definitions in Appendix A is used consistently in all chapters, although I recognize that each museum has its own nuanced version of such terms as *visitor* and *outreach*. Because the lack of shared language and definitions is one of the museum field's main obstacles (Lee and Linett 2013), I have taken care to base my terms on the field's most tested and accepted definitions where available. These definitions are strongest when specific, like *site visitor*, but we also need more inclusive terms, like *program participants*, and as yet unmeasured terms, like *dwell time*.

Yet museums are not engineered entities with precise edges, and some definitions have fuzzy borders. Museums are organic, fluid, and changing—or at least the survivors are. Many lofty terms like *value*, *impact*, *performance*, and *benefit* elude precise definitions and measurements. Many terms are roughly synonymous, but with different baggage. A particularly freighted group of synonyms includes *ends*, *purposes*, *mission*, *goals*, *outcomes*, *perceived benefits*, *impacts*, and *values*. A museum may want all of these to result from its activities, but each term carries somewhat different expectations, resulting in confusion that impedes collaboration and improvement.

THE ORGANIZATION AND SEQUENCE OF CHAPTERS

This book, divided into two parts, addresses the fundamental questions about the why and how of museums. How can museum leaders make sense of their wealth of data, opinions, and suggestions? Then, how can they go on to use that understanding to develop more effective and efficient museums? Specific questions lead off each chapter.

The two parts of the book are written in different styles. "Part 1: Theory" is scholarly in tone and builds its cases with citations of established authorities; part 1 uses gerunds for chapter titles to emphasize the research and analysis processes used to build the evaluation framework. "Part 2: Practice" is more conversational and instructive. Part 2 is addressed to you and uses active verbs for chapter titles to emphasize the actions you can take.

THE ORGANIZATION AND SEQUENCE OF CHAPTERS

Part 1: Theory

Chapter 1: Finding the Museum Theory of Action: *How does a museum move from its intentional purposes to its actual results?*

Chapter 2: Identifying Potential Museum Impacts: *What potential impacts and benefits can museums provide for their communities and their audiences and supporters?*

Chapter 3: Measuring Impact: *What are some of the implications and logical corollaries of the Museum Theory of Action and the analysis of MIIP 1.0 on measuring impact?*

Part 2: Practice

Chapter 4: Shift from Theory to Practice: *How can museum professionals apply these theories to museum practice? How do we go about measuring impact and performance?*

Chapter 5: Prioritize Your Museum's Purposes and Impacts: *How do your current audiences and supporters benefit from your museum? Given an understanding of what they want, how does your museum select and prioritize its intentional purposes and desired impacts?*

Chapter 6: Determine Your Museum's Performance Metrics: *How does management select indicators to measure impact and performance? How does a museum periodically test the validity of its indicators?*

Chapter 7: Compare Your Museum to Your Peers': *How does a museum compare its performance to peer museums in similar contexts?*

Chapter 8: Report Changes in Your Impact and Performance: *How does a museum develop a data-informed culture?*

Summary

Chapter 9: Summary and Future Potentials: *What has been accomplished? How do you further advance the museum field, your museum, and your profession? What lies ahead?*

Both parts use MIIP 1.0, an Excel database available to all for free (see the web link on the copyright page). Part 1 uses it for research, and part 2 allows you to use it as a starting pool of suggestions and as a listing of some established indicators ready for adoption.

ADAPT THIS THEORY AND TOOLKIT TO YOUR NEEDS

The second part of the book has several how-to processes; they try to balance brevity and detail. You are likely to skip some steps and add others, and such adaptations are desirable; the process and results must become yours.

The process of selecting and then analyzing the right metrics to measure a museum's impact and performance takes time, management focus, and leadership guidance. It takes math skills; metrics are ultimately numbers and KPIs are formulas. It takes both creativity and humble patience. The sixteen pairs of worksheets at the end of this book (one filled in for a "Sample Museum" and the other blank for you to adapt) may seem daunting, but the intent of the worksheets is to illustrate many possible steps and variables. Each museum can decide which steps are right for them.

This process analyzes ideas by tagging and sorting many options from several sources in progressive cuts using an Excel database, but there are other ways, like concept mapping or walls full of stickies. You should adapt this book's suggestions to your needs.

You will desire data that do not yet exist. You may find that some of your ideal KPIs depend on at least one data field that your museum is not collecting. Perhaps you have not kept track of which teachers repeat, or have no system for distinguishing tourists from residents in the attendance count, or have not been consistent in how you track visitor satisfaction levels. While the quality and quantity of museum data are increasing, this book sets up a demand for some data ahead of supply, and in these cases you will need to adapt to existing data, or set up new data collection processes.

The amount of time and resources required to do a proper job of KPI selection, along with the operational logistics of collecting some desired data, are potential challenges. However, we have to start somewhere with what we have. Plus, there are factors that could mitigate these issues: The amount of work that a museum currently dedicates to strategic planning can be shifted to this process for one cycle, as it covers the same territory differently with the added benefit of a measurable plan that accounts for all the museum's impacts and benefits. DataArts and the museum associations are working to develop demand from managers for the data they collect; data quality, transparency, and quantity are increasing; and time- and resource-challenged managers can select some KPIs intuitively and just start using them, evolving better choices as they go.

Fortunately, we have a solid foundation to build upon in the prior work of museum associations, museum leaders, and scholars. By giving you access to large samples of this work, MIIP 1.0 saves you a huge amount of time in researching potential indicators.

CONCLUSION

I look at museums differently from many others. As a museum planner, I have to take the long, integrated view in the master plans we create for our museum clients. As a servant of many museums over many decades, I see the rich diversity of museums, but I also see our shared patterns of professional practice linking a wonderfully varied collection of museums. All museums seek to "change lives," but each museum has its own goals, ways, resources, activities, audiences, supporters, and impacts. Given the need to account for museum impact and performance, it is no longer a question of avoiding metric measurements, but rather one of selecting the right metrics—the metrics that most closely get at what you are trying to achieve.

The museum field needs to adopt a shared framework and language because the field still lacks accepted ways to measure impact. I believe we have indicators of impact and performance if we (a) adjust our thinking about museums to evaluate them as multiple-purpose, community service institutions rather than solely as mission-focused institutions; (b) recognize that in addition to public impact, museums also create private, personal, and institutional impacts; (c) admit that for museums some key performance indicators (KPIs) may also be evidence of impact; and (d) accept that there is no one standard to measure all museums, but that each museum will need to declare its own intentional purposes, theories of action, and evaluation indicators.

This framework does not provide one scale to judge all museums. On the contrary, I believe the diversity of "whys" and "hows" are the field's wealth and innovation hotbed, and that the field is richer by being inclusive and diverse. This framework allows others, such as the AAM's accreditation commission and the Association of Art Museum Directors, to set finer membership filters, and critics and commentators can weigh in with what they think museums should do or be like, but I don't think society will benefit from a single scale. In time some shared indicators might arise, most likely as indicators of the changing scale of a museum's vitality and impact. Yet now is not the time to set up a single system to score all museums, and perhaps that goal is neither advisable nor possible.

Now is the time, however, to set up a framework for each museum to measure changes in its own impact and performance. Museums need to evolve in response to their changing communities. This book offers theory, tools, and processes to help museums respond to the demands for metrics from our authorizing and funding sources, and to benefit from using KPIs to measure and improve impact and performance. By understanding how and why museums do what they do, we can make museums even more valuable.

NOTES

1. In 2014, the IMLS released a new estimate at 35,000, but that figure is based on a database including duplicates and museum-related organizations that are not museums.
2. The original article cited the following sources at this point: (Ebrahim & Weisband 2007; Gibelman & Gelman 2001, 2008; Kearns 1996; Panel on the Nonprofit Sector 2005, 2007; Young, Bania, & Bailey 1996).
3. The original article cited the following sources at this point: (Brest & Harvey 2008; Crutchfield & Grant 2008; Monitor Institute 2009; Paton 2003).
4. I was an adviser to this study by Slover Linett for DataArts (formerly the Cultural Data Project).
5. Audited financials are not required below a certain annual budget size.
6. MODS was an AAM and White Oak Institute joint initiative; both the author and Ford W. Bell, DVM, participated.

REFERENCES

Berger, Ken, Robert M. Penna, and Steven H. Goldberg. "The Battle for the Soul of the Nonprofit Sector." *Philadelphia Social Innovations Journal* (May 1, 2010). Accessed October 8, 2014. http://www.philasocialinnovations.org/site.

Ebrahim, Alnoor, and V. Kasturi Rangan. "The Limits of Nonprofit: A Contingency Framework for Measuring Social Performance." *Harvard Business School*. May 2010. Accessed October 29, 2014. http://www.hbs.edu/faculty/Publication%20Files/10-099.pdf.

Gates, Bill. *Annual Letter*. January 2013. Accessed October 21, 2014. http://www.gatesfoundation.org/Who-We-Are/Resources-and-Media/Annual-Letters-List/Annual-Letter-2013.

Hein, George E. "Museum Education." In *A Companion to Museum Studies*, by S. MacDonald. Oxford: Blackwell, 2006.

Jacobsen, John W. "The Community Service Museum: Owning up to our Multiple Missions." *Museum Management and Curatorship* 29, no. 1 (2014): 1–18.

———. "A Research Vision for Museums." *Curator* 53, no. 3 (July 2010): 281–89.

Korn, Randi. "The Case for Holistic Intentionality." *Curator* (April 2007): 255–64.

Lee, Sarah, and Peter Linett. "New Data Directions for the Cultural Landscape: Toward a Better-Informed, Stronger Sector." *Cultural Data Project* (now DataArts), December 2013. Accessed October 8, 2014. http://www.culturaldata.org/wp-content/uploads/new-data-directions-for-the-cultural-landscape-a-report-by-slover-linett-audience-research-for-the-cultural-data-project_final.pdf.

Legget, Jane. "Measuring What We Treasure or Treasuring What We Measure?" *Museum Management and Curatorship* 24, no. 3 (2009): 213–32.

Merritt, Elizabeth E., and Philip M. Katz. *Museum Financial Information 2009*. American Association of Museums, August 1, 2009.

Museums Association. "Museums Change Lives." *Museums Association*. July 2013. Accessed November 4, 2014. http://www.museumsassociation.org/download?id=1001738.

Persson, Per-Edvin. "Rethinking the Science Center Model." *Informal Learning Review* no. 111 (November–December 2011): 14–15.

Peysakhovich, Alex, and Seth Stephens-Davidowitz. "How Not to Drown in Numbers." *New York Times*, May 3, 2015, SR 7.

Raymond, Susan U. *Nonprofit Finance for Hard Times: Setting the Larger Stage*. Hoboken: Wiley, 2010.

Semmel, Marsha. "How Do We Prove the Value of Museums?" *AAM Annual Meeting*. Institute of Museum & Library Services, 2009.

Weil, Stephen E. "Beyond Big & Awesome Outcome-Based Evaluation." *Museum News* (November/December 2003): 40–45, 52–53.

———. "Beyond Management: Making Museums Matter." *INTERCOM: International Committee on Management*. 2000. Accessed 2015. http://www.intercom.museum/conferences/2000/weil.pdf.

PART I

THEORY

How and Why Do Museums Do What They Do?

CHAPTER 1

FINDING THE MUSEUM THEORY OF ACTION

How does a museum move from its intentional purposes to its actual results?

Before we can start to measure impact and performance, we need a theory to test and measure. All museums, and most other organizations, operate on a theory of change: If we do these actions, then these outcomes and impacts should occur. If we do an exhibition about infectious disease, then visitors should increase their awareness and change their behaviors. We can then test the theory by measuring whether they do. Or, at an organizational level, if the Wing Luke Museum of the Asian Pacific American Experience (Seattle) generates its exhibits and programs within its communities, then the museum should be seen as part of the whole community, and the community's social capital and sense of identity should be strengthened.

These are theories of action. Is there an underlying theory of action that applies to all museums? Yes, at the simplest level: If a museum is achieving its intentional purposes, then the museum should see indications of its desired impacts. However, this start-finish simplification ignores all the steps between intent and result. What theory of action connects a museum's intent with its result? How do museums do their job? How will the exhibits in the Science Museum of Virginia (Richmond) engage and inspire youth? Only when we incorporate our processes and activities—how museums actually work to achieve their ends—can we start to measure impact and performance in ways that help management improve both.

This chapter develops the Museum Theory of Action as a way of organizing any museum's measurements and actions. There is no need to reinvent the wheel; we can build on considerable prior work. There is a need, however, to synthesize aspects from these many theories and evaluation frameworks to accommodate the rich diversity of museums.

THE NEED FOR ACCOUNTABILITY

The emphasis on accountability and evaluation from public funding agencies and from private donors and foundations has resulted in considerable discussion about a nonprofit's public value. As a sector within the nonprofit category, the museum field has also focused on value, adding our own academic literature, museum association surveys, and dashboards of useful indicators created by individual museums and their leaders.

The need to measure impact and performance is developed in the introduction, citing calls for action from Harvard Business School and Charity Navigator for all nonprofits, DataArts for cultural nonprofits, and the Institute of Museums and Library Services and Stephen E. Weil for the museum sector.

From the business world, Peter Drucker, Peter Senge, and Jim Collins have each proposed ways to manage organizations through the use of strategic indicators. These can be further organized using Kaplan and Norton's balanced scorecard.

Fortunately, many actual and suggested ways of thinking about and measuring museum impacts now exist in the global literature, museum practices, and museum associations as well as in existing demographic and social data. There is considerable international research on learning in informal settings. *Learning Science in Informal Environments* (Bell et al. 2009) is an excellent aggregation of knowledge about informal STEM (Science, Technology, Engineering, and Mathematics) learning in museums and other non-school settings. Studies have been conducted on the impact of museums on their audiences, communities, and economies (Bradburne 2001; Garnett 2001; Science Centre Economic Impact Study 2005; Museums Association 2013).

At least three scholarly journals have devoted issues to museum public value and economic factors: *Journal of Museum Management and Curatorship* 24(3), September 2009; the *Journal of Museum Education* 35(2), Summer 2010 and 35(3), Fall 2010; and *The Exhibitionist* 31(2), Fall 2012.

The September 2009 *Museum Management and Curatorship*'s 24(3) special issue on museum value includes Carol A. Scott's "Exploring the Evidence Base for Museum Value." Scott's later book, *Museums and Public Value: Creating Sustainable Futures* (C. A. Scott 2013), organizes eleven articles, and her introduction covers many perspectives on museum value. While there are previous efforts to establish frameworks for museum evaluation (Friedman 2007; Falk and Sheppard 2006; D. Anderson 1997; Baldwin 2011), the data infrastructure to support such frameworks has not been in place until recently. Achieving this goal is now possible because of increased transparency of museum operating data (M. L. Anderson 2004; Stein 2009); the growing body of evaluation findings and evidence posted on http://www.visitorstudies.org/, http://informalscience.org/, and NSF's Online Project Monitoring System; and new national data compilations of museum operating data, such as the Association of Children's Museums' (ACM) online database, DataArts, Guidestar's collection of IRS 990 data forms, and other online museum data.

This discussion about a museum's value is also a discussion about a museum's impact. The value of a museum lies in its contributions—how have we changed someone's life? How have we changed our world? This book focuses on measuring the value/impact of the museum as a whole, and not of its many individual programs. What impacts did the museum achieve this year? For whom? And at what cost/value to whom?

EXPLORING EXISTING EVALUATION FRAMEWORKS FOR COMMON, UNDERLYING ASSUMPTIONS

The literature also suggests ways of evaluating museums and other nonprofits, and ways of organizing and using indicators.

The following eleven sources suggest how indicators might be organized into an evaluation framework for museums. All share these basics: There is a need; there is an organization and resources to address the need; and there is an audience that benefits. In more technical terms, there is external input to a means, which then has an audience interface resulting in ends. Further analysis of these overlapping frameworks reveals a more detailed and useable underlying theory of action.

Mark Moore's Strategic Triangle and Public Value: The Nonprofit World has widely adopted Moore's strategic triangle (Weinberg and Lewis 2009), intended for use in government-funded social services. Moore's triangle involves an authorizing environment that works with the operating environment (the institution) to produce the public value desired by both. The most efficient value is created when all three components are aligned. Given his focus on government-funded agencies, Moore's perspective was that "politics remain the final arbiter of public value just as private consumption decisions remain the final arbiter of private value" (Moore, as cited in Alford and O'Flynn 2009, 177). This may apply to government and university museums, but most North American museums are funded by combinations of public, private, and personal sources and need to pay attention to politics, social forces, and the consumer marketplace.

Public value is central to Moore's approach, and it has also become central to the museum literature on value, as noted earlier, so it is worth being clear about its meaning. Writing about Moore's work, Alford and O'Flynn observe that public value is greater than public good or public interest in that "it connotes an active sense of adding value, rather than a passive sense of safeguarding interests" (2009, 176). They also note that public value is temporal and harder to pin down than consumer value:

> A policy or purpose is valuable in the context of the material and social problems that arise in that environment. Public managers may not be able to define what is valuable in absolute terms, but they can seek to decide (or enable the determination of) whether a given goal is more valuable than another in a particular circumstance. In the process, they can rely on policy analysis tools such as program evaluation or benefit-cost analysis, but these are aids to understanding, not arbiters of policy. (Alford and O'Flynn 2009, 176)

This caution reminds us that indicators are not policy, but only inform policy choices and management decisions. A warning should accompany the use of any indicator: "This indicator is intended for information only. May be hazardous if taken as instruction." Indicators are not marching orders or compensation indexes, but informational perspectives on current positions and recent trends. To be progressive in a rapidly changing world, a museum's selection of indicators should help its leaders make visionary choices and evolutionary changes; the selection should not become just a report card, and the selection should evolve as well.

For nonprofits, including museums, impact and value must be evaluated both quantitatively and qualitatively—numbers and stories, and, in the hearts of nonprofits, it is the emotional story and theory of action narrative that drives support and engagement. According to Moore, "For an enterprise to succeed in producing value, the leaders of the enterprise have to have a story, or an account, of what value or purposes the organization is pursuing" (cited in Alford and O'Flynn 2009, 177). In the best of worlds, indicators illuminate the way there, and provide the authorizing environment with collateral evidence that the museum's story rings true.

Others have expanded Moore's strategic triangle into evaluation frameworks, such as Cole and Parston's Public Service Value Model (PSVM) methodology that "measures how well an organization, or series of organizations, achieves outcomes and cost-effectiveness year after year. The methodology gives public managers a way to evaluate an organization's performance in relationship to the organization's average performance over a series of years" (Cole and Parston, as cited in Alford and O'Flynn 2009, 185).

Theory-Based Evaluation: Birckmayer and Weiss, in their "Theory-Based Evaluation in Practice: What Do We Learn?" in the journal *Evaluation Review* observed, "All programs have a theoretical basis, no matter how weakly the assumptions are articulated. Program people make some assumptions about why the set of activities they plan will lead to desirable outcomes" (Birckmayer and Weiss 2000, 426). If a museum wants to change the world in some way, what are its theories about how it will bring about and measure those changes? Their approach relates to museums:

> Theory-Based Evaluation in Practice (TBE) is an approach to evaluation that requires the assumptions on which the program is based in considerable detail: what activities are conducted,

what effect from each activity, what the program does next, what the excepted response is, what happens next, and so on, to the expected outcomes.[1] The evaluation then follows each step in the sequence to see whether the expected ministeps actually materialize. (Birckmayer and Weiss 2000, 408)

TBE is based on a theory of change and/or a theory of action, which may be synonymous to some. Others draw a level distinction, meaning that a theory of change covers the big picture (e.g., museums use their resources to change lives, while a theory of action details the pathway, steps, and actions the museum takes to effect its desired changes. Writing in *The Evaluation Exchange*, the Harvard Family Research Project periodical on emerging strategies in evaluation, Claudia Weisburd and Tamara Sniad from Foundations, Inc., further clarify the distinction: "A theory of change identifies the process(es) through which a given type of social change is expected to occur. A theory of action maps out a specific pathway in that theory of change, or an organization's role with respect to achieving that change, based on an assessment of how it can add the most value to the change process" (Weisburd and Sniad 2005/2006, 3). The more detailed and therefore more observable theory of action is the more useful of the two terms to address the complexity of the museum field and to provide a meaningful framework for evaluation, particularly TBE.

Logic Models: Very similar to theories of change and action, logic models add definition to the steps. The W. K. Kellogg Foundation, in its evaluation handbook for grant applicants, defines logic models as "a picture of how your program works—the theory and assumptions underlying the program. . . . This model provides a road map of your program, highlighting how it is expected to work, what activities need to come before others, and how desired outcomes are achieved" (Kellogg 2006, 1). This traditional, one-way logic model is a way of connecting a project's goals to resource investments, to activities, to outputs, then to outcomes, and finally to impacts and social values. Kellogg diagrams it as a left-to-right sequence, shown in table 1.1, that horizontally connects the boxes in each step of the logic model in order to evaluate and measure a program's effectiveness and efficiency in transforming a funder's grant award into community impacts and public value.

It is tempting to use logic models to evaluate entire museums as well as their individual grant-funded programs. However, a one-way logic model approach assumes the museum vs. the world, where the intention of the museum (us) is to improve the world (them), and the museum is judged and valued on how well it succeeds in improving them. The richer and more socially beneficial reality recognizes the symbiotic relationship between the museum and the world: The world also wants to make us different. It has every right to: The world—our audiences, donors, society, city, culture, community, and/or market—is paying our bills. A museum logic model needs to be looping or two-way.

Table 1.1. The Basic Logic Model

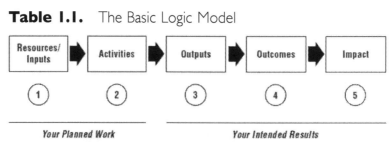

Source: W. K. Kellogg Foundation, Logic Model Development Guide, 2004

Jim Collins and the Hedgehog Concept: In his *Good to Great and the Social Sectors: A Monograph to Accompany Good to Great*, business analyst Jim Collins adapts his framework developed for the business sector for the nonprofit social sector. He says:

> Greatness comes about by . . . understanding three intersecting circles: what you can be the best in the world at, what you are deeply passionate about, and what best drives your economic or resource engine. (Collins 2005, 34)
>
> A fundamental difference between the business and social sectors [is that] . . . the critical question is not "How much money do we make? But How can we develop a sustainable resource engine to deliver superior performance relative to our mission?" (18)

Museums adopt business bestsellers when their board members suggest approaches that they find effective in running their own organizations. In addition to Jim Collins, two other business gurus, Peter Drucker and Peter Senge (Jacobsen 2014, 2), influenced museums to adopt focused missions, vision statements, core values, and decision frameworks, collectively a museum's core ideology, as called by the late organizational coach Roy Shafer.

The problem for museums, however, is that most mid to large museums do not have the luxury of focused missions as they also have to serve their funders' and customers' missions. Jim Collins advised organizations to be like hedgehogs and do one thing well (roll into a spiky ball), rather than be like its enemy, the wily jack-of-all-trades fox. In free-choice marketplace economies, museums have evolved to be more like the fox than the hedgehog, and so museums with multiple funding sources may be better off thinking like a fox rather than acting like a hedgehog.

Museum Theory: We also need to establish the conceptual framework for museums, beginning with our concepts and assumptions about what museums are, why they exist, and for whom. This book builds on the ICOM definition of museums[2] and on four concepts that museums in North America, the United Kingdom, and the Eurozone might agree with, though the implications may not be clear:

1. Stephen Weil's introduction to John Cotton Dana's selected writings from the 1920s quoted Dana's maxim that museums should find what the community needs and fit the museum to those needs (Peniston 1999, 16).
2. Weil's own Theory of Museums bases a museum's worth on the good it has accomplished; the museum's resources are the means to that end. The performance evaluation is then of the museum's effectiveness at achieving its purposes and of the efficiency of its resource use (Weil 2002; 2005).
3. John Falk and Lynn Dierking, in describing their Contextual Model of Learning, place emphasis on museums' unique business model of free-choice learning that meets personal and sociocultural needs in physical contexts (Falk and Dierking 2000, xii; Falk and Sheppard 2006; Falk and Dierking 2012, 33). Free choice means museums are in a competitive marketplace controlled by the consumers. No one has to visit. No one has to give museums money. This is a fundamental difference in our business model from schools and other formal educational institutions. We have to attract and benefit our audiences and supporters.
4. George Hein builds a wide mission on John Dewey's progressive education that is sharable by all museums: The mission of building a better and more democratic society (Hein 2006, 349).

These conceptual foundations have implications for today's museum leaders:

- Dana's Implication: Museums are responsible for offering their communities services that address their needs and aspirations.

- Weil's Implication: Museums should use their resources (means) to achieve their purposes (ends), and be evaluated on how effectively and efficiently they do that (performance).
- Dierking and Falk's Implication: Museums operate in a competitive, free-choice marketplace by offering physical and social services valued by their audiences and supporters.
- Hein's Implication: Museums aspire to make the world better and more democratic, such as advancing community development and social good.

Synthesized, these concepts underlie museum economic theory: The community funds the museum to use its resources to provide effective services back to the community. The museum provides these services efficiently and, instead of privatizing its net revenues, contributes to community development and social good.

Project Evaluation Frameworks: In its *Framework for Evaluating Impacts of Informal Science Education Projects*, the National Science Foundation's Informal Science Education program (NSF-ISE, now NSF-AISL) established a logic model-based methodology for their own work that links, left to right: the intended impact; to the inputs needed; to the activities generated; to the outputs or through-puts of the activities; to the individual outcomes; and finally, to the project's strategic impacts, which loop back to the beginning to compare to the project's objectives (Friedman 2008, 36).

This framework synthesized earlier evaluation experience, and has been a factor in establishing a language and set of expectations shared widely in the informal learning evaluation field, represented by the Visitor Studies Association (VSA) and the AAM's Committee on Audience Research and Evaluation (CARE). One of the NSF contributions has been to establish categories of informal learning impacts, such as changes in levels of "awareness, knowledge or understanding, engagement or interest, attitude, behavior, abilities, skills, and other" (21). Given these categories of impacts, the NSF asked evaluators to state what indicators they will use to monitor whether the impact is happening as well as what kinds and level of indicator responses might show evidence (23). This way of categorizing and assessing the impact of individual projects on their target audiences establishes language and precedents that might be useful in thinking about other kinds of outcomes.

However, the distinctions between evaluating a project and a museum are important, in order to avoid importing inappropriate expectations or methodologies. The NSF's framework and many of the evaluation studies conducted by members of VSA and CARE are of projects, not of museums as institutions. Compared to projects, institutions are more complex. More than the sum of its yearly projects, an active museum has a long-term impact on and a relationship with its community and its audiences and supporters. Projects have clear objectives, some of which can attract continuing funding as long as evaluation certifies the results against the expectations. A museum can have multiple missions, multiple audiences, and multiple funders. Projects can have outcomes with their individual participants, as documented by surveys. Museums, on the other hand, have impacts on their cumulative audiences and their communities that might better be evaluated at a systems and societal level: The project and its participants (units) operate at a different scale than the museum and its communities (aggregated).

This suggests that museum evaluation should look at operating data and market demographics in addition to evaluations of its projects. Evaluating a museum on the results of a year's worth of operation is very different from evaluating a single project, but institutional evaluation may be able to use some project evaluation methodologies and language with caution.

Infrastructure Model: In an NSF-funded convening of the Association of Science-Technology Centers (ASTC) leaders two decades ago, Mark St. John and Deborah Perry in their *Investments in Informal Science Education: A Framework for Evaluation and Research* (Perry, Huntwork, and St. John 1994), reflected on a different approach to museum evaluation:

We see grants for exhibit development and other investments in informal science education as investments in infrastructure. Consequently, these investments should be evaluated against a set of criteria that are appropriate for evaluating infrastructure, not against criteria that assume direct and immediate "impacts" on the visiting public. (Perry, Huntwork, and St. John 1994, 6)

This museums-as-infrastructure model suggests that museums be evaluated by how well they fill their niche within a community's cultural, educational, civic, and economic systems: Does the city have enough quality leisure attractions? Are there enough interactive galleries for children? Do we have venues for blockbusters that draw tourists? Do we have enough trusted places for community gathering and celebration? Measuring fit can be a quantitative evaluation: A museum or a city can compare data on its assets—total amount of exhibit space, number of program spaces, collection size, staff count, endowment, etc.—to peers in other communities to identify areas where they can expand to fill a niche pioneered by their peers, thereby adding to their community's infrastructure.

Scott's Typology of Values: The previous frameworks look at museum purposes expressed by museum professionals. Museum researcher Carol Scott also looked at the end results—the values end-users believe museums offer. Scott's research had two cohorts and sought the common ground of values shared by both the public using museums and the professionals working in them and how those shared values might relate to a typology of values.

Public and funder surveys reveal a museum's perceived values in the eyes of their audiences and supporters. There have been various efforts to categorize perceived values, also known as end-users' and customers' benefits and outcomes. The Museums Association (United Kingdom) recently grouped the results of a public survey by Britain Thinks into three broad categories of perceived benefits: Enhance well-being; create better places; and inspire people and ideas (Museums Association 2013, 5). David Stevenson conducted a survey about the perceived value of the Scottish national museums to Scottish citizens; he asked what they valued about their museums, whether they used them directly, and how much they would be willing to add to their yearly taxes to cover the national museums if their funding disappeared. Using a methodology called contingent evaluation, Stevenson monetized the value of those museums to Scottish citizens, which was higher than the government's actual support for the museums.

Scott, in her "Advocating the Value of Museums," reported on the results of her literature review and observed:

In the burgeoning literature on this subject, value is described across a variety of dimensions and three main beneficiary groups. The dimensions include instrumental, intrinsic, institutional, and use values. The beneficiaries of these values can be individuals, communities and the economy. (C. Scott 2007, 4)

Scott tests the evidence base for each of these four dimensions [author's formatting and excerpts]:

Instrumental Value describes the utilitarian and instrumental benefits . . . through economic benefits such as civic branding, tourism, employment and the multiplier effect on local economics, through social benefits including increased social capital, inclusion, social cohesion, tolerance for cultural diversity, urban regeneration and civic participation and through benefits to individuals such as learning, personal wellbeing and health. (C. Scott 2007, 4)

Intrinsic Value gets to the heart of the intangibles of museum experiences. For individuals, intrinsic values are experienced as a "state of absorption . . . and . . . deep satisfaction" that the "pleasure" of seeing an artwork or having a cultural experience that is moving and meaningful, can engender . . . explore "personal meaning," the discovery of "personal beliefs in amongst universal truths" experiences that address our needs to experience "the religious, the numinous and the sublime." (McCarthy et al. 2004 as cited in C. Scott 2007, 4)

Other intrinsic benefits are experienced collectively. Symbolic value . . . the "creation of social bonds" that "make connections between people" and "reinforce a sense of unity and identity." (C. Scott 2007, 4)

Use and Non-use Value: Direct use of cultural services is a key indicator in determining public value. Willingness to give something up, to spend money, to commit energy and to spend time visiting, using, enjoying and traveling to and from cultural activities are tangible demonstrations that the public values culture. (C. Scott 2007, 5)

However, a growing body of literature suggests that the absence of direct use does not preclude attribution of value and that non-use values such as option, future and bequest value are significant dimensions of the total value of culture. (C. Scott 2007, 5)

Institutional Value: Public Value refers to the value created by government through services, laws, regulations and other public institutions. Holden argues that public institutions are integral to building public confidence. He argues that well-run public agencies that are ethical, fair and equitable in their dealings with the public and transparent in their practice generate trust in the public realm. (Holden 2004, 44 as cited in C. Scott 2007, 5)

Scott's testing of a model combining Moore's (1995) triangle (authorizing, operational, and public environments), which Holden adopted to three types of value (instrumental, institutional, and intrinsic) with a wide range of use "values," widens the scope of what we understand as museum value. Her research and writing make a strong case that museums offer value not just in what they do, but in what they mean, in how they are used, and in their very existence as public assets.

Mulgan's Indicator Types: Geoff Mulgan, policy director for Prime Minister Tony Blair, observed in the *Stanford Social Innovation Review* that nonprofits often measure and report on value in three different ways to different audiences: External advocacy and validation; internal management metrics; and impact evaluation studies for specific funders. Different methodologies are used for each; these different ways of counting and describing also complicate the way toward clear and meaningful measures of value (Mulgan 2010, 8).

Mulgan's division of the three different ways nonprofits report on value is similar to the categories of purposes, key performance indicators (KPIs), and outcomes, as used by museums:

a. "External advocacy and validation" indicators tend to fall into the institutional purposes and guiding principles categories where mission statements, strategic objectives, corporate values, marketing promises and other intentional purposes are expressed and used in external case statements and marketing materials intended for generating support and earned revenue. These indicators are primarily qualitative statements.
b. "Internal management metrics," which count both capital assets and operating outputs and costs, align with the categories of resources, activities, operating data, and key performance indicators for measuring efficiency and performance. These indicators are primarily quantitative data.
c. "Impact evaluation studies" fall into the perceived value category of indicators for assessing effectiveness at achieving desired outcomes and impacts. These indicators include both qualitative and quantitative data.

Mulgan's three categories also align with the left, center, and right portions of a classic logic model and theory of action discussed above.

Operating and Evaluation Data: Jay Rounds, in his article "The Museum and Its Relationships as a Loosely Coupled System" (Rounds 2012), observes the complexity of the museum context when he proposes a loosely coupled relationship between a museum's intentions and its individual outcomes due to a museum's lack of control over the many variables that affect each end-user's experience and perceived benefits—how the individual feels that day; what is in the news; how crowded it is, etc. Rounds's work questions the validity of methodologies that assess outcomes based on surveying a sample of individuals. In response, perhaps it is worth trying a socioeconomic methodology that looks not at the individual outcomes, which Rounds proves are hard to predict, but at the annual aggregated evidence from a museum's total audiences and stakeholders—its annual operating data, which may provide more meaningful and actionable data. By looking at all of a museum's activities and engagements over a full year, we may average out the uncoupled and unpredictable individual responses.

The White Oak Institute's "Review Guide of Existing Museum Databases" aggregated the survey questions of ten museum associations (AAM, ASTC, etc.) that regularly collect operating data into a database of 1,082 data collection fields.[3] These indicators record yearly or year-end status of seven different aspects: Institutional information (8 percent of the indicators); engagement counts (16 percent); resources: physical (9 percent); resources: collections (3 percent); resources: HR (7 percent); finance (55 percent); and other (3 percent) (White Oak Institute and the American Alliance of Museums 2011, C, 3–1).

In addition to operating data coming mostly in numbers from the administration department, museum leaders also receive evaluation data coming from a wide variety of sources: board member suggestions, visitor comment cards, exhibit time and tracking studies, visitor satisfaction surveys, and formal evaluation studies to name a few kinds of evaluation data that managers might see.

A large professional community of evaluators has developed since the founding of the Visitor Studies Association in 1990, on the theory that evaluation can be used to prove and improve a project or program, such as an exhibition or after-school workshop. Summative evaluation has accepted methodologies to measure how well an intentional objective was achieved, and this evidence is important to the funders. Developmental evaluation has approaches to improve a project over time with its evolving objectives and audiences, and these course corrections are important to developers.

Once a museum's activities are operational—the galleries are open, the outreach bus is touring, or the summer camp is under way—operating and evaluation data can start coming in, informing management adjustments. Often the squeaky wheel, particularly revenue shortfalls and attendance drop-offs, gets frenzied attention, due to looming payroll issues if not solved. While such quick action is often justified, if any one of a museum's multiple revenue sources gets disproportionate attention for too long, the other revenue sources will eventually erode.

A balanced and prioritized dashboard of operating and evaluation data will help managers keep the museum's full range of values in mind. For a dashboard to be meaningful, the museum must decide its priorities—which impacts and performances, and then find ways to evaluate how each is doing as well as how they interact.

Accounting Definitions: Note that over half the aggregated museum survey questions in the "Review Guide of Existing Museum Databases" deal with finance. Museum financial statements are another perspective to inform a theory of action for museums. Unrestricted operating revenues are divided by revenue categories using well-established accounting definitions. Support and earned revenue, plus income from institutional assets (endowment, land use, royalties), are three categories that make up the majority of a museum's operating revenue. Support revenue is subdivided between private (businesses, donors, and private foundations) and public (government taxpayer funds). Earned revenues are subdivided in many different ways; this book considers visitors and program participants as the two main sources of personal earned revenues.

Money received from a museum's audiences and supporters in return for services benefiting them directly (gallery admissions, program fees, retail purchases, etc.) is considered earned revenue, while revenue from donors, foundations, and government agencies is considered support revenue; their motivation is supposed to be altruistic for the benefit of others. In practice, the lines are fuzzy: Members, who are really buying discount admissions, believe they are supporting a good cause, while corporate donors may negotiate direct benefit and visibility packages.

To summarize, a museum's potential revenue sources are public, private, personal, and institutional. In order to continue receiving revenue from the external markets, the museum must provide public, private, and personal benefits at least equal to the value of the revenues received. Museums are marketplace institutions competing for both earned and support revenues while at the same time sustaining, evolving, and growing the museum. Accounting data track these key revenue sectors and the museum's operations and assets.

ANALYZING EVALUATION FRAMEWORKS TO REVEAL COMMON GROUND

These eleven frameworks, concepts, and definitions drawn from the literature provide a foundation and guidance for developing an institutional evaluation framework for museums.

- Moore's Strategic Triangle establishes a way to evaluate the relationship among a government agency, its authorizing environment, and the value they create together. Producing public value is the purpose and desired outcome of the relationship. In Moore's approach, value is political, not market based, and that value is judged by the authorizing environment when the government or foundation decides on funding and other types of support and authorization. For museums, the triangle needs to be expanded, given their provision of both political and market-based values.

- Theory-Based Evaluation and Logic Models recognize that producing value needs a theory of how the intention will beget the outcomes: What is the sequence of actions we believe will have the results the museum wants? The linear sequence of left-to-right boxes, marching from purpose to value, provides both managers and evaluators with the ability to look at the steps: The needs translate into intentional purposes, then input and resources are invested, resulting in activities that generate outputs and hopefully outcomes, also known as value.

- Collins's Hedgehog Concept, adapted for the social sector, looks for an alignment among three institutional attributes: passion, unique capability, and a sustainable, improving resource. In museum terms, this translates into a museum's mission and guiding principles, its unique museum services, and its assets and revenues.

- Museum Theory assumes that museums should use their resources efficiently to deliver effective services that respond to their community's needs and aspirations, and that the museum's revenues are related to its provision of those services, plus the museum's re-investment in its community's development and social good.

- Project Evaluation Frameworks provide methodologies, standards for evidence, and language for project evaluation that can inform institutional evaluation.

- St. John and Perry's Infrastructure Model looks at the role museums play in their overall educational, cultural, and economic infrastructure, and recognizes that museums add value simply by existing and operating—what accountants call capital assets and resources.

- Scott's Typology reveals a wide range of perceived values among the public, and she establishes categories of values: Institutional, instrumental, intrinsic, and use and non-use values.

- Mulgan's Indicator Types relate to the different kinds of indicators nonprofits use for different audiences: evidence of effectiveness to funders, internal operating metrics, and end-user assessments.

- Operating and Evaluation Data provide management with information they can track over time and combine into meaningful KPIs, some of which may indicate outcomes and impacts.
- Accounting Definitions provide a well-established set of definitions for the revenues a museum receives from its community in return for its services/values. Accounting terms recognize public and private support revenues, and private and personal earned revenues, with an additional category coming from income earned by institutional assets, like endowment.

When these evaluation frameworks are collected and aligned in their intent, the synthesis reveals a comprehensive theory of action sequence that addresses the complexity of museum evaluation by accommodating many perspectives into a combined framework and underlying structure. The steps move from desire to result, from purpose to impact, and from left to right with evaluation indicators along the way to help improve the fit. They flow from purpose to impact through an underlying Museum Theory of Action in a series of overlapping steps shown in the bottom collected row of table 1.2 and directly in table 1.3. As the next chapter describes, each step has its own family of indicators.

THE MUSEUM THEORY OF ACTION: FROM INTENDED PURPOSES TO PERCEIVED VALUES

The Museum Theory of Action, built on the bottom row of table 1.2, assumes that a museum produces its impacts and benefits through a sequence of steps. In this theory, a museum produces its values through iterations of a sequence of logic model-like steps as described in the following constructed narrative: (1) Museum leadership (and/or other forces), in response to perceived community needs and aspirations, determine the museum's *intentional purposes*; (2) leadership and staff filter the many possibilities for achieving those purposes by the museum's *guiding principles* to select the museum's

Table 1.2. Alignment of Eleven Evaluation Frameworks to observe that the categories collect (next-to-last row) into seven action steps (last row).

	EXTERNAL INPUT →			MEANS →		AUDIENCE INTERFACE →		ENDS
Moore's Strategic Triangle	authorizing environment		organization or agency					public value
Theory-based Evaluation (Action Steps)	desired outcomes			activities				actual outcomes
Logic Models				resources & inputs	activities	outputs		outcomes impact
Hedgehog Concept			passion	unique capability	drive the resource engine			superior mission performance
Museum Theory	community needs		purpose	business model				progress and social justice
Project Evaluation	intended impact			inputs needed	activities generated	outputs		outcomes strategic impacts
Infrastructure	infrastructure needs			museum investments				increased social infrastructure
Value Typology				institutional values	use & non-use values			intrinsic values instrumental values
Indicator Types	external advocacy & validation			internal metrics				impact evaluation studies
Operating Data				resources	engagements	finance	KPIs	exchange value
Accounting Categories				capital assets balance sheet	expenses	revenues	net	net contribution
Collected Categories	community needs (desired benefits)	intentional purposes	guiding principles	resources	activities	operating data	KPIs	perceived benefits & values
Action Steps	0	1	2	3	4	5	6	7

Source: The White Oak Institute

desired impacts and their target audiences and supporters; (3) staff, with their knowledge of the museum's *resources*, produce (e.g., plan, design, test, fabricate/create, market, deliver, and operate); (4) the museum's *activities*, using a constantly iterative cycle of; (5) *evaluation and operating data* that feed into; (6) the museum's *key performance indicators* that monitor; (7) the *impacts* and *benefits* the museum is providing its audiences and funders, which feed back to the beginning as one source of their perceived community *needs* and aspirations (see table 1.3).

The Museum Theory of Action follows the sequence of a classic logic model, revised to loop back to the beginning. There are feedback cycles even within the seven steps. The museum evaluates the outputs and outcomes of all its activities in order to prove and improve their efficiency and effectiveness at delivering the museum's intentional purposes.

Of course, audiences and funders have other ways of voicing their needs and aspirations, and museum practice often veers from this linear sequence. In practice, decisions and actions within the museum culture seem more web-like than linear: The marketing department wants to engage teens, development is courting a collector of animation cels, education wants to script some teen workshops, and a curator has been itching to do a popular culture show. Such webs of interest can drive decisions that escape the Theory of Action's intentional sequence, particularly when staff initiates activities ahead of leadership, but this theory of action intends to reflect the fullest, most responsible and thoughtful sequence.

USING THE MUSEUM THEORY OF ACTION

Is Moore's strategic triangle an "empirical theory of what public managers actually do, or a normative prescription of what they should do?" (Alford and O'Flynn 2009, 174). This question also applies to the Museum Theory of Action. Moore was attempting to do both, and there is a third use as a research framework (Alford and O'Flynn 2009, 175). This museum theory should also be useful in those three ways: (1) Provide a framework to see what a museum is actually doing now, and evaluate the alignment between intentions and results ("documentation"); (2) provide guidance to museums for decisions about the future ("planning"); and (3) provide researchers and evaluators with a shared framework for evaluating the impact and performance of museums ("evaluation").

Many museums are already using several of the eleven evaluation frameworks, such as accounting statements, project evaluations, and visitor surveys. These evaluations can continue, as they are embedded within the Theory of Action, and can feed into a comprehensive institutional evaluation.

Table 1.3. The Museum Theory of Action: Logic Model Version

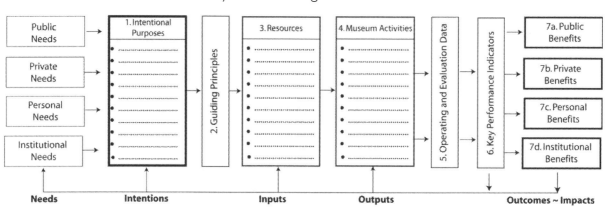

Source: The White Oak Institute

While developed to accommodate the most complicated business models, the theory must work for any museum, from fully government-funded museums, to entrepreneurial museums, and to the multi-funded museums common in U.S. cities. Individual museums and career professionals can use the Theory of Action to get more specific about their intentions, guiding principles, resources, and activities, and they can select indicators using their operating and evaluation data in KPIs that monitor the impacts they desire.

CONCLUSION

The Museum Theory of Action assumes that the community's needs drive a museum's intentional purposes, and that the museum, honoring its guiding principles, uses its resources to deliver its programs and other activities, which generate operating and evaluation data, and, if all goes well, result in outcomes, impacts, and perceived benefits by the museum's community and its audiences and supporters. This sequence loops back to the museum's intentions, as the community and its audiences and supporters express their needs through their votes of time, effort, and money, which influence the museum's decisions, starting the cycle over again in a constantly evolving alignment of museum purposes and community needs. Key performance indicators (KPIs) evaluate the efficiency and effectiveness of the cycle.

The Museum Theory of Action may begin to address museum complexity. It allows for multiple needs, purposes, impacts, and benefits to multiple end-users and beneficiaries. It organizes the "how" of the museum's actions into seven steps synthesized from other evaluation frameworks. The analysis of the 1,025 indicators discussed in the next chapter finds alignment between the potential indicators and each step in the Theory of Action; all fit, and no step is unpopulated.

NOTES

1. The original cited Suchman 1967; Weiss 1972, 1995, 1997, 1998; Bickman 1990; Chen 1990; Chen and Rossi 1987; Costner 1989; Finney and Moos 1989 at this point.

2. The ICOM definition: "A museum is a non-profit, permanent institution in the service of society and its development, open to the public, which acquires, conserves, researches, communicates and exhibits the tangible and intangible heritage of humanity and its environment for the purposes of education, study and enjoyment" (ICOM 2007).

3. This is a different database from MIIP 1.0, although the fifty-nine indicators distilled from it as recommendations for the IMLS's Museums Count are #131–209 (some indicators had sub-questions, which were split out).

REFERENCES

Alford, John, and Janine O'Flynn. "Making Sense of Public Value: Concepts, Critiques and Emergent Meanings." *International Journal of Public Administration* 32, no. 3–4 (2009): 171–91.

Anderson, David. *A Common Wealth: Museums in the Learning Age.* London: DCMS, 1997.

Anderson, Maxwell L. *Metrics of Success in Art Museums.* Los Angeles: The Getty Leadership Institute, J. Paul Getty Trust, 2004.

Baldwin, Joan H. "The Challenge of 'Value': Engaging Communities in Why Museums Exist." A Museum Association of New York | Museumwise White Paper. October 2011.

Bell, Philip, Bruce Lewenstein, Andrew W. Shouse, and Michael A. Feder. *Learning Science in Informal Environments—People, Places, and Pursuits.* Washington, D.C.: National Academies Press, 2009.

Birckmayer, Johanna D., and Carol Hirschon Weiss. "Theory-Based Evaluation in Practice: What Do We Learn?" *Evaluation Review* 24, no. 4 (August 2000): 407–31.

Bradburne, James M. "A New Strategic Approach to the Museum and Its Relationship to Society." *Museum Management and Curatorship* (2001): 75–84.

Collins, Jim. *Good to Great and the Social Sectors: A Monograph to Accompany Good to Great.* New York: HarperCollins, 2005.

Falk, John H., and Lynn D. Dierking. *Learning from Museums: Visitor Experiences and the Making of Meaning.* Walnut Creek: AltaMira, 2000.

———. *Museum Experience Revisited*. Walnut Creek: Left Coast Press, 2012.

Falk, John H., and Beverly K. Sheppard. *Thriving in the Knowledge Age: New Business Models for Museums and Other Cultural Institutions*. Lanham, MD: AltaMira, 2006.

Friedman, Alan J. "Framework for Evaluating Impacts of Informal Science Education Projects." *informalscience.org*. March 12, 2008. Accessed November 4, 2014. http://informalscience.org/documents/Eval_Framework.pdf.

———. "The Great Sustainability Challenge: How Visitor Studies Can Save Cultural Institutions in the 21st Century." *Visitor Studies* 10, no. 1 (January 2007): 3–12.

Garnett, Robin. "The Impact of Science Centers/Museums on Their Surrounding Communities: Summary Report." *The Association of Science-Technology Centers (ASTC)*. July 12, 2001. Accessed October 8, 2014. http://www.astc.org/resource/case/Impact_Study02.pdf.

Hein, George E. "Museum Education." In *A Companion to Museum Studies*, by S. MacDonald. Oxford: Blackwell, 2006.

Holden, John. "Capturing Cultural Value." *Demos*. 2004. Accessed November 4, 2014. http://www.demos.co.uk/files/CapturingCulturalValue.pdf.

Jacobsen, John. "The Community Service Museum: Owning up to Our Multiple Missions." *Museum Management and Curatorship* 29, no. 1 (2014): 1–18.

Kellogg, W. K. "Logic Model Development Guide." *W. K. Kellogg Foundation*. February 2, 2006. Accessed October 21, 2014. http://www.wkkf.org/resource-directory/resource/2006/02/wk-kellogg-foundation-logic-model-development-guide.

Mulgan, Geoff. "Measuring Social Value." *Stanford Social Innovation Review* (Summer 2010). Accessed November 4, 2014. http://www.ssireview.org/pdf/2010SU-Feature_Mulgan.pdf.

Museums Association. "Museums Change Lives." July 2013. Accessed November 4, 2014. http://www.museumsassociation.org/download?id=1001738.

Peniston, William A. *The New Museum: Selected Writings by John Cotton Dana*. American Alliance of Museums Press, 1999.

Perry, D., D. Huntwork, and Mark St. John. *Investments in Informal Science Education: A Framework for Evaluation and Research*. Inverness: Inverness Research Associates, 1994.

Rounds, Jay. "The Museum and Its Relationships as a Loosely Coupled System." *Curator: The Museum Journal* 55, no. 4 (October 2012): 413–34.

Science Centre Economic Impact Study, Questacon—The National Science and Technology Centre. "Making the Case for Science Centers." *Association of Science-Technology Centers*. February 2005. Accessed November 3, 2014. http://www.astc.org/resource/case/EconImpact-whole.pdf.

Scott, Carol A. "Advocating the Value of Museums." *INTERCOM*. August 2007. Accessed November 4, 2014. http://www.intercom.museum/documents/CarolScott.pdf.

———. *Museums and Public Value: Creating Sustainable Futures*. London: Ashgate, 2013.

Stein, Rob. *Transparency and Museums*. November 3, 2009. Accessed October 21, 2014. http://www.imamuseum.org/blog/2009/11/03/transparency-and-museums.

Weil, Stephen. *Making Museums Matter*. Washington, D.C.: Smithsonian Institution, 2002.

———. "A Success/Failure Matrix for Museums." *Museum News* (January/February 2005): 36–40.

Weinberg, Mark L., and Marsha S. Lewis. "The Public Value Approach to Strategic Management." *Museum Management and Curatorship* 24, no. 3 (2009): 253–69.

Weisburd, Claudia, and Tamara Sniad. "Theory of Action in Practice." *Harvard Family Research Project*. Winter 2005/2006. Accessed October 21, 2014. http://www.hfrp.org/evaluation/the-evaluation-exchange/issue-archive/professional-development/theory-of-action-in-practice.

The White Oak Institute and the American Association of Museums. *Review Guide of Existing Museum Surveys*. Institute of Museum & Library Services, 2011.

CHAPTER 2

IDENTIFYING POTENTIAL MUSEUM IMPACTS

What potential impacts and benefits can museums provide for their communities and their audiences and supporters?

Museums provide services to their communities, audiences, and supporters. Weil observed that "museums can provide forms of public service that are all but infinite in their variety" (Weil 2002, 89).

The Guggenheim Museum in Bilbao attracts tourists. The British Museum cares for civilization's treasures. The Texas State History Museum tells their story. Yad Vashem Holocaust History Museum (Jerusalem) establishes a global symbol. The Monterey Bay Aquarium protects the ocean. The Museum of Art and History (Santa Cruz, California) gathers the community. The Lawrence Hall of Science (Berkeley, California) develops curriculum materials, and the District Six Museum (Cape Town) preserves heritage.

Of course, all these museums also do more. They provide visitor experiences; they create jobs; they inspire innovation; they offer respite and beauty; they preserve memories and objects; and they communicate regional identity. Each of these museums has a business model—the people, agencies, and organizations that pay the museum the money needed to provide these services.

What potential impacts and benefits can museums provide their communities, and for which audiences and supporters? The quest to answer this research question is told in this chapter, from the methodology, to the findings, and to their implications.

As discussed in the previous chapter, the research question is important because of a lack of appreciation for how many contributions museums can make, which comes at a time when museums need to justify their support. Museums lack a framework for communicating their contributions and value, and the public lacks an understanding of all the ways a museum could serve them. How can museums serve? The research question seeks to list the main Categories of Potential Museum Impacts.

As used in this book, *impact* and *benefit* are both words for the outcomes of a museum's activities. They may describe the same outcome but recognize a difference in perspective: Impacts are what the museum wants to accomplish; benefits are what the community, audiences, and supporters want from the museum. If a museum is providing a benefit, then it can decide if it wants to have that as an impact or not—potentially, any benefit the museum field provides could be selected by a museum as one of its desired impacts. Because this book is written to help museum professionals improve *impact*, that word is used in preference, but *benefit* could also have been used from the community, audience, and supporter perspectives (see also Appendix A, Definitions and Assumptions).

The museum field's rich literature and existing work on impact and performance offers a thoughtful and varied sample of existing and proposed indicators of museum impact and performance. The research project conducted by the White Oak Institute set out to map the current range of museum services, benefits, beneficiaries, and supporters. This chapter describes the Museum Indicators of Impact and Performance (MIIP) 1.0 database and the analysis process, and presents the findings—fourteen Categories of Potential Museum Impacts, sorted by their audiences and supporters.

THE RESEARCH METHODOLOGY: ANALYZING MIIP 1.0

In order to analyze how thoughtful museum professionals globally have been thinking about impacts and performance, the White Oak Institute collected fifty-one systems of museum indicators of impact and performance (MIIP) into an aggregated database (MIIP 1.0) of 1,025 indicators. The goals of the analysis were to identify categories of museum impacts and to see if the 1,025 museum indicators of impact and performance supported the Museum Theory of Action documentation, planning, and evaluation framework.

With these goals in mind, the collection is intentionally diverse rather than comprehensive. For instance, inclusion of different perspectives from around the world and from the major disciplines of museums and their authorizing environments was important, as was paying attention to peer-reviewed journal articles and museum association task forces that have proposed field-tested ways to evaluate museums and to measure their value. The diversity of the fifty-one sources for MIIP 1.0 (see Appendix B) increased the likelihood that a category important to some sector of the museum field would appear at least once.

The collection also uses a wide definition of *indicator*: MIIP indicators include data collection fields and responses (routinely asked formal questions and surveys), evaluation criteria, institutional success measures, foundation objectives, management resources, proposed indicators, and research findings. They are either quantitative or qualitative, and may indicate to some expert audience potentially meaningful data related to measuring museum impact and performance.

While MIIP 1.0 may not be complete, it is representative. At this point, it does not include other worthy sets of indicators such as the American Association for State and Local History's (AASLH's) proprietary StEPs assessment program, DataArts new data fields, and the Association of Art Museum Directors' (AAMD) confidential survey. Perhaps these will be added to a MIIP 2.0; perhaps a museum wants to expand MIIP 1.0 with their favorite indicators. Later iterations are likely to evolve the categories and analysis presented in this book. However, MIIP 1.0 is large and representative enough to get started.

MIIP 1.0 was developed by the White Oak Institute and is available for free to everyone, along with the Museum Theory of Action diagrams. To download copies, go to the website listed on the copyright page or search for "MIIP 1.0," or "Museum Indicators of Impact and Performance."

ANALYSIS OF THE DATABASE OF MUSEUM INDICATORS OF IMPACT AND PERFORMANCE (MIIP 1.0)

The research analyzed 1,025 indicators related to museum impact and performance drawn from fifty-one sources (see Appendix B). The research findings include:

- All the indicators fall into at least one of the seven steps of the Museum Theory of Action, with none that do not fit.
- There are at least twelve categories of external impact and two of institutional impact.
- These can be sorted by their beneficiaries, also known as the museum's audiences and supporters: Public impacts, private impacts, personal impacts, and institutional impacts.
- The MIIP database offers museum managers and evaluators a robust and diverse menu that they can filter to select the indicators most meaningful to their purposes.

Fit with the Museum Theory of Action

There are kindred groups of indicators within MIIP 1.0—attendance, learning outcomes, purposes, and collections are a few of the sixty data topics identified. The purpose of identifying and tagging

CATEGORY OF SOURCE DOCUMENTS

MIIP 1.0 has 1,025 indicators from fifty-one sources. The sources and the indicator numbering system are listed and referenced in Appendix B. The sources represent the following categories:

- Data Collection Fields (2 sources with 209 indicators total = "2/209")
- Evaluation Criteria (9/113)
- Institutional Evaluation (4/153)
- Foundation Objectives (4/20)
- Management Resources (2/56)
- Proposed Indicators (16/136)
- Research Findings (14/339)

MIIP 1.0 has the following fields filled in with information provided by the source, including the indicator itself:

- Source: Author
- Source: Date
- Source: Title of book, report, survey, or document containing the indicators (51)
- Source: Organization or Publisher
- Indicator text and number (#1–#1,025)
- Source's Indicator Category (if used)
- Source's Indicator Sub-Category (if used)

these common grounds is to see the big picture of the museum field's potential impacts. The explorations involved tagging each indicator with its:

- Step Location: Where the indicator lies along the Theory of Action by one of the seven steps. These tags are mostly determined by the source (e.g., public survey results are in Step 7: Perceived benefit, while financial data are in Step 5: Operating data), and otherwise by judgment;
- Potential Museum Impact: The category of potential museum result, service, benefit, or impact the indicator is monitoring; and
- Indicator Content: The topic or content of the data being collected.

A lengthy and iterative process of tagging the 1,025 indicators revealed similarities and patterns. There were indicators that related to collections, and others to human resources, but where should those that related to curators go? There were indicators that related to the purpose or why of the museum, and those that related to the what, how, and for whom. Smaller groupings were merged with similar indicators under umbrella terms, and early outliers formed categories of their own. Individual judgment was certainly a factor in this round of tagging the indicators, since some indicators could fit in several categories, and because the categories have transitional and not sharp boundaries. The goal was to help filter the database to identify the main groupings and to be useful to later users. It was also important to be as inclusive as possible in order to accommodate the widest definitions of nonprofit "museum,"[1] and to avoid promoting one kind of idealized museum.

As an example, "Total on-site free attendance" (#129) is tagged as Operating data (Step 5), and its data content is Attendance: Free; it may be useful as an indicator of Broadening participation, one of twelve areas of potential external museum impacts.

The Theory of Action is intended to handle the global museum field's rich diversity of purposes, guiding principles, resources, activities, supporters, and audiences. The categorizing begins to picture that diversity of benefits—all that museums can be—but even these 1,025 indicators are just a beginning. With the inevitable growth and change of the field, new museum impacts will appear on the radar of indicators, further increasing the field's potential worth to our communities.

Step Location of Each Indicator along the Theory of Action

Every indicator in the MIIP database is tagged with one of the seven steps in the Theory of Action: intentional purposes; guiding principles; resources; activities; operating data; key performance indicators; and perceived benefits. These are dimensional and sequential categories and not strict non-overlapping categories—intentional purpose indicators (Step 1) start to look like guiding principles (Step 2), and vice versa, while, at the other end of the action sequence, some key performance indicators (Step 6) start to look like perceived benefit indicators (Step 7), which loop back to the start as they look like intentional purposes (Step 1).

The 1,025 indicators fall along the seven sequential steps of the Museum Theory of Action:

1. **Intentional Purposes** (95 indicators) come from museum leadership as statements about what the museum intends to accomplish. Mission and vision statements, objectives, goals, charters, manifestos, and policy directives from authorizing agencies all contain *intentional purposes*. "Inspire learning," "Bridge cultural divides," "Support the pre-K–12 system," and "Spark workforce development" are examples of intentional purposes (IPs). Though they appear at the start of the sequence, these purposes often come from the community, most clearly communicated by the perceived benefits at the end, making a loop from Step 7. Intentional purposes are the "whys" of the museum; they are the reasons the museum deserves its nonprofit privileges.

2. **Guiding Principles** (53) also come from leadership as statements about the organization's beliefs, credos, character, core values, corporate culture, aesthetic, style, learning approach, priorities, and brand identity. Guiding principles are the fundamental "hows" of the museum, stipulating the ethical and quality terms for producing its exhibits and programs. Common *guiding principles* include authenticity, diversity, accuracy, sustainability, and respect.

3. **Resource Indicators** (98) come mainly from museum association surveys as listings and quantifications of a museum's long-term assets and capital, broadly defined to include its community reputation, staff expertise, collections, exhibits, facilities, endowment, etc. Resources tend to be capital, long-term considerations. Some resource indicators are directly quantitative, such as square feet of gallery space, number of collection objects, and endowment size. Other resources are inherently qualitative, such as the museum's reputation, identity, and expertise, yet selected quantitative indicators can monitor changes in these qualitative resources, such as the number of external requests the curators receive annually for their expertise.

4. **Activity Indicators** (51) come mainly from museum association surveys as listings and sometimes quantifications of a museum's operating programs, broadly defined to include gallery visits, exhibitions, programs, membership, events, classes, festivals, outreach, web, and social media, etc. Activities tend to be operating, periodic considerations, such as a summer camp, the year's slate of traveling exhibitions, governance meetings, outreach programs, and other operational activities covered by the operating budget.

5. **Evaluation and Operating Data** (213) come from formal evaluation studies, from accounting as quantifications of a museum's outputs, and from external sources as quantifications of the museum's service market and community. These indicators provide managers and funders with qual-

itative and quantitative data about the activities. Data can vary widely in source and objectivity: Ticketing system data are numeric, consistent, and objective, while suggestion box comments are words, sporadic and highly subjective. *Operating data* are generated routinely and comprehensively. *Evaluation studies* are periodic or occasional, ranging in incremental effort from one or two questions asked of exiting visitors by staff or volunteers over a weekend to costly, long-term formal research projects run by professional researchers.

6. **Key Performance Indicators** (155) are quantitative formulas such as ratios, averages, and benchmarks that measure the effectiveness and efficiency of the activities. KPIs typically use evaluation and/or operating data in formulas that are meaningful to managers. KPIs use the data generated by the previous step in formulas selected by leadership to inform them about the museum's impact and performance and its operations. *Impact and performance KPIs* (Step 6b) such as teacher renewal rates and published articles per curator are the focus of part 2 of this book. *Operational KPIs* (Step 6a) such as average salary and energy costs per square foot are established already in many museums. There are bound to be overlaps between the two categories of KPIs.

7. **Perceived Benefits** (360) come from the end users and *beneficiaries* of a museum's activities: the community and its audiences and supporters. End users can be audiences, such as visitors and program participants, or supporters, such as government agencies, grant funders, and corporate sponsors that fund the outcomes they desire. Data can come from surveys, admissions, revenues, accounting, grant reviews, opinion polls, and many other methodologies for gathering both qualitative and quantitative data. Benefits perceived by the community include social goods such as community gathering, support for education, and preserving heritage. Benefits perceived by audiences include spending quality time with friends and family, gaining insight and inspiration, making new social connections, and learning something. Benefits perceived by supporters include achieving their philanthropic goals such as addressing social issues, advancing understanding, changing attitudes or behavior, reaching underserved audiences, and supporting a community asset.

FOURTEEN CATEGORIES OF POTENTIAL MUSEUM IMPACTS

Impacts can be grouped under broad content umbrellas, such as preserving heritage, which covers more specific impacts such as collection conservation, cultural identity, and access to history.

How can we best organize this variety of impacts, benefits, and services? They can be most usefully organized by who they benefit: the community and its audiences and supporters. Given a specific impact, who are the audiences that benefit from that impact, and who are the parties that tend to fund the process?

Impacts currently being delivered by museums have precedented funding sources that range from the most socially beneficial (broadening participation), funded by governments and foundations, to the most individually beneficial (personal leisure), funded by visitors. An actionable way of organizing a museum's potential impacts is to sort them by the kinds of funders that have supported them in the past. This perspective helps management connect ideas for impacts with potential funding sectors.

Based on this economic approach, on the definitions in Appendix A, and on the accounting discussion in the previous chapter, the impact areas are divided into Public Impacts (seven categories), Private Impacts (two), Personal Impacts (three), and Institutional Impacts (two). *Public impacts* benefit the public as a whole, and tend to be funded by government and private philanthropy; *private impacts* tend to benefit businesses and corporations; *personal impacts* benefit individuals, families, and groups, and *institutional impacts* benefit the museum. Analysis of the MIIP 1.0 indicators reveals twelve broad areas of external impact and two of internal impact. The direct beneficiaries are not always the funders.

A foundation might pay for a teen workshop, benefiting teens directly while benefiting the foundation indirectly by serving its mandate. Internal impacts benefit the museum, either helping with operations or building capital resources.

Because MIIP 1.0 sought to be representative of many perspectives, the list of potential museum impacts and their data content topics, itemized in Appendix C, provides museums with a large selection. Naturally, there will be additions, both from omissions and from the recognition of new kinds of museum impacts. Appendix C allows museum leaders to ask: How many of these community benefits do we offer in some degree? Which impacts reflect our missions? Which are important to our audiences and supporters? Should we make adjustments? Table 2.1 is a summary of the fourteen potential impact areas.

Categories and definitions of the fourteen impact areas organized by their precedented funding sources and kinds of impact follow. For examples of specific indicators in each category, see Appendix C.

Public Impacts—Benefits to Society and the Public at Large

A. **Broadening participation** (85 indicators) address the public benefit of increasing social justice and inclusion. These indicators cover audience diversity, access policy, inclusivity, community connections, management culture, universal design, and approach to learning. Museums can be public resources that welcome all; they can also set examples of respect and inclusion.

B. **Preserving heritage** (47) indicators cover the public benefit of caring for and interpreting our past, both physically and culturally, through stewardship of collections, historic sites, and cultural neighborhoods. Heritage preservation contributes to a sense of belonging and where we come

Table 2.1. Categories of Potential Museum Impacts.

		# of MIIP indicators
Public Impacts		
A	Broadening participation	85
B	Preserving heritage	47
C	Strengthening social capital	76
D	Enhancing public knowledge	43
E	Serving education	56
F	Advancing social change	40
G	Communicating public identity & image	27
Private Impacts		
H	Contributing to the economy	85
I	Delivering corporate community services	9
Personal Impacts		
J	Enabling personal growth	147
K	Offering personal respite	4
L	Welcoming personal leisure	11
Institutional Impacts		
M	Helping museum operations	308
N	Building museum capital	87
Total indicators in the MIIP 1.0 database		1,025

Source: The White Oak Institute

from; a place for communal archives, lessons of history, display of property and collections, and the preservation of memory. This curatorial and stewardship role has a long legacy in museum history, and for some museums, taking care of their collections is their highest priority.

C. **Strengthening social capital** (76) indicators monitor the potential contributions a museum makes to the health and social networks of its greater community through forming community connections and partnerships; serving as a public gathering place; providing the means for communication and debate in a trusted, neutral environment; serving as an honest broker; facilitating events; and collaborating with other organizations on community projects. Museums are part of a community's capital assets and add to its cultural, educational, and economic infrastructure. Museums and other cultural facilities add public value and build public trust (Holden 2004) by creating museum-quality brand relationships. As capital-intensive, physical structures open to the public, they add to a city's balance sheet. As collectors and stewards of a community's material culture, they maintain its valuable objects.

D. **Enhancing public knowledge** (43) indicators monitor the research contributions a museum makes to the body of public and professional information, innovation, and scholarship, and its access by individuals, the community, and the economy. Fifteen of the indicators refer specifically to a museum's contributions to scholarship. Reputation refers to the museum's trusted expertise and the quality of museum staff, exhibitions, and collections. Research museums have contributed knowledge to art history, biology, botany, history, and anthropology for a long time. More recently, museums have been researching learning in their informal environments and publishing their results.

E. **Serving the educational system** (56) indicators monitor potential museum impacts to both formal education (schools) and museum professionals through student programs, educational initiatives and campaigns, STEM (Science, Technology, Engineering and Mathematics) learning, literacy, school partnerships, and resources for educators. Most museums have relationships with schools, and students represent some share of their audience.

F. **Advancing social change** (40) indicators monitor a museum's potential impacts in leading people and communities to make changes deemed beneficial by society, such as addressing social problems, health initiatives, global environmental conservation, education initiatives, social justice, human rights, tolerance, fairness and equality, anti-discrimination, poverty, and reflecting on lessons from the past to envision new ways of living in the future (Museums Association 2013). Because museums are well respected and trusted, taking a stand on an issue has impact: When the Peoria Riverfront Museum chose to build adhering to LEED environmental standards, the Caterpillar Visitor Center, built adjacent to the museum, followed its example.

G. **Communicating public identity and image** (27) indicators monitor potential museum impacts that help a region, a community, or individuals think about, discuss, develop, and communicate their desired identity and image. At the city level, a museum can serve as a symbol, a statement of pride, an affirmation of a culture, and a reflection of local priorities. At an individual level, a museum can become an important personal relationship, a symbol of who we are, a part of our identity, and a brand we trust. The Tech Museum of Innovation is a symbol for Silicon Valley, and its members and supporters include individuals who identify with technology.

Private Impacts—Benefits to Businesses, Government, and the Economy

H. **Contributing to the economy** (85) indicators monitor the museum's contributions to the regional and local economy by motivating tourism, increasing land and tax values, direct spending, neighborhood development, providing jobs, and developing the workforce and the quality of life. Workforce development (e.g., inspiring tomorrow's scientists, building twenty-first-century skills, priming the pipeline, and attracting and retaining a qualified workforce) is a driver of corporate partnerships for STEM and youth museum projects. Blockbuster touring exhibitions can have an impact on a city's tourism economy, and new museums have improved neighborhoods. Generally, a museum's economic impact supports businesses and governments, and, in a ripple effect, generates jobs and incremental taxes.

I. **Delivering corporate community services** (9) indicators monitor potential museum impacts to businesses that are fulfilling their community service responsibilities, networking with other civic leaders, or associating their brand with the museum through sponsorships, and providing value to their employees by giving them museum access privileges. Corporations want improvements in the quality of life, and they collaborate with others to address significant social problems; museums can be effective partners to implement defined programs to address these needs.

Personal Impacts—Benefits to Individuals, Families, and Social Groups

J. **Enabling personal growth** (147) indicators monitor the benefits individuals and families get from their museum engagements that help them grow in abilities, awareness, and understanding. Enabling personal growth has the most indicators of the twelve external potential museum impacts, reflecting the museum field's focus on providing value to its free-choice audiences. Personal growth in museums can happen in many ways, and the most pervasive indicators in this category relate to learning, again reflecting the field's commitment as places of informal learning and to AAM's priorities for education (Hirzy 2008). Museums can help people learn and develop their capacities, knowledge, perspectives, sense of relevance, and social and family insights. This area also includes the intrinsic benefits a museum can provide its visitors and program participants, such as affirmation, belonging, enlightenment, excitement, awe, insight, joy, perspective, reflection, satisfaction, and meaning. Museums can engage individuals in worthy purposes through volunteer opportunities.

K. **Offering personal respite** (4) indicators monitor the benefits individuals and families get from museum engagements that help them find comfort, spend time alone safely and quietly, or get away from their daily pressures.

L. **Welcoming personal leisure** (11) indicators monitor the benefits individuals, groups, and families get from their museum engagements that help them relax, have fun, and be entertained. These services are also offered by theme parks, movie theaters, and other entertainment centers.

Institutional Impacts—Benefits to the Museum Itself

M. **Helping museum operations** (308) indicators monitor the museum's yearly operating activities. Some are used for accounting and for assessing performance and efficiency. The data in these indicators tend to change periodically, and are reported on at least yearly; some are reflected in a museum's statement of activities for a fiscal year. There are more indicators monitoring museum operations than any other area, reflecting a natural preoccupation with how the museum and its staff, collections, facilities, and budgets are running. Revenues, expenses, human resource data, attendance, activity listings, management culture, marketing, performance, and value judgments characterize this area of indicators.

N. **Building museum capital** (87) indicators monitor the museum's long-term resources and assets, both tangible (facilities, endowment) and intangible (brand reputation, type of museum, long-term partnerships); these categories list what the museum is and has. Some of these indicators are reflected in balance statements. These indicators tally capital assets, listings of community resources, and public impact components; track capital campaigns, governance and parent organizations, institutional data (address, formal name, tax code) long-term community trust, in-house expertise, and management culture; and provide counts of collections, square feet of space, acres of land, and dollars in reserve.

DATA CONTENT TOPICS

MIIP can also be analyzed by looking at the content of the indicators. Among the 1,025 indicators, there are also sixty data content topics, many with sub-topics—what data is this indicator measuring? There are data content topics with many indicators, such as the sixty-nine indicators of learning, and yet others where a few indicators are the sole evidence in the sample of a potential museum service, such as mourning. This distinctive impact only needs to show up once to be listed, though its degree of pervasiveness in the sample will be low; mourning is an intentional purpose for some museums, such as memorials, and many other museums have instances where they have helped people in grief. Learning, however, is much more pervasive as a museum impact in MIIP 1.0 than mourning. In Appendix C, the data content topics are shown under each impact. The top ten, starting with the most frequently appearing data content, are: revenue; learning; economic impact; resources; value judgment; attendance; intrinsic value; management culture; collection objects, and community connections.

CONCLUSION

This chapter follows a research question—what potential impacts and benefits can museums provide their communities and for which audiences and supporters?—from the research methodology to the findings and to an organizing framework.

How can museums serve? The research question reveals a wealth of precedented impacts across a spectrum of beneficiaries. Analysis of the indicators reveals many potential benefits and impacts collected into fourteen broad, umbrella Categories of Potential Museum Impacts. This finding and the summarization of the many into manageable categories provide museums with a way to think about their desired impacts and the public with a way to appreciate a museum's many possible contributions.

The second part of this book turns the MIIP database from a research and analysis resource into a practical tool for museum professionals. A word of caution in this respect. Several of the sources propose ready-made packages of indicators for institutional evaluation, such as the "25 Indicators of Success" used by the Indianapolis Children's Museum in 1999 (Source #13). "Number of objects from the total collection used in any media during the year" (#443) and "Number of trustees/advisors who attend board meetings" (#444) are two examples from those twenty-five indicators that indicate activity and operating data, respectively, but that could become planning objectives once a base year is established and staff are expected to better last year's results: more objects from the collection; higher trustee attendance.

However, achieving certain metrics should not become the de facto purposes of a museum. Rather, the museum needs to actually improve the world, and to select metrics that are meaningful indicators of its achievements. Museums should also use other ways of assessing their results periodically as a double check. The Theory of Action allows a museum to track its purposes through to its impacts, selecting indicators to monitor each step along the way, and the Categories of Potential Museum Impacts offer museums reminders of the many ways they could have impact.

The next chapter connects the Theory of Action with the Categories of Potential Museum Impacts both to integrate Part 1: Theory, and to provide the foundation for Part 2: Practice.

NOTE

1. The ICOM definition used in this book specifies nonprofit, which excludes commercial, for-profit museums.

REFERENCES

Hirzy, Ellen Cochran. *Excellence and Equity Education and the Public Dimension of Museums*. American Alliance of Museums, 2008.

Holden, John. "Capturing Cultural Value." *Demos* (2004). Accessed November 4, 2014. http://www.demos.co.uk/files/CapturingCulturalValue.pdf.

Museums Association. "Museums Change Lives." July 2013. Accessed November 4, 2014. http://www.museumsassociation.org/download?id=1001738.

Weil, Stephen. *Making Museums Matter*. Washington, D.C.: Smithsonian Institution, 2002.

CHAPTER 3

MEASURING IMPACT

What are some of the implications and logical corollaries of the Museum Theory of Action and the analysis of MIIP 1.0 on measuring impact?

This chapter applies the concepts in the previous two chapters to the question of how to measure impact, setting the stage for the next part of the book. After a review of the last two chapters, this chapter considers evidence of value, distinguishes between value and worth and between impact and benefit, explores free-choice exchanges of time, effort, and money as measures of impact, describes the benefits of tracking measurements, and explores using quantitative key performance indicators to evaluate qualitative impacts. While consistent with the theory developed in chapters 1 and 2, some of these thoughts may be challenging to conventional museum practice.

Measuring impact, while an appealing goal conceptually, is challenging to do head-on, as the basic definitions and methods have eluded the museum field: What impacts? On whom? How do we quantify and then measure impacts?

Because these challenges are real, this evaluation framework does not attempt to measure impact directly, but instead to observe quantitative indicators that an impact might be occurring and then track changes to those indicators over time and in comparison to peer museums. The process suggests periodic evaluations to validate or amend the meaningfulness of a measure as an indicator of an impact.

REVIEW OF THE MUSEUM THEORY OF ACTION

The previous chapters and their detailed appendixes B and C show the results of tagging each indicator with its step location, its primary potential impact, and its data content.

The Museum Theory of Action diagram in chapter 1 follows the sequence of a classic logic model (see table 1.3). In table 3.1, the Theory of Action is revised to loop back to the beginning, with feedback cycles even within the seven steps; this two-way version puts more emphasis on the value exchanges between the museum and its audiences and supporters.

The museum evaluates the outputs and outcomes of all its activities in order to prove and improve their efficiency and effectiveness at delivering the museum's intentional purposes. The theory assumes that the community's needs drive a museum's *intentional purposes*, and that the museum, honoring its *guiding principles*, uses its *resources* to deliver its programs and *activities*, which generate *operating and evaluation data*, and, if all goes well, result in outcomes, *impacts*, and *perceived benefits* by the museum's *community* and its *audiences* and *supporters*. This sequence loops back to the museum's intentions, as the community and its audiences and supporters express their needs through their votes of time, effort, and money, which influence the museum's decisions, starting the cycle over again in a constantly

Table 3.1. Museum Theory of Action: Two-way Version

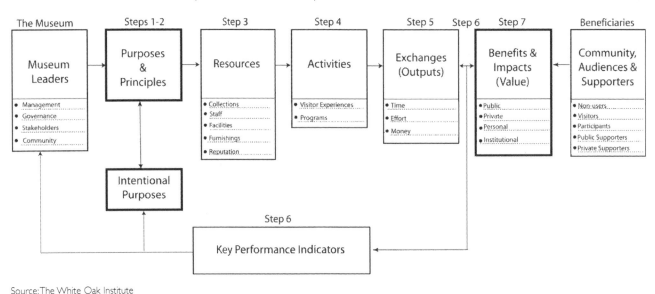

Source: The White Oak Institute

evolving alignment of museum purposes and community needs. *Key performance indicators* (KPIs) evaluate the efficiency and effectiveness of the cycle.

Step 7, at the far right of the action line, contains the results of the museum's activities. These are also called *ends*, *outcomes*, *impacts*, and *benefits*. In Step 1, the museum states its *intentional purposes* and lists the *desired impacts* it hopes to find at the end of the Theory of Action, in Step 7. Step 7 also contains the community's, audiences', and supporters' *perceived benefits*. In short, Step 7 indicators hold both the museum's desired impacts and the beneficiaries' perceived benefits. Management can investigate the alignment between these two subsets. Because of the looping aspect of the Theory of Action, all Step 7 indicators could align back to Step 1, the museum's purposes. For instance, if your museum is delivering some significant perceived benefit such as popular traveling exhibitions, but your purposes seem to be ignoring it, you can decide whether you should become less or more intentional about delivering that benefit.

The listing of a museum's potential impacts in chapter 2—fourteen areas of impact organized into four markets (see table 2.1) with sixty data content topics (see table C.2 in Appendix C), organized into seven steps along the Museum Theory of Action—illustrates the complexity Weil discusses in the quote opening chapter 1. Yet even this long listing will never be complete.

MIIP 1.0 does not claim to be comprehensive; its fifty-one sources and 1,025 indicators are a generous sampling of the museum field's best indicators, but there are many others. This analysis makes no judgments about the quality, usefulness, or practicality of the indicators, though they all come from reputable expert sources. Hence, some of the indicators may be meaningful and others not, and there are bound to be many missing indicators. Research and experience will assess the usefulness of any indicator, and new, better indicators will be developed. In time, MIIP 1.0 can grow, and museums can refine their indicator selection. The evaluation framework itself—the Museum Theory of Action—is also likely to need adjustment:

Discovering that a theory is not quite right should not discourage program personnel. A program theory serves many purposes. It helps clarify how a program is expected to work, it helps focus the evaluation on key results, and it provides structure to the interpretation of results. In the end, whether or not the theory is right, it will have provided a framework for thinking about how the program is working. (Birckmayer and Weiss 2000)

EVIDENCE OF VALUE

The call for evidence of the value of museums as a way to defend traditional revenue sources and attract new ones has led key museum thinkers to keep up the pressure on empirical evidence of our outcomes and cumulative impact, and to change the game from judging worthiness to measuring value:

> Pressured into delivering against social and economic policy objectives and required to justify their existence in terms specified by funding bodies, the museum sector has often found itself in a reactive position, struggling to articulate the value of museums amidst pressures to define it in the utilitarian terms of economic and social policy. (Scott 2007)

Many relevant efforts deal with measuring value in other fields. For instance: the Library Use Value Calculator, first developed by the Massachusetts Library Association; the Strategic Triangle (Moore 1995); the Balanced Scorecard (Kaplan and Norton 2001), and the program evaluation criteria of major funders such as NSF, NIH, NEA, Kresge, and IMLS. Public tax records, such as the U.S. federal tax 990 forms and the requirement for audited financial statements, may offer ways to measure impact and performance if adapted to the museum field's unique needs for institutional measurement.

WORTH AND VALUE

Merriam-Webster defines *worth* as "a fair return or equivalent in goods, services or money for something exchanged; the monetary worth of something: market price." Michael Porter's concept for an organization's unique value proposition (UVP) equates market price, value, and intrinsic worth (Porter 1985). Other definitions also equate economic value, worth, and price, but for many, these are loaded terms with different meanings in different contexts for different viewpoints.

Weil focused on *worthiness* with the strong feeling that some museums were more worthy than others because they were more purposeful and better performing at achieving their purpose (Weil 2005).

However, worthiness is tricky territory. Are art museums more worthy than sports halls of fame? Is support for schoolchildren more worthy than support for tourism? Is a Bible-based creationist museum more worthy than a science-based natural history museum? Your answers will be shaped by your world view, and other world views may define worthiness differently.

Fortunately, this rancorous and groundless argument is neither necessary nor useful to the process because we can measure impact, benefit, and performance without trying to judge worthiness. Both the art museum and the sports museum need ways to measure their impacts; others can decide on the relative worthiness of those impacts.

Instead of worth, this book considers the *value* of a museum's impacts and benefits. A discussion of value has to start with the question "of value to whom?" For instance, a visitor's experience in a museum exhibition has a value to that visitor, and exposing that visitor to the content of that exhibition has a value to some supporters and possibly to the greater community.

Value is in the eye of the beholder, not in the mind of the owner. A museum cannot set its own value, but it can measure indicators of its value to its community, audiences, and supporters.

A museum's value lies in its impacts, says Weil (2005). However, the museum's value is actually expressed in terms of the value of the benefits. Since value is in the eye of the beholder, any valuation must first track the value the community and its audiences and supporters place on their perceived benefits, and then see if those findings relate to measuring the museum's desired impacts.

MUSEUMS ARE OF VALUE BECAUSE OF THEIR IMPACTS AND BENEFITS

Museums spend $21 billion annually in the United States and employ 400,000 people (Merritt and Katz 2009). This outflow of money can also be viewed as a roughly equal inflow, since museums tend to zero out differences: The United States receives enough benefit from the activities generated by 400,000 museum professionals to value the collective impact of U.S. museums at $21 billion annually. Doing the math using IMLS's last trustworthy museum count of 17,500, the economic value of an average museum's annual impacts was at least $1,200,000 in 2009.

There is now sufficient data on U.S. museums that quantitative assessments of changes in some values to some of the markets can be measured. The tangible aspects of a museum's value can be measured even if the intangible aspects remain immeasurable.

We can never know, much less measure, a museum's total impact or its total value. We can, however, measure many of its outputs and some of its outcomes, and identify indicators of the value of its impacts and benefits to different markets. Once we accept the assumption that a museum has some total value, even if we can't measure all of it, then we can search for change indicators, and, by observing those change indicators over time, use that information to manage a museum's evolving value proactively.

IMPACT AND BENEFIT

The activities the museum operates may result in *impacts on others* and *benefits to others*. Most impacts, we hope, will be beneficial, but others, such as a museum's carbon footprint, may not be.

Outcomes, ends, and impacts are words for the changes that the museum is making (or wants to make) in individuals and in society, with the underlying hypothesis that the museum is the active agent implementing these changes. Prepositions matter in their distinction: Outcomes result *from* the museum's activities, and impacts are *on* the museum's community, audiences, and supporters.

A museum aspires to have *impacts* on its community, audiences, and supporters. The community, audiences, and supporters receive *benefits* from the museum. The benefits can be different from the impacts: A family visiting an aquarium receives the benefit of a quality family experience, while the aquarium's impact on the family is to heighten their awareness of conserving biodiversity. Or, the benefits and impacts can be aligned: New parents bring their toddler to a children's museum to see her develop and learn with new kinds of challenges; the children's museum's mission is child development. Studying the alignment between a museum's benefits and impacts may illuminate potentials and inefficiencies. It is useful to remember the distinction, which hinges again on their prepositions: Society, individuals, and organizations receive benefits *from* the museum. The museum has impacts *on* society, individuals, and organizations. Benefits are in the eyes of the beneficiary; impacts are in the desires of the museum. When the desired impact is the same as the perceived benefit, such as the children's museum example where both the museum and the visitor want child development, the impact and the benefit are aligned. When they are different, such as the aquarium example, they are unaligned.

When the perceived benefit aligns with the museum's desired impact, then the value of the benefit is proportional to the value of the impact, and measures of changes to the value of the benefit may also indicate changes to the value of the impact. How does the children's museum measure its desired impact on child development? If the museum knows its family audience visits the museum in part to develop their children and that they leave satisfied that the visit helped their children develop, then the museum can track changes in audience behavior—more or less visits, repeats, time on-site, spending, etc.—as indicators of changes to the museum's impact on child development.

What about the aquarium, where the visiting family's benefit is different from the aquarium's desired impact? In this case, audience behavior data alone does not indicate that the museum is having any impact on conserving biodiversity. However, if formal evaluation studies determine that some portion of the sample audiences experience biodiversity attitude and awareness impacts, then changes in attendance and dwell time may indicate changes in biodiversity impact.

MUSEUM ENGAGEMENTS AS EXCHANGES OF TIME, EFFORT, AND MONEY

Museums are free-choice options in a busy and highly competitive market. While there are certainly some museum engagements where people are forced to visit, such as students on school field trips and subordinate employees attending a corporate event, most people and organizations freely choose to engage with a museum. Even line-item funding established by legislation is open to legislators' votes and, hence, to the swings of politics and the economy, as many museums found during the Great Recession (2008–2009). Because so many other leisure-time options are available to residents of the world's cities, the choices to visit count as a kind of evidence, what Scott and Holden call *use value*, whereby the simple fact that people use public institutions is evidence of their public value (Scott 2007, 5).

Money is not the only currency in the marketplace, and the time and effort spent by the museum's visitors, participants, and supporters are also indicators of the value they place on the benefits they receive from their museum engagements. Our community and its audiences and supporters exchange their money, effort, and time for museum engagements that result in *perceived benefits*.

Money has its limits as an indicator of value. Many of the world's great museums are free to visitors, and many other urban museums offer free days and access policies. Free access is a clear public value. Museum expert Elaine Gurian makes a compelling social justice argument that museums should be free if we truly want to remove barriers to universal access and to claim that we are community gathering places, which we cannot claim if it costs money (Gurian 2005). Progressive museums like the Exploratorium (San Francisco) treasure and support their free-access audiences as closest to their mission. During a 2013 ASTC session, Dennis Bartels, head of the Exploratorium, explained their strategy of high prices for tourists that offset their subsidized prices for residents and free access programs for underserved audiences.

Free admission in return for consumer data is an Internet business model that might benefit some museums. In a *Fortune* article, Amy Langfield reported: "The Dallas Museum of Art eliminated its $10 general admission . . . and saw annual attendance jump to 668,000 from 498,000. . . . The museum has seen a 29% increase in minorities visitors" (Langfield 2015). Admissions revenue must have declined, though clearly the museum's public value increased.

Time and effort are particularly important for museums and can be more challenging to attract than money. The indicator that free access is a public value is that the public actually uses the privilege to visit the museum. The indicator that the Dallas Museum of Art's public value increased is that 34 percent more people made an effort to visit. All museum engagements require time, and all physical museum engagements require effort. The time is indicated by the total minutes of a museum engagement. The effort embraces all the logistics and stress of traveling to the museum or to a museum-sponsored off-site program. The cumulative number of person-trips provisionally indicates effort. "Provisionally" recognizes that each person-trip involves different amounts of effort, and that we need to search for better metrics. It takes much more effort for an immigrant, multi-generational family living in the fringes of a foreign city to travel to a museum than it takes the tourist couple staying at a nearby hotel.

Time is also valued differently by these two audiences: An immigrant family may have only their Sunday together, and the traditions that affirm their culture take up much of the day, leaving precious little time for museum visits. The retired couple has time on their hands. Effort and time can be barriers as well as money.

One of the great promises of museums on the Internet and mobile devices is the significant reduction in the amount of money, effort, and time needed for virtual museum engagements. Outreach programs bring the museum out to neighborhoods and schools, reducing barriers. The challenges lie in physical engagements within museums; these real-time encounters with unique collection objects and museum staff require audience time, effort, and often money. What do our audiences get in exchange? The proof that they get benefits of some sort is if they keep coming and keep spending their time, effort, and money.

In order to understand the simple numbers of our annual exchange totals—the amounts of money, effort, and time that our community and its audiences and supporters devote to a museum's activities each year in return for the benefits they receive—we need evaluation studies, surveys, and conversations to understand why each of the main sectors made those exchanges.

In a competitive, free-choice marketplace, these exchanges are evidence of the value a museum's community and its audiences and supporters place on their museum engagements in comparison to all the other competing visitor experiences, program studios, volunteer opportunities, charitable causes, and grant applications out there. Museums have to compete by offering activities that attract money, effort, and time. This is hard work and requires the best talents and other resources to deliver compelling benefits and competitive value.

This imperative that museum engagements must deliver value to our community and its audiences and supporters can be restated more constructively: The amounts of money, effort, and time that our community and its audiences and supporters spend on us are evidence and indicators of our value to them. A track record of such exchanges proves that a museum delivers competitive perceived benefits. Of course, these exchange numbers get more revealing when we can look at changes in these amounts over time and in comparison to peer museums. Such processes are the focus of the second part of this book.

WHO PAYS FOR COMMUNITY IMPACT?

Of the 660 indicators of external impact in MIIP 1.0, 404 relate to public values from impacts that museums want to have on their communities at large; impacts on the community get twice the attention paid to audiences and supporters combined. When the museum authors mentioned in chapter 1 write about museum value, they are writing about *public value*, or the value of a museum to society and its community. In the Categories of Potential Museum Impacts (see table 2.1), the public impacts include broadening participation, preserving heritage, strengthening social capital, enhancing public knowledge, serving education, advancing social change, and communicating public identity and image.

These seven categories of public impacts are like motherhood and apple pie, but who pays for them?

There are some museum governance structures where the answer is direct. In government-, tribal-, and university-owned museums, where the community is defined by the funding source, the annual value of the museum's community impacts is supposed to be at least what the community is putting in. Muzeo (Anaheim, California) is a municipal museum funded by the city to attract vitality downtown and to add quality of life for the city's residents. The Hood Museum (Hanover, New Hampshire), run by Dartmouth College, serves teachers and students as an educational resource and enriches the cultural life of this college town. The Smithsonian plays a central role in U.S. and even global culture, preserving heritage, enhancing public knowledge, and building national identity; it is funded primarily by federal tax dollars. These funding sources are committed to serving their communities as a whole; often laws or policy preclude them from benefiting individuals or private parties, so their funding must be dedicated to the greater social good.

Many museums, however, are independent 501(c)(3)s without a university, tribe, or government to underwrite operations. While some of these independent museums have had public taxpayer funds, AAM graphs the share of all museums' operating budgets that comes from public sources as line declining since at least the 1970s (Merritt and Katz 2009). Independent museums are caught in a squeeze: declining public funds at a time of increasing demands for public impacts and benefits to the community as a whole.

The same AAM graph shows that private support funds have made up the difference, and museums have turned to their private supporters (donors, corporate sponsors, private foundations, fundraising events, etc.) to pay for community impacts, while continuing to advocate for their remaining public funds. Together, a museum's private and public supporters pay for the museum's community impacts and benefits.

The business sector, including regional corporations, businesses, and their supporting government agencies and NGOs, funds museum community impacts that support their larger interests: contributing to the economy and delivering corporate community services.

Audiences also help, but their value exchanges with the museum are primarily for personal benefits and impacts: enabling personal growth, offering personal respite, and welcoming personal leisure.

If a museum runs on only earned revenue from its audiences, does it still have an obligation to deliver community impacts? Technically, yes: The nonprofit status comes with an obligation to provide public service, but if no one is funding public impacts, then the spirit to make the world better loses to the marketplace realities of providing valued personal benefits to the museum's only paying audiences. Yet even the mythical all-earned-revenue museum could have enough impacts on its audiences that the greater community may come to benefit, or, inspiring just one Nobel Prize winner may transform a region's economy.

Pursuing unfunded mandates can be presumptuous of museum leadership: How can they be certain they know what impacts the community needs unless they are getting some verification in the form of community support? Exploris opened in Raleigh (North Carolina) in 1999 as a new $40 million museum and global learning center. Its founder had served in the Peace Corps before running a successful business. The purpose was to increase understanding of global cultures, with the desired impact that visitors, especially teens, would develop respect and empathy for peoples around the world. This noble cause was able to raise the capital, but the audience did not show up (teens are very hard for any museum to attract), and other supporters found other causes more pressing. Exploris closed in 2007.[1]

Said another way, the community did not sufficiently value Exploris's impacts or benefits to sustain its operation. Conversely, a museum that *does* sustain funding from public and private supporters has evidence that experts (donors, grant officers, legislative staff, etc.) believe the museum is having a valuable impact on the community.

BENEFITS OF MEASUREMENT

How will measurements be useful? The benefits of defining ways to measure changes to the value of a museum's impact on others and its benefit to others, and of assessing performance by the museum can be understood by taking a leap of imagination over the hurdles of logistics, politics, and established procedures to a bright future when:

- Museums will have hard data and clear evidence of the annual changes in their impact, benefits, and performance measured by their selection of key performance indicators (KPIs).
- Museums will have dashboards of their unique mix of key performance indicators with reliable, meaningful data that management can use to constantly tune and steer the institution's resources to more effectively and efficiently achieve the museum's evolving purposes.
- Museums will share data with their comparable peers, which will help identify and celebrate best practices, provide motivation and role models for low-performing museums to improve, and establish networks for sharing practice, programs, and exhibitions.

While this rosy future drives us forward, what can we do now? This is frontier territory for museums. We will not have all the tools we want, and we already have a lot to do just to survive. However, we are resourceful, and museums now have enough data and networks to start developing a culture of measuring and demonstrating our public, private, and personal values. The measurements we already have can help us improve both impact and performance.

Jim Collins, the business guru and author of *Good to Great*, when he addressed the Association of Children's Museums Conference in 2008, observed that like great corporations, great museums will be the ones that set goals and measure results, achieving sustainability and growth by managing KPIs. Without KPIs, museums will not be able to move with assurance from good to great, advises Collins.

Some reliable indicators of museum impact already exist. We have economic impact studies, visitor satisfaction surveys, and many summative evaluation studies that document evidence of learning outcomes from specific exhibitions, films, after-school workshops, and other programs. A national study by Britain Thinks conducted with the Museums Association (UK) found that Britons valued their national museums for a wide range of benefits (MIIP 1.0 indicators #698–#706). Many respondents saw museums as beneficial both to them as individuals and to society (Britain Thinks 2013).

Standardization is most needed at the data field level—museums should agree on the definition of such data fields as on-site visits, full-time equivalent employees (FTEs), and facility size, for example. However, museums do not yet need to agree on KPIs, which are calculations and formulas involving data fields. As we move toward the evident benefits of meeting Weil's challenge to agree on ways to measure our impact, we must also pay attention to his warning: "One caution should be noted: a museum might be better off with no system in place for gauging its impact than with a bad one that uses an inappropriate set of measures" (Weil 2003, 53). To avoid this, each museum needs to support data field standardization, but thoughtfully decide which of those data fields are important to them and select its own set of appropriate KPIs, lest others impose bad ones. For instance, museums should count on-site visitors the same way, but each museum has to decide if that count is important to them and whether they want to include that data field in any of their KPI calculations.

USING KEY PERFORMANCE INDICATORS (KPIs) AS INDICATORS OF IMPACTS

The number and variety of a museum's social outcomes are too daunting to count from the bottom up. It is impractical to conduct evaluation studies of every program the museum runs every year, but we can look at the totality and at the institutional impact. This shifts the evaluation process from "what is the outcome of a program on each individual?" to "what is the impact of a museum on its society?"

We can look at how the museum performs as a community resource in total—all its exhibits and other programs—by looking at its overall institutional operating data.

A careful selection of key performance indicators can become a meaningful management dashboard. KPIs can combine quantitative operating, evaluation, and market data into formulas that track the relationships of data fields over time. For instance, the number of teachers electing to bring their students to a museum (operating data) divided by the teacher population (market data) results in a market index KPI; factor that by the ratio of repeating teachers to get a satisfaction KPI. Of course, many other factors may be at work, and periodic evaluation needs to test the validity of such indicators.

Some KPIs may be able to indicate that the museum is achieving its desired impacts, even though the KPIs are based on output counts from activities. Using the previous example, if we assume teachers are expert educators, then their repeated selection of the museum is an indicator of an expert community's assessment of the museum's educational value compared to their other options. KPIs that might act as impact indicators are potentially new evaluation tools for measuring impacts.

Some KPIs in MIIP 1.0 can be restated as desired impacts. "Ranking by schoolteachers as important to them in the classroom" (#393) is a perceived benefit that can be restated as a desired impact: "We desire to be important to schoolteachers." The Net Promoter Score (#641) is an indicator of visitors' perceived benefits that can be restated as a desired impact: "We desire visitors to recommend us to others."

As discussed in chapter 1, the Theory of Action is continuous, and the indicators in the border zones are worthy of study. This is particularly true of the border between Step 6 KPIs and Step 7 perceived benefits. The examples below are in this interesting border zone where output numbers from certain sources may indicate benefits and impacts. These borderline KPIs are labeled "Step 6b KPI: May indicate impact." Step 6a KPIs tend to be purely operational, like the ratio of child to adult ticket sales, but Step 6b KPIs, while still quantitative calculations based on operating data, may indicate impacts and performance. The number of peer-reviewed journal articles per museum curator is mathematically a KPI based on output counts, but changes in the number may also be a good indicator of changes to the museum's contributions to public knowledge, one of the fourteen impact categories.

The Step 6b subset of indicators may be promising ways to evaluate outcomes and impacts using quantitative evaluation, operating and market data. Once we respect the professionalism and responsibility with which our community and its audiences and supporters make their decisions, and once we accept that we must compete for their decisions, then some of the following KPIs might be found to be valid indicators of outcomes and hence, impacts in their expert eyes, despite the KPI's reliance on numeric data. A selection from the seventy-seven indicators in MIIP 1.0 tagged as "KPIs that may indicate impact" follows (see Appendix B for indicator sources, listed by number).

KPIs such as these are based on annual operating data and quantitative surveys. In many cases they count the actual behaviors of experts at what their constituents need, be they teachers, foundation program officers, partner organizations, or committed member parents.

While changes to these and similar KPIs hold promise of measuring changes to impacts, this big data needs small data. The validity of output-based indicators (big data) must be tested periodically by evaluation studies (small data) to make sure changes they record are due mostly to changes in the intended impact, rather than mostly to marketing promotions, new competition, or school budget changes. Realistically, a change in any one indicator is influenced by several factors. Volunteer hours may be up because of the increased perceived value of the museum's volunteer opportunities, but some part of the increase may be due to a new shuttle from a senior center. Managers need sensitivity to accommodate external factors and take care not to assume full responsibility for a changed indicator. KPIs are only indicators of impacts, and then they are open to external variables, hence imperfect.

KPIs THAT MAY INDICATE IMPACT

Broadening Participation

"Percentage of employees from minority groups managing two or more staff members" (#327)

"Extent of alignment of visitor demographics with demographics of local population" (#382)

Strengthening Social Capital

"How many partnerships with other organizations do you manage simultaneously?" (#544)

"How much time per month does your professional staff spend on community affairs as members of service organizations, municipal boards, nonprofit boards, or volunteer organizations?" (#557)

Enhancing Public Knowledge

"Articles per staff member—2.73 at NHM" (#997)

"Number and value of museum/university projects funded by research grants" (#659)

Serving Education

"Ranking by schoolteachers as important to them in the classroom" (#393)

"How many calls or after-school visits per month do you receive from schoolchildren working on school assignments?" (#522)

"Teacher professional development offered by the center is in demand" (#640)

Contributing to the Economy

"Number of international tourists annually" (#657)

Enabling Personal Growth

"Percentage of visitors who would rank visit as exceeding expectations" (#390)

"Net Promoter Score—likelihood to recommend" (#641)

"Number of visits per visitor per year" (#667)

"Diligent visitors (%DV) is the percentage of visitors in the tracked sample who stopped at more than one-half of the exhibit elements in the exhibition" (#681)

"Sweep rate index (SRI) is calculated by dividing the exhibition's square footage by the average total time spent there for a tracked sample of casual visitors" (#685)

Building Museum Capital

"Endowment change through new gifts and endowment growth" (#433)

"Changes in unrestricted net assets after depreciation" (#829)

Surveys and focus groups also have their issues, as do all methods of social outcome research (Mulgan 2010).

To mitigate these issues, museums need checks and balances, such as using open-ended evaluation to illuminate quantitative operating data. The processes in this book urge you to use multiple perspectives and multiple measures in order to accommodate the complexity of museum impacts and the likelihood that any single perspective or measure may be misleading in some degree. We need to test each KPI (big data) periodically using evaluation studies (small data) to see if changes in the big data actually correlate with changes in the impact. This distills to a mantra for museum evaluation: *Measure constantly; validate periodically.*

Key performance indicators are accepted as indicators of performance in the corporate world and in other nonprofit fields, but in the museum field, using KPIs as indicators of impact will be innovative (Lee and Linett 2013). While evaluation is still the most trusted way to measure a specific program's outcomes against its objectives, KPIs may be better at measuring the volume of outcomes and at observing and documenting trends and changes in a museum's annual impacts.

CONCLUSION

People and organizations pay money, spend time, and make efforts to engage with a museum in return for the impacts and benefits they receive. The cumulative exchanges of their time, efforts, and revenues are indicators of the cumulative value received.

Of these three value indicators, the money exchanges are most thoroughly and accurately counted. This does not mean that revenues are better indicators than time or effort, or more meaningful, but it does mean that revenue data are more consistent, accurate, third-party verified, and comparable than data tracking effort and dwell time. Data about the effort our audiences and supporters spend on museums is improving in quality and consistency. Attendance, as an indicator of effort, has long been used to rank a city's museums in popularity, and attendance is a driver of many other museum programs, like membership and retail sales. It is not the only metric, however.

A thoughtful process of harnessing operating data to evolve and improve museum impact and performance will have many benefits for a museum, for its professional staff, and for the museum field as a whole: evidence of changes in impact and performance, a dashboard of KPIs to inform decisions, and a network of museums sharing data and best practices.

Key performance indicators, based on operating, evaluation, and market data, are promising indicators of impact, provided they are periodically tested and evaluated for accuracy and meaningfulness.

Part 1 of this book explores the museum field's rich literature and wisdom to find an underlying Theory of Action, to identify fourteen categories of potential impact, and to observe some corollaries and implications. Of what practical use is the analysis and theory developed in this part 1? What are the next steps? Part 2 of this book transitions from the theory in part 1 to the practice in part 2 with its step-by-step process for using these tools. MIIP 1.0 was developed for the research, but it can also serve you as a tool, and the Theory of Action can serve as your organizing and evaluation framework.

NOTE

1. The building was converted into a children's museum in 2007—the Marbles Kids Museum (Raleigh, NC). The author's company consulted briefly with Exploris to try to adjust their budget expectations.

REFERENCES

Birckmayer, Johanna D., and Carol Hirschon Weiss. "Theory-Based Evaluation in Practice: What Do We Learn?" *Evaluation Review* 24, no. 4 (August 2000): 407–31.

Britain Thinks. *Public Perceptions of—and Attitudes to—the Purposes of Museums in Society.* Britain Thinks for Musuems Association, 2013.

Gurian, E. H. "Free at Last: A Case for Eliminating Admission Charges in Museums." *Museum News* 84, no. 5 (September/October 2005).

Kaplan, R., and D. Norton. *The Strategy-Focused Organization: How Balanced Scorecard Companies Thrive in the New Business Environment.* Boston: Harvard Business School, 2001.

Langfield, Amy. "Art Museums Find Going Free Comes with a Cost." *Fortune,* June 1, 2015. http://fortune.com/2015/06/01/free-museums.

Lee, Sarah, and Peter Linett. "New Data Directions for the Cultural Landscape: Toward a Better-Informed, Stronger Sector." *Cultural Data Project* (now DataArts) December 2013. Accessed October 8, 2014. http://www.culturaldata.org/wp-content/uploads/new-data-directions-for-the-cultural-landscape-a-report-by-slover-linett-audience-research-for-the-cultural-data-project_final.pdf.

Merritt, Elizabeth E., and Philip M. Katz. *Museum Financial Information 2009.* American Association of Museums, August 1, 2009.

Moore, M. *Creating Public Value: Strategic Management in Government.* Cambridge: Harvard University Press, 1995.

Mulgan, Geoff. *Measuring Social Value.* Summer 2010. Accessed November 4, 2014. http://www.ssireview.org/pdf/2010SU-Feature_Mulgan.pdf.

Porter, Michael E. *Competitive Advantage: Creating and Sustaining Superior Performance.* New York: Simon and Schuster, 1985.

Scott, Carol. "Advocating the Value of Museums." *INTERCOM.* August 2007. Accessed November 4, 2014. http://www.intercom.museum/documents/CarolScott.pdf.

Weil, Stephen. "Beyond Big & Awesome Outcome-Based Evaluation." *Museum News* (November/December 2003): 40–45, 52–53.

———. "A Success/Failure Matrix for Museums." *Museum News* (January/February 2005): 36–40.

PART II

PRACTICE

How Do You Measure Your Museum's Impact and Performance?

CHAPTER 4

SHIFT FROM THEORY TO PRACTICE

How can museum professionals apply these theories to museum practice? How do we go about measuring impact and performance?

This second part of the book presents ways to measure changes in impact and ways to compare performance. Both parts share theory, data definitions, and museum-wide frameworks, and both parts are content neutral, allowing a museum to count what it believes is important and to weigh performance scores according to its priorities.

This chapter establishes foundational definitions and research processes in preparation for the next four chapters about specific practices. The chapter provides you with an overview of key performance indicators (KPIs); an understanding of the quality limits of the evaluation and operating data you will be using; instructions for using MIIP 1.0 and the Museum Theory of Action as your planning tools; and a starting process for your museum to select your own set of KPIs to measure your desired impacts and performances.

Jason Saul has written an excellent manual, *Benchmarking for Nonprofits*, which provides rationale for using benchmarking as a means of institutional advancement, as well as worksheet templates to conduct the assessments. Saul uses benchmarking to identify best practices and then sets objectives to decrease the gap between that goal and the current data. He says, "Benchmarking empowers any organization to make today's state-of-the-art tomorrow's industry standard" (Saul 2004). This practice part of the book seeks to provide you with step-by-step processes and sample worksheet templates designed for a museum context.

The methods and formulas developed in this book can be used by any museum that fits the wide definition in Appendix A. As each museum has unique purposes, resources, and communities, each museum should define what measurements are most appropriate.

ESTABLISH GROUND RULES FOR MEASURING INDICATORS

Based on Weil's theory as developed in chapter 1, the value of a museum is equal to the value of its impacts. We can observe changes to the perceived value of a museum's impacts and benefits once we make some basic assumptions and rules:

- Museum engagements include all physical encounters between the public and the museum, whether on site or in off-site programs, and whether with visitors, program participants, donors, advisers, volunteers, or other members of the community. A museum engagement is defined as one physical person-trip to a museum or to a museum-sponsored program off site by a person not employed or contracted by the museum. The person-trip is a measure of *effort* spent by the person (time and often money are also spent). Virtual engagements can be added once physical engagement data reporting is established. The individual museum engagement (aka, person-trip, site visit) is the unit of measure.

- Audiences and supporters spend *time* in their museum engagements. Dwell time is measured in minutes from arrival to departure. Although we know time is also spent in preparation, travel, and follow-up, the number of on-location minutes is all we can hope to measure, and even that data is seldom measured. Some museums, like the Museum of Science (Boston, Massachusetts) with its time-stamp parking lot, can easily calculate car arrivals and departures to look for trends. However, most museums do not have such timing mechanisms in place and rely on assumptions about the duration of visits or the program's run time. Technology may be on the way with gallery sensors that keep track of people movement and crowdedness; such a system could calculate dwell time, identify the areas of the museum with the longest and shortest dwell times, and troubleshoot bottlenecks. For now, however, even the most basic information—average visitor dwell time—is not widely collected, much less standardized in definition. This book, therefore, relies primarily on money and effort indicators.

- Annual operating revenues refer specifically to the *money* received during an operating year that addresses operations and ongoing grant-funded programs related to operations. Endowment income and other non-outcome-based revenues are not good indicators of the changing value of a museum's social outcomes because they are not current free-choice "purchases" of the museum's social outcomes, and such non-social-outcome revenues should be excluded from calculations of social value. Funds intended for capital projects or other anomalies should also be excluded.[1]

- Annual data consistent with the museum's fiscal year is the most stable and reliable period of assessment, and is assumed to be the time period covered for any data field.

- Resource indicators, like number of staff and square feet of a gallery space, report status at the end of the fiscal year, with an explanation of any significant changes in status.

USE MULTIPLE KINDS OF KEY PERFORMANCE INDICATORS

Indicator is the generic, encompassing term. A mission statement is an indicator of the museum's purpose; its annual budget is an indicator of the scale of operations, and its visitor satisfaction level and supporter repeat level are indicators of its results. *Key performance indicators (KPIs)* are a subset of all indicators in MIIP 1.0. They are tagged Step 6a and 6b. Most of these KPIs are mathematical formulas that incorporate two or more *data fields*. A data field can have *data entries* for different terms, like this year and last year, and come from different sources, like peer museums and market data.

Your museum probably collects KPIs already. Efficiency indicators like cost of utilities per square foot, cost per visitor, ratio of marketing cost to earned revenue, and capture ratio of school population are common KPIs that management monitors to assess efficiency. But can KPIs measure your intentional purposes and your effectiveness? Only you and your stakeholders can answer this, and then only after a thoughtful selection process and a few rounds of testing and evolving. The process described in chapter 5 starts with prioritizing your intentional purposes (IPs) and their desired impacts.

The museum can quantify its selected KPIs from its evaluation and operating data, its community's socioeconomic data, and the average and/or median of a sample of comparable peer museums. When a museum's intangible values remain roughly constant at a unit level, then changes in the number of units provide museums with ways to measure changes in the value of their cumulative impact and to compare their performance with their peers.

These numbers indicate changes in impact and relative performance; they are not calculations of total value, nor are they some absolute performance specification. The museum still has its uncounted intangible values and its worthiness, which we set aside in this special theory. These intangible values and the museum's worthiness are what motivate support funds and provide brand assurance to earned revenue sources. KPI numbers are calculated on the museum's tangible values only, but when the intangibles remain roughly constant, changes to these tangible values may be actionable indicators of changes in effectiveness, efficiency, and performance, and can be used by museum managers to expand outcomes in volume, improve community services, and increase impact and performance.

Performance measures can be mathematical calculations of efficiency and effectiveness measures. Stephen Weil observed that a museum uses its resources as a means to achieve its ends, and that measurements of a museum's performance need to include both how effectively it achieves its ends and how efficiently it uses its resources to do the job. He goes further to observe that there is no point in measuring efficiency if you are not being effective (Weil 2005).

Jeanie Stahl[2] has spent decades developing and working with KPIs to help museums assess their operating performance compared to peers and to inform the operating implications of capital projects, such as expansions and new museums. Stahl created her menu of KPIs from her work on many museums' projects, her role as a committee member on the Association of Science-Technology Center's Analysis and Trends Committee, her work on the recommended survey questions for the IMLS's museum census, and as the contractor for the development of the Association of Children's Museum Online Benchmark Calculator.

Stahl finds that performance indicators are useful for a variety of purposes: Peer reviews, self-assessments, impact indicators, market indexes, unit costs, change measures, and target figures are among common categories already in use.

Peer Reviews

Several museum associations offer formal institutional assessments conducted by peer museum managers. These follow an established protocol, such as reviewing the museum's code of ethics, financial statements, and planning documents, including emergency plans to protect collections. Some offer accreditation, like AAM and AZA; others offer templates, like the AASLH's StEPs program and the ACM's Online Benchmarking; others offer private consultations like AAM's Museum Assessment Program (MAP). The documents that result from these peer reviews can be the foundation for forward planning.

Self-assessments

Opinions abound in and around most museums. Opinions about what should be done, what is wrong, and how to fix it are not limited to the chain of command, nor should they be. Most museums are public institutions and should welcome opinions from internal and external sources. Do not attempt to deal with every opinion as it comes in, thereby having to tell many of them "no"; rather, add opinions to a wish list, which will become a database of potential ideas for the museum to consider in upcoming planning. SWOT (Strength, Weakness, Opportunity, Threat) exercises are excellent self-assessments that collect inside opinions, each of which can be imported into a database of ideas for sorting and grouping. Performance and space-use assessments that compare your operating numbers and space assignments to those of your peers look at your current business model and how you are using your building. The assessments will highlight areas of excellence and opportunity.

Impact Indicators

Museums need evidence of their impacts. Over the last thirty years, this need has established a professional community of museum program evaluators producing a growing body of accessible evidence of learning and other social outcomes.

Much of this evaluation is objective driven by funders wanting confirmation of the intent of their award; however, museums also need different impact evaluation methods to measure a much wider array of museum impacts as perceived by families, schools, teens, young adults, seniors, businesses, private foundations, government agencies, and neighbors. Economic impact studies and fund-raising audits are a well-established measurement, but we need more methods for other impacts, like community building and quality-of-life enhancement. Not every impact will be positive. Not every impact will fit the museum's brand, and not every impact can be promised, but a full list of a museum's impacts will indicate the range of benefits perceived by the museum's community, audiences, and supporters.

Impact Change Indicators

If previous evaluation studies or reasonable assumptions have validated that a museum has some starting level of a particular impact, say *building social capital*, then the museum can track quantitative changes to its impact by following selected KPIs for social capital, such as growth in museum partnerships, increase in facility use by community groups, and growing social media engagements. If a museum starts with some level of impact, then it can monitor changes to indicators of that impact.

Market Indexes

Market indexes are fractions with the museum's number on top, and a community or market number on the bottom. The results are in percent and are most useful as indicators of comparable performance within a market: Is your market index of your community's schoolchildren growing or declining? How about your share of the region's philanthropic spending?

Market indexes account for changes in the community. A museum should not be too proud of a growing attendance number until it factors in the market's growth.

Market indexes are analytic but not service models because the denominator—typically some existing resident demographic population number—does not include the museum's users who live outside that demographic, like tourists and distant school groups. An attendance-to-market population index of 32 percent does not mean that 32 percent of the resident population was served since tourists are included in attendance but not in the resident population. Among peer museums, differences are proportional and roughly cancel out—by definition, peers have similar social contexts with similar shares of tourists and distant school groups. Caution should be used with tourism; Omaha and New Orleans have very different tourism profiles, and a museum in New Orleans may show a higher market index of its metro population than a similar museum in Omaha because there are more tourists from outside the metro population in the New Orleans visitor count. This may not be a factor for children's museums geared for residents, but it is a factor for large aquariums, which tend to draw tourists. Another anomaly is the inverse ratio between population size and the attendance-to-population ratio: The larger the population, generally the smaller the attendance ratio. This may be due to a disproportionately larger number of competing leisure options in larger cities.

The source of the market population data should be stable and accessible in consistent ways and for the same year as the museum's annual operating data. This consistency is a high enough priority to merit some compromise on ideal definitions. For instance, the Association of Children's Museums' (ACM's) KPI on school attendance uses the city's "Metro or Micro CBSA" population as the denominator rather than the arguably more meaningful school populations because the school districts vary in territory from city to city and do not always align with geo-demographic data, whereas metro or micro population are nationally aligned standards.

Examples of potentially useful market index KPIs include (see also examples in Appendix D):

- Total museum engagements/Metro population
- Earned revenue per cap/Metro median household income
- Energy consumed per square foot/Metro average for public assembly buildings
- School districts served/Total regional districts
- Public funding share of revenue/National average for museum sector

Unit Costs

Unit costs are typically fractions using internal operating data with a dollar amount on top and the number of units on the bottom, resulting in dollars per unit. Average ticket price (ATP) is a commonly used KPI that divides the total admission revenue by total admissions attendance, including free. Other useful money-based KPIs are visitor spending per capita in the museum store, earned revenue per on-site visit, operating expenses per square foot of facility, HR costs per employee, and funds raised per development dollar spent.

Unit costs can also apply to non-money-based units, like gallery visits per square foot of galleries, metro population per square foot of building, and visits per full-time equivalent (FTE) employee. Comparing such unit costs to peers is very helpful to planning as it identifies costs that may need investigation.

For instance, a relatively high number of visits per gallery square foot compared to peers can indicate overcrowded galleries. In the hands-on galleries popular in science centers, the ratio of annual visits divided by gallery square feet is a good indicator for crowdedness; crowdedness factors over eight or ten may indicate a need for gallery expansion. A high metro population to building size ratio may also indicate a need for expansion, and a high ratio of engagements per employee might indicate an efficient staff, a stressed staff, and/or lower levels of public service compared to your peers.

Given the right metrics and consistent data—two significant challenges—a museum might be able to calculate its unit cost efficiencies: What do we collect in total revenues per average annual museum engagement? What is the average dwell time per museum engagement? While such total calculations may be impractical until we can count total museum engagements, we can start with subsets of unit costs, such as the earned revenue per site visit.

Change Measures

Change measures are fractions with the increase or decrease on top, and the previous year's figure as the denominator. For instance, the percentage change in yearly school group revenue is calculated by dividing the amount of the change from last year to this year by last year's total, and the resulting percentage can be negative or positive. The change can also be calculated as an index simply by dividing this year's total by last year's. Results over 1.00 show increases; those below 1.00 show decreases. Some KPIs are mathematical formulas involving other KPIs, and so are layered formulas drawing from several data fields across different years, such as a five-year rolling average of corporate membership plus sponsorship revenues, factored by regional corporate earnings and inflation.

Change measures are very useful for setting and monitoring planning goals, such as increasing learning outcomes, increasing private support revenue, decreasing energy costs, and increasing membership retention rates. Change measures are the foot soldiers of a museum's campaign to increase its effectiveness and efficiency because leadership can set specific percentage change goals that can be measured at the end of the year. Data comparisons often need algorithms to adjust for inflation, economic conditions, and geographic differences in economic indexes.

Target Figures

Target figures are fixed objectives against which the museum can measure actual results. Diversity in cultural identity, economic strata, gender, etc. as reported by the U.S. Census Bureau can be target percentages, against which the museum can compare its actual diversity and set new objectives. Budgets are fixed numbers against which spending and revenues are judged. Ideal KPIs can be used as target figures to measure progress, such as a museum's target share of an audience to be engaged.

Community-Scale Metrics—Fertile Areas for Exploration

Museums should think of their indicators and operating data in the context of existing and emerging social and cultural evaluation metrics at a community or market level. There are popular indexes for community health such as *Forbes*'s Most Livable Cities (Levy 2010) and the Creative Economy (Florida 2002). There are already well-established national-level regional science indicators (National Science Board 2012), humanities indicators (American Academy of Arts & Sciences 2010), and the Artists for the Arts Foundation's National Arts Index (Cohen and Kushner 2014). These are possible sources of relational data, along with demographic and psychographic data from subscription sources such as Demographics Now. The free online U.S. census–based resource, American FactFinder, is a good source for U.S. demographics, as are local or state government online sites. At a more nuanced and thorough analysis level, innovative work is happening in such multidisciplinary research centers as the Urban Institute, NORC at the University of Chicago, the Voinovich School at Ohio University, and the Center for the Study of Philanthropy at the University of Indiana.

The relationship between a community's well-being and its collected and totaled museum resources may also be observed by the ratio of all of their museums' annual engagements to population, the square-foot total of free and subsidized public space to population, the number of all museum volunteer hours per capita, and the share of disposable income spent on the community's museums.

Comparing those indicators to similar populations or to the same population over time may show a correlation between civic well-being and investment in community service institutions. Are there correlations between quality-of-life indexes and a city's use of its museums? Do innovation indicators correlate with above-average cultural infrastructure measures? If any such correlations are found, then theories about potential causal relationships can be developed and tested. The explorations may also uncover indicators of other museum impacts, such as museum roles in developing a region's economy, cultural identity, and workforce.

Social Media and Digital Data as Indicators of Use and Value

The digital data available to museums are increasing in scope and information. Patterns of use, references to the museum, attitudes expressed about the museum, images shot and questions asked on mobiles are some of the kinds of data museums might access to observe behaviors, monitor opinions, and understand impacts, as well as to hear what visitors and program participants say they get from their engagements.

Data may also become available on site from sensors and visitor input stations. A network of people sensors could lead to measurements of traffic routes through galleries, dwell time per component, crowdedness, visitor inputs at digital interactives, satisfaction ratings, and value perceptions.

UNDERSTANDING THE QUALITY
LIMITS OF EVALUATION AND OPERATING DATA

There is very high-quality evaluation data on learning outcomes at a program level, and some longitudinal studies of learning impacts at an intuitional level. Much of this evaluation has been driven by funders that stipulate independent evaluation of whether the program achieved its goals. The Center for the Advancement of Informal Science Education (CAISE) maintains an evidence base that tracks what we have learned about informal STEM learning. You can go to informalscience.org and search for what studies have found about cyberlearning, for instance. Most of this evaluation data is focused on learning outcomes, broadly defined.

Evaluation studies that solicit individual users through surveys, focus groups, and interviews have their limits and biases, as do other data collection methods. Social value expert Geoff Mulgan lists issues with all methodologies: "Many social value metrics are inherently unreliable" (Mulgan 2010, 40). Of Stated Preferences, the data collection method including studies like these, he says, "Stated preferences often do not correlate with actual behaviors" (41). Direct interface with respondents often means that both the respondent and the interviewer/survey introduce variables that can subtly sway results: Respondents in museums want to seem smart and want to please, but they also have time limits; and evaluators need to enlist a number of respondents in a limited time and hope to get more work from their clients. Evaluation is typically done on a sample, not on all visitors or participants. Is that sample representative? Was the sampling day different? Can the results be generalized? These and other factors make such *small data* not as generalizable as annual operating *big data* that by definition measures the whole audience, and measures them by their actual behavior and not by their expressed opinions. Evaluation studies are strongest when used qualitatively.

In addition to evaluation studies, individual museums have marketing studies that track visitor and participant satisfaction, likeliness to recommend, motivation for visiting, zip code, and more. These studies are typically held in confidence, so it is hard for you to benefit from marketing studies done by others. In practice, museum staff members exchange studies among peers, which is another benefit of forming a peer museum network.

Of Revealed Preferences, of the data collection method including operating data, Mulgan says, "Few fields have enough viable data" (Mulgan 2010, 41). While this is still true of the museum field, museum operating data is emerging from a past of inconsistent data definitions and a legacy of opacity. Despite Mulgan's apparent antipathy to any social metric source, we must start with the data we have and can trust the most, being very cautious and humble before drawing conclusions.

Museums are moving toward more transparency. In the United States, nonprofit 501(c)(3) museums with annual revenues over $50,000 (2015) have to file either IRS Form 990 or 990-EZ disclosing revenue sources and expenses, including high-paying salaries. Companies like Guidestar publish this public data in searchable and accessible ways. Many larger museums post their annual reports on their websites; some publically share their audited financial statements. The Dallas Museum of Art goes further by posting selected KPIs to allow public monitoring. The museum is no longer the only party with access to its measurement data; funders and stakeholders can invent and populate KPIs of their own, using your public data.

We have solid financial data for larger nonprofits, and we have this data in-depth for those grant-seeking museums in states covered by DataArts. We now have good data on revenues—the money aspect.

Engagement counts are the second most reliable source of operating data, after financials, but they still have a long way to mature before they can become truly reliable evidence. Politics and spin control lead to ways of reporting engagement data for advocacy purposes that is not useful for research and planning purposes. It is important both to count accurately and to count every engagement by shared definitions. Counting accurately means honesty, documentation, strict adherence to reporting standards, and transparent reporting of fiscal year counts. For instance, ASTC and Appendix A define a visit as one person visiting the museum's site (a person-trip or site-visit). If that visitor buys a combination ticket once there, some science centers report combo tickets to their IMAX® and their exhibit galleries as two visits; this double-counting makes their attendance data look higher than their ASTC-conforming peers. ASTC has neither the power nor the resources to maintain and enforce data reporting standards. However, a change in counting policy may have the net effect of decreasing the museum's perceived attendance numbers, requiring adjustments in expectations. Sometimes public funding subsidies are tied to the old numbers, requiring renegotiations. There can be resistance to aligning definitions.

On the plus side, counting engagements comprehensively should increase a museum's total. Behind-the-scene engagements with supporters, foundation staff and donor meetings, volunteer shifts, advisor interactions, board meeting participants, opening galas, and press tours are also museum engagements in addition to visitors and program participants.

We have less data, unfortunately, for the amount of time that individuals, partner organizations, and supporters choose to spend in museum engagements such as board meetings and in-kind advisory roles, as well as the participations in all of the museum-branded offerings off site and virtually.

In time, perhaps more sectors of the museum field will settle on shared definitions for how to track attendance, dwell time, and other forms of museum engagements, and data from those domains may get the robustness currently enjoyed by revenue data. Then we will able to record and follow shifts among the amounts of time, money, and effort that our audiences and society invest in us. Museum associations can play an active role in establishing consistent counting definitions and categories.

USING THE MUSEUM THEORY OF ACTION AND MIIP 1.0 AS RESOURCES AND TOOLS

The Museum Theory of Action and MIIP 1.0 and their subsequent versions are available publicly on a free access link listed on the copyright page.

MIIP 1.0 is an interactive Excel database searchable and filterable for many uses: Museum leaders can sort through and prioritize their options for mission and purposes; fund raisers can search by funding cases; evaluators can find existing data collection fields with track records and comparable data; researchers can look for patterns in the indicators; and you can look for options for your museum.

For instance, a museum may decide to move *broadening participation* higher in its priorities, and it can look to MIIP 1.0 for many ideas about how to achieve and measure that goal. The museum may notice the number of indicators related to management culture, and awake to the notion that broadening participation has to start at home. They will notice many ways to broaden participation—free entrance, universal design, language, organization chart diversity, learning styles, outreach, etc., and decide which ways and activities to pursue based on their guiding principles and resources. Once the museum has put a theory of action in place to broaden participation in its own way, then it can go back to MIIP 1.0 to select indicators (or collaborate to develop missing ones) that provide data about how well they are broadening participation.

Accessing MIIP 1.0 and the Museum Theory of Action

MIIP 1.0 was developed by the White Oak Institute[3] and is available free to everyone, along with the Museum Theory of Action diagram. To download copies, go to the website listed on the copyright page or search for "MIIP" or "Museum Indicators of Impact and Performance." The MIIP database is read-only, so that the original version remains intact online; however, you can rename and save the file with your initials and go to work adapting it to your needs offline.

The processes in this part of the book assume familiarity with the use of Excel's database features. MIIP 1.0 is an Excel database designed to be filterable by you. There are 1,025 indicators, and the sheer number can be daunting. However, if you use the drop-down filter arrows at the top of each column, you can select parameters that narrow your search. You can also add columns (aka data fields) for your own tagging, as well as insert new rows (aka indicators), if you have some favorites not explicit in MIIP 1.0.

The filters you may find most useful are:

- Category of Potential Impact and Benefit (Column H) tags every indicator with one of fourteen categories of potential impact and benefit. These categories, listed in table 4.1, are organized by market sectors: Public Support, Private Support, Personal Earned Income, and Institutional Operations and Capital. This filter is helpful in focusing the content of the indicators at the big-picture level. Use a version of Worksheet 4.1, "Matrix of Impacts and MIIP Categories" in Appendix E to decide on the categories relevant to your desired impacts.
- Content of Indicator (Column I) is a finer-grain filter that is also useful to track aspects that cross over several impact categories, like "collections" and "learning." The sixty content topics are listed in table C.2 in Appendix C.
- Step or Kind of Indicator (Location of indicator along the Theory of Action) (Column G) helps you filter by what step you are looking for. In chapter 5, when you develop a list of potential purposes and desired impacts, you can filter by "Step 1 Intentional Purposes" and "Step 7 Perceived Benefits." In chapter 6, when you select KPIs to measure those selected impacts, you can filter

Table 4.1. Categories of Potential Museum Impacts

		# of MIIP indicators
Public Impacts		
A	Broadening participation	85
B	Preserving heritage	47
C	Strengthening social capital	76
D	Enhancing public knowledge	43
E	Serving education	56
F	Advancing social change	40
G	Communicating public identity & image	27
Private Impacts		
H	Contributing to the economy	85
I	Delivering corporate community services	9
Personal Impacts		
J	Enabling personal growth	147
K	Offering personal respite	4
L	Welcoming personal leisure	11
Institutional Impacts		
M	Helping museum operations	308
N	Building museum capital	87
Total indicators in the MIIP 1.0 database		1,025

Source: The White Oak Institute

Table 4.2.   The Museum Theory of Action: Logic Model Version

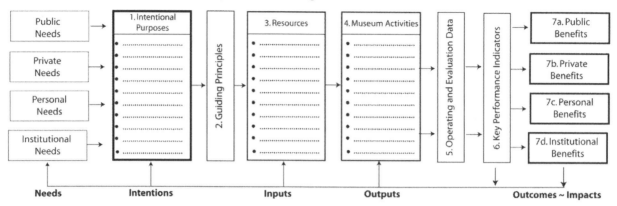

Source: The White Oak Institute

by "Step 6 KPIs," while also checking Steps 3–5 ("Resources," "Activities," "Output counts and evaluation studies") for any data fields you might want for new KPIs.

- Blank Data Fields 1–3 (Columns D–F) allow you to add your own tags, such as your selection, priority, content group, etc. You can always add more blank columns if you wish, but you must first turn off the data-filtering drop-down menu function until you have added the new columns.

Identifying a First-Cut Selection of MIIP 1.0 Indicators

Even after filtering, you are likely to have a large number of MIIP indicators, perhaps as many as several hundred, and the sheer size of the database may be daunting. Do not try to read, much less code, the whole list at one sitting.

Take the time to read all the indicators suggested for each of your desired impacts. Ignore the differences in syntax to focus on the idea. This is an opportunity to see what other great minds suggest to address your desired impact. Some ideas will be familiar, but others will open new possibilities of achieving your impact and may spark ideas for new museum audiences, supporters, and services. Read with your creativity turned on: "How can we adapt and use this indicator?"

However rich the full list may be, it needs to be pruned radically before distribution. In essence, the steps are about a progressive selection sequence that edits and pares down the "Full List of Potential Indicators," which may number in the hundreds, to the "Final Cut," which might include sixteen to twenty-four carefully considered and widely accepted indicators of your museum's desired impacts.

Once you have filtered for one of your desired impacts, use one of the blank data fields to tag them with that desired impact.

Look for and tag related indicators. Invent short tags for those *content groups* of related indicators such as "partnerships" and "operating culture."

Review the indicators beside each desired impact and ask which of these get closest to what your museum could use or address. Are there any content groups in each desired impact that are primary or more important/relevant than others? Can you cut and combine more?

Favor the larger ideas, and try to delete sub-ideas. If you want to combine indicators, add a new row for the combination and use Column B to identify the source (you), perhaps also tracking the original indicator numbers. Delete all the dupes and lesser indicators.

Keep editing down until you have a manageable number that you are comfortable sharing with the rest of your Core Team. This will take time and patience, but you will learn much and focus your thinking in the process. Copy the First Cut filters and paste them into the main Potential Purposes and KPIs databases that you will set up in chapters 5 and 6.

ORGANIZING AN INCLUSIVE AND TRANSPARENT SELECTION PROCESS

To succeed in establishing your museum's selection of purposes and KPIs as described in chapters 5 and 6, you should involve others in a consensus-building process that engages all stakeholders and yet is accomplished smoothly by limited resources. The parties typically include:

- Museum Governance: the board of directors or trustees in nonprofit museums, the chancellor or departmental office in university museums, or the public funding agency for government museums. These are examples of the ultimate authorities for setting the museum's policy using the Policy Governance Model (Carver and Carver 2006).
- Museum Leadership: the museum's executive team, typically the top lines of an organization chart, or the museum's managers, directors, and vice presidents, all led by the museum's staff CEO or director. In smaller museums, some board members take on management roles.
- Core Team: the collaborative group that will develop a slate of potential purposes and recommend KPIs for adoption by governance. This ad hoc group will meet periodically, review drafts, make suggestions, and provide guidance on key choices and priorities. The Core Team should include both governance members and museum managers for a total of four to twelve people, depending on the size of the museum. For this process, the Core Team must include the staff heads of finance, operations, and evaluation, or their equivalents in smaller museums.
- Project Leader: a CEO, senior manager, or knowledgeable contractor who will do or delegate the work, feed the Core Team with drafts, and facilitate their meetings, leading up to writing and editing the final "Key Performance Measures." In part 2 of this book, "you" refers to the Project Leader. The Project Leader should be comfortable with math and analyzing quantitative data and qualitative ideas. MIIP 1.0 is an Excel database, and the project needs skills in sorting and filtering Excel databases and analyzing the results. Either the Project Leader or a team member needs to be able to categorize, collect, and synthesize similar ideas under broader umbrellas.

The Project Leader should be a champion for the museum's adoption of purposes and KPIs. A can-do attitude, leadership qualities, delegation authority, and creative energy will be needed to get through the issues that are bound to crop up.

CONCLUSION

The objective of this Part 2: Practice is to help museums determine their purposes, select KPIs, and measure changes in impact and performance. The process needs to be inclusive to succeed, and deserves leadership time and attention.

This part of the book has several step-by-step how-to processes. They try to balance brevity and detail. You are likely to skip some steps and add others, and such adaptations are desirable; the process and results must become yours.

This book's processes analyze ideas by tagging and sorting them in progressive cuts using an Excel database, but there are many other ways, like concept mapping or walls full of stickies.

Because many museums have free-choice business models competing in their marketplace for their audiences' and supporters' discretionary money, effort, and time, and because many museums serve multiple audiences, supporters, and purposes, this process can get complicated if you don't boil down the choices into a few big-picture groups.

Use MIIP 1.0 as a reminder of potential purposes and KPIs. It is useful to align to MIIP when selecting your indicators, but your museum's prioritized purpose statements may need to reflect the unique intersection of your intentions and passions, your museum's resources, and your community's needs in new or adapted indicators.

Ultimately, the adoption of metrics to inform decisions is a cultural change. The change may have been driven by donors and market competition, but in time, museum leaders and managers can embrace this approach to think through their intentions by expressing their theories of action and desired impacts, and by using their own selection of indicators to observe the changes and see if their action theories are on track, and if not, make modifications.

NOTES

1. They are, however, additions to the museum's capital assets.
2. Ms. Stahl is the author's partner in museum analysis and planning and at White Oak.
3. The author is CEO of the White Oak Institute, a nonprofit museum research initiative.

REFERENCES

American Academy of Arts & Sciences. *Humanities Indicators*. February 2010. Accessed December 1, 2014. http://www.humanitiesindicators.org/content/document.aspx?i=108.

Carver, John, and Miriam Carver. *Reinventing Your Board: A Step-by-Step Guide to Implementing Policy Governance*. San Francisco: Jossey-Bass, 2006.

Cohen, Randy, and Roland J. Kushner. *National Arts Index: 12-Year Span of 2001-12*. 2014. Accessed December 1, 2014. http://www.americansforthearts.org/sites/default/files/pdf/information_services/art_index/2014-NAI-Full-Report.pdf.

Florida, Richard. *The Rise of the Creative Class: And How It's Transforming Work, Leisure, Community and Everyday Life*. New York: Basic, 2002.

Levy, Francesca. "America's Most Livable Cities." *Forbes*, April 29, 2010. Accessed December 1, 2014. http://www.forbes.com/2010/04/29/cities-livable-pittsburgh-lifestyle-real-estate-top-ten-jobs-crime-income.html.

Mulgan, Geoff. "Measuring Social Value." *Stanford Social Innovation Review* (Summer 2010). Accessed November 4, 2014. http://www.ssireview.org/pdf/2010SU-Feature_Mulgan.pdf.

National Science Board. *Science and Engineering Indicators 2012*. Arlington, VA: National Science Foundation (NSB 12-01), 2012.

Saul, Jason. *Benchmarking for Nonprofits: How to Measure, Manage, and Improve Performance*. Saint Paul: Fieldstone Alliance, 2004.

Weil, Stephen. "A Success/Failure Matrix for Museums." *Museum News* (January/February 2005): 36–40.

CHAPTER 5

PRIORITIZE YOUR MUSEUM'S PURPOSES AND IMPACTS

How do your current audiences and supporters benefit from your museum? Given an understanding of what they want, how does your museum select and prioritize its intentional purposes and desired impacts?

This chapter addresses these questions with a step-by-step process for prioritizing your museum's intentional purposes and desired impacts. The process is informed by your community needs and aspirations, by your audience and supporters' choices, by your recent planning, and by the suggestions you add from MIIP 1.0.

This chapter is the first of four chapters focused on step-by-step processes. The sequence starts in this chapter with selecting your museum's *intentional purposes* and *desired impacts*—the "why?" of the museum. The next chapter outlines a process to assess how well you are achieving these goals by selecting and measuring your unique dashboard of *key performance indicators* (KPIs). Together, chapters 5 and 6 enable you to measure changes to your impact and performance relative to your recent past. Chapter 7 enables you to compare your impact and performance to your peer museums, and chapter 8 integrates your selected measurements into reports and dashboards.

THE COMMUNITY MUSEUM AND ITS MULTIPLE PURPOSES

In "The Community Service Museum: Owning Up to Our Multiple Purposes," published by the *Journal of Museum Management and Curatorship*, I concluded:

> The current reality is that many US museums already operate as community service museums and pursue multiple purposes, which result in multiple kinds of outcomes. . . . This is good, and we should not feel guilty about it, but listen harder to our operating data, and then look creatively for the common ground between the museum's intentions and our audiences' and supporters' intentions. We can track our changing impact through our operating numbers, and observe the shifting ratios among our multiple revenue sectors to inform planning and to keep the museum responsive to its external market and economy. (Jacobsen 2014)

This chapter builds on this conclusion by assuming that your museum might pursue multiple purposes and deliver multiple outcomes and impacts desired by multiple audiences and supporters. Collectively, these main revenue, effort, and time sectors are your *key service markets*. The process still works for a single-purpose museum, but this process accommodates multiple purposes and allows for more layered business models.

Do you still categorize some revenues or audiences as "mission critical" and others as "mission enabling"? Is this still a useful class distinction?

Perhaps it is time to think anew about your museum's operating revenue and attendance sources, aka your museum's lifeblood. Emotions, tradition, and risk are involved, which makes this step political and potentially divisive. As discussed in chapter 3, revenue, effort, and time are free-choice exchanges that indicate perceived value. All these are won by your museum in a competitive economy: There are plenty of alternative missions, programs, and leisure activities competing for your audiences and supporters. Look strategically at each revenue and attendance stream as an expression of some audience or supporter's interests, but do it with caution and deliberation: Do we wish to serve these beneficiaries? Are we proud of the service? Is it branded and consistent with the museum's guiding principles? Can we layer on content or learning outcomes? Does it have a neutral or net positive impact on other revenues and stakeholders?

If the answer is "yes" to such questions, but "no" to "Is it central to our mission and core business?" then consider expanding the definition of your mission and core businesses before relegating the revenue stream and its funders to second-class, "ancillary" status.

A workable option is to side-step the mission question and go directly to purposes by asking: What individual or societal benefits do we provide to each key service market? Are those benefits we wish to continue providing? If so, how can we be more purposeful, effective, and efficient at providing them? In the evening, the New England Aquarium (NEAq) screens Hollywood hits in its Simons IMAX® 3D Theatre; these screenings are "non-mission," but they bring nighttime vitality to Boston's urban waterfront. Would NEAq provide more value downtown if they became more intentional about delivering that service?

The Maryhill Museum of Art, located on a large, remote tract of land in Washington State, has leased some land to a wind farm operator, with revenues of about $250,000 per annum. Is this to be treated like endowment income and excluded from MMA's tally of its mission outcomes? Or does the museum decide to become intentional about promoting environmental projects like wind farms? The second choice of making environmental action an intentional purpose is likely to increase the effectiveness, efficiency, dollar volume, and quality of the museum's environmental benefits to its revenue partners and to society.

The Rochester Museum and Science Center's (RMSC) 2008 mission statement was: "stimulates broad community interest and understanding of science and technology and their impact." In 2011, a master planning process,[1] informed by operating data, resource assessments, and community needs analysis articulated three prioritized purposes: science learning; community gathering; and regional economic development.[2] All are now intentional purposes tied to planning objectives. The mission statement remains in place, and the highest priority purpose is the mission purpose; however, day-to-day management and the staff culture can now move toward these multiple purposes. For instance, RMSC has many spaces within its buildings available for meetings and receptions. RMSC can now host weddings, festivals, events, and community celebrations that do not involve science learning without the off-mission stigma.[3] Such events gather the community, make more use of the museum's resources, and advance the second of the museum's multiple intentional purposes.

The processes described in this chapter involve building a list, modeled here as an Excel database, of potential indicators of possible purposes, impacts, perceived benefits, and community needs that you and the rest of your museum's leadership should consider before formalizing your intentional purposes and desired impacts. The foundation of the list/database comes from your museum's previous community, audience, and donor research, your strategic planning, plus suggestions for additional possibilities drawn from the 1,025 indicators suggested by the field and filterable by downloading MIIP 1.0. This description covers a full process, but you may wish to short-cut through several steps. This is manageable as long as the main goal is kept in sight: to develop for leadership's consideration a short list of potential purposes and their desired impacts that represents all key stakeholders and that takes advantage of what other museum professionals have learned.

The balance of this chapter focuses on (1) assessing your audiences' and supporters' *perceived benefits*; and (2) selecting and prioritizing your museum's *intentional purposes* and *desired impacts*.

ASSESS YOUR AUDIENCES' AND SUPPORTERS' PERCEIVED BENEFITS

This process will provide your museum with a quantified list of your operating audiences and supporters in subtotals of key service markets listed by share of operating revenues and engagements. A museum's financial statements show who is paying for the museum's operation, and the operating revenues and attendance breakdowns are a good place to start research for long-range planning.

1. Start an Excel worksheet modeled on Worksheet 5.1, "Operating Revenue Comparisons" and another modeled on Worksheet 5.2, "Key Audience and Supporter Segments."
2. Review recent internal operating and financial statements to understand the sources of your museum's yearly operating revenues; note any anomalies in each year that might have affected operations, like a blockbuster exhibition, or the opening of a new wing. Record the annual operating revenues for at least one recent year without major anomalies ("Base Year"), and categorize them by sources, using standard definitions (see Appendix A). The main sources that provide most of your annual revenues are your museum's *key service markets*, such as visitors, grant-making foundations, corporate members, etc.
   a. Use the most recent audited financial statement to identify revenues received from operations during the fiscal year, and, for comparison, one or more years before. Exclude capital asset additions such as endowment income. In this exercise, the museum is trying to identify and study the external operating revenues it receives in return for its annual activities.
3. Do the same for your engagement counts. Most museums keep track of the visitor attendance part of a museum's annual engagements; some keep good track of some of their program participations, but none keep track of and report on all their engagements. Use what engagement counts you have by the definitions shared by others and calculate your on- and off-site attendance. Recognize that this is only a subtotal of the museum's annual engagements. One engagement is one person-trip to a museum site or to a museum-produced off-site program or exhibit. Focus first on physical engagements; add virtual engagements later.
4. Do the same for your dwell-time tallies, if you have them. What is the amount of time an average individual spends per average museum engagement? Which audience segments exchange the most of their discretionary time in return for the benefits they receive from their museum engagements? There is currently insufficient data on dwell time to use annual totals as meaningful indicators; hence, the processes in this book rely primarily on money and effort exchanges.
5. Once you know the relative shares of revenue and engagements by service market, adopt a framework of nested categories for thinking about and monitoring your community and its audiences and supporters, ideally aligned with your counting and accounting systems and with museum operating data standards. The framework should include all who support, interact, and/or use the museum through museum engagements. Table 5.1 shows a full picture that you can adapt to your stakeholders.

   In addition to those who engage with the museum, there are also non-users who still perceive benefits from museums; such non-users value their museums as options to visit, as contributors to a community's quality of life, and as stewards of the legacy of their times (Scott 2007).

Table 5.1. The Community and Its Audiences and Supporters

The Community and Its Tourists

Audiences & Supporters — *Total Engagements* — Non-Users

Public Supporters — Private Supporters — *Total Support Engagements* — Visitors — *Total Visitor Engagements* — Program Participants — *Total Program Engagements*

Key Visitor Segment	Exhibit Galleries	Feature Theater	Other Venues	Gift	Café
General Visitors					
Adults w/Children	•	•	•	•	•
Adults w/Adults	•	•	•	•	•
Young Adults	•	•	•	•	•
Teens	•	•	•	•	•
Solo Visitors	•	•	•	•	•
Group Visitors					
School & Youth	•	•	•	•	
Bus Tours	•	•	•	•	•

Total Venue Visits

Program Participants:

On-Site
— Individuals
— Organizations
— Professionals
— Hobbyists
— Groups
— Teachers
— Households

Off-Site
— Students
— Teachers
— Organizations
— Passers-by
— Other Museums
— Fairs & Festivals

Virtual
— Individuals
— Social Groups
— Linked Partners

6. Import your operating revenue totals, engagement counts, and dwell times (if available) from each sector (visitors, program participants, private and public supporters) into the Excel worksheets. Make sure they total the amounts in the audited financial statements for consistency of data, or annotate differences. Calculate the annual shares from each sector over several past years.

   a. Annotate the yearly numbers to explain anomalies, and start to look for deeper trends. Develop a base year data portrait of normalized operating revenues and engagements, adjusted for inflation and population growth; the museum will use these figures as benchmarks to set planning objectives for change. Add your current year (or budget forecast).

7. Quantify changes among the sources of revenues. Once you have identified what shares of the annual revenues and engagements were provided by each key service market for both your base year and current year, compare changes in relative market shares. Have total revenues and engagements increased or decreased? Have the market shares changed? Which sectors are growing or declining? Why?

   a. Assess the relative volatility of each service market. Is this a steady source of quiet support funds, or an entrepreneurial sector requiring constant attention?

8. Assess who is getting what *perceived benefits* from the museum. Who is currently funding and attending the museum's activities, and why? What do they think they are getting that is valuable to them? Is the cost sufficiently worth it to them that they want to keep doing it?

   a. Group the categories that account for most of the museum's operating revenue and annual engagements by similar interests and business models, like school groups and corporate sponsorships, adhering to standard definitions that also line up with your current data collection.

   b. Use both qualitative and quantitative surveys to ask what *perceived benefits* each key service sector thinks it gets from its museum experiences. Put more emphasis on qualitative methods, principally focus groups with public audiences and personal interviews with representative supporters, stakeholders, and community spokespeople. Perhaps visitor studies and program evaluations already exist, but have event planners been surveyed? For a first pass, the museum's development office can report what attracts supporters, and the marketing office can report what attracts audiences.

9. Set up a Word document called "Perceived Benefits," and import into it quotes from community needs interviews (see 2.b in the next section), focus groups, SWOT exercises, evaluation findings, and opinions from managers that list all the benefits that the community and its audiences and supporters are currently getting, or hope to get, from the museum. After clustering similar benefits, give each distinct benefit cluster a two- or three-word descriptor, and copy all descriptors into a new Excel worksheet "Potential Purposes and Impacts" following Worksheet 5.3.

10. Add indicators of other potential perceived benefits, using MIIP 1.0 filtered for Step 7 as a source of ideas that might have been missed but should be considered by the museum.

11. The database should now have a row per benefit descriptor; tag all as *potential benefits*. Also tag each with its source and type of audience or supporter.

12. Test the database by filtering by "Private Supporter" or another of your tags. Are there blanks that need to be tagged? Does filtering bring together benefits from different sources? Can you go back to the original order with everything in place?

The above steps identify the museum's key service markets and what they want for their money; planning can be focused on providing them with higher value outcomes and impacts more effectively and efficiently.

SELECT AND PRIORITIZE YOUR MUSEUM'S INTENTIONAL PURPOSES

1. Brief governance on the need for your museum to establish prioritized *intentional purposes* and *desired impacts*. Describe your proposed process to return to governance with a short list of potential purposes and desired impacts for them to select and prioritize. Invite suggestions, discussion, and participation in the Core Team that will be guiding the process. Obtain any necessary approvals to proceed, including resource approvals. During the process, provide governance with status updates.

2. Review your museum's most recent strategic planning.
   a. Build on previous museum planning to honor and take advantage of all the research and thought that went into your museum's most recent planning exercise. You need a set of purposes and desired impacts to start this process, and your museum's *recent planning* is the most defensible set of starting assumptions. A museum's strategic master plan typically includes mission, vision, guiding principles (aka core values), objectives, strategies, tactics, and timelines. You and your museum's governance may reinforce, update, or change these during this process. Update these to respond to recent changes.
   b. Research your *community's needs and aspirations*. What do community leaders and spokespeople list as the community's needs? How do they think the museum might help add more value? Who might pay for it? This process can be as simple as reviewing regional visioning documents and your city's master plan, or as thorough as a multimodal process involving those documents plus interviews with community leaders and spokespeople, demographic and psychographic market analyses, off-site intercept surveys, and other means of finding out: "What are the region's needs and aspirations? What are [the interviewee's] needs and aspirations? What might our museum do to help?"
   c. Highlight all phrases from your recent planning and community needs that read like purposes and aspirations for the museum. Include the mission and vision statements, and most likely the summary objectives (usually three to eight at the summary level, with detail underneath). Also, include quotes from the community needs that evoke the museum's impact, such as "The museum has transformed the waterfront." Err on the side of inclusion, but do not bother

repeating ideas or getting into the detail. Avoid concrete plans about means, like expanding a gallery. Your collected highlights should be a top-level list of ten to thirty of the museum's previously desired ends and intentional purposes plus the community needs.

3. Add indicators of other potential purposes and desired impacts, using MIIP 1.0 as a source of ideas that might have been missed but that should be considered by the museum. Tag them as "Intentional Purpose: MIIP" or "Desired Impact: MIIP."

4. Import (a) your list of community needs and aspirations; (b) your intentional purposes and desired impacts, and (c) your audiences' and supporters' perceived benefits that you set up in the previous section into a combined database "Potential Purposes and Impacts" (see Worksheet 5.3).

    a. Together, these are indicators of your potential purposes and desired impacts and benefits. Each can be located along the Museum Theory of Action by what kind of indicator it is—where it came from and what it is trying to do. Tag each row with one of the following seven steps in the Theory of Action: "Purpose, Principle, Resource, Activity, Data, KPI, and Perceived Benefit" (see chapter 1 for definitions). At this stage, most will be Purposes and Perceived Benefits, but you are likely to find outliers and step-boundary questions. Use "???" for the outliers. The edge questions are more interesting, as they highlight the continuous nature of a theory of action. A purpose like "diversify our audience" can also show up as a guiding principle like "we celebrate diversity." A supporter can state their desired benefit in what sounds like a purpose: "The museum should be a portal for regional organizations to reach the public."

    b. Your desired impacts and their perceived benefits are both in Step 7, as the results or ends of the museum's activities. The difference is one of perspective: *your* desired impacts and *their* perceived benefits. An impact can be a benefit; an impact can happen but not be perceived as a benefit; and audiences and supporters can get benefits that you did not desire.

5. Analyze the alignment between your recent planning purposes and your audiences' and supporters' perceived benefits. Start to group purposes, desired impacts, and benefits that are alike into several umbrella groups, using your best judgment. For instance, you might have listed a purpose to "further the understanding of your region's history," and teachers may see benefit in your ability to "engage their students in history." These two could be grouped under "history education." Look at the twelve MIIP categories of external impact (see table 2.1) for ideas for group names.

    a. Sort your database to collect like impacts into *content groups* (e.g., family learning, tourism, civic pride, etc.). Look at the kinds of indicators in each grouping. Are there significant differences among the sources for any of the content groups? Does a content group like "community identity" have an equal number of purposes and benefit indicators? Are some groups primarily from audience sources? Or from supporters or internal planning? Are there benefits valued by audiences or supporters that museum planning seems to be ignoring? Conversely, are there desired impacts that few audiences and supporters are valuing? What do the revenue and engagement numbers say about the size of the benefit markets? Are there common grounds where all parties are represented and after the same purposes and benefits?

    b. Draft an internal report for leadership's consideration called something like a "Study of the Alignment of our Purposes to our Audiences' and Supporters' Perceived Benefits."

6. Convene the Core Team to review the draft and discuss the implications. This is not yet the time to act on these findings, but it is a chance to test the waters for possible shifts in priorities and additions to the museum's intentional purposes.

    a. Let the Core Team decide on further drafts and larger circulation of the study.

7. Consolidate and synthesize the content groups down to eight to twelve big ideas where the museum might serve a purpose.

a. Your database now has a large list of indicators grouped by similar content. Each content group may contain a number of indicators, mostly purposes and benefits.

b. Review the relative shares of revenue and engagements among your key service markets. Which content groups are most valuable to the museum? Tag the content groups with phrases about their relationship to revenues and engagements.

c. Once you understand what your community and its audiences and supporters value from their exchanges with the museum, the museum can decide whether those purposes are beneficial and appropriate, reverse-engineer purpose statements intended to result in those revenues, and adopt them among the museum's intentional purposes.

d. This step activates the return direction and two-way aspect of the Theory of Action; the community, through its exchanges of money and effort, is shaping the museum's intentions.

8. Convene the Core Team to review and short-list the content groups and to brainstorm possible language for summary purpose statements and desired impacts for each content group in their short list. End the meeting with a short list (eight±) of potential purposes and desired impacts, using Worksheet 5.4, "Potential Purposes and Impacts—Short List" as a model.

9. Write up your museum's potential purposes and desired impacts.

a. For each short-listed content group, translate and synthesize the indicators in that group into the following written statements: An intentional purpose and its desired impacts, and a theory of action that describes how the museum will use its resources to achieve those desired impacts for which audiences and supporters. This states the Why? So what? How? and Who? Use Worksheet 5.5, "Theory of Action Rationale" as a model.

b. Summarize these in a draft report, "Potential Purposes and Impacts." Use the narrative to explain the sources and rationale behind each potential purpose. Treat each candidate equally, allowing governance to be the judge of relative importance.

c. Finalize the draft with the Core Team, and then circulate it to leadership.

10. Prioritize your museum's purposes and impacts by convening leadership in a facilitated workshop, like a board retreat, to wrestle with the museum's most important questions: "What are our main purposes, and what are we trying to achieve?" Starting with the short-listed potential purposes and impacts, leadership should either combine or select the museum's top two to five intentional purposes, and then assign to each a percentage priority, adding up to 100 percent.

a. Keep the revenue and attendance analysis in mind as leadership weighs the choices: Which purposes relate to the funding and engagements from which audiences and supporters?

11. Formalize, circulate, and pursue your museum's prioritized purposes and impacts.

a. Write up the workshop's results as the museum's "Intentional Purposes and Desired Impacts."

b. Present the document and its story to governance with a recommendation to formally adopt the results of their workshop and this process.

c. Once that formal ratification is accomplished, circulate the document widely among staff and contractors, followed by discussion groups and then planning sessions.

12. Periodically review and update the museum's prioritized purposes and desired impacts.

NOTES

1. Disclosure: The author facilitated this process through his company, White Oak Associates, Inc.
2. These titles cover more detailed sub-purposes and specifics.
3. Each museum needs to investigate the tax implications of this approach in its own jurisdiction; earned revenue for some secondary purposes may be deemed taxable.

REFERENCES

Jacobsen, John. "The Community Service Museum: Owning up to Our Multiple Missions." *Museum Management and Curatorship* 29, no. 1 (2014): 1–18.

Scott, Carol. "Advocating the Value of Museums." *INTERCOM*. August 2007. Accessed November 4, 2014. http://www.intercom.museum/documents/CarolScott.pdf.

CHAPTER 6

DETERMINE YOUR MUSEUM'S PERFORMANCE METRICS

How does management select indicators to measure impact and performance? How does a museum periodically test the validity of its indicators??

In this chapter, you will build on the accomplishments of the previous chapter—prioritizing your museum's intentional purposes (IPs) and their desired impacts—to select, record, and eventually test and monitor your Key Performance Indicators (KPIs). Your goal is to find meaningful indications of some aspects of your museum's performance (effectiveness and/or efficiency) in achieving your intentional purposes. You will use the middle steps of the Museum Theory of Action to help you find your museum's performance metrics.

The Theory of Action assumes that your museum pursues its *intentional purposes* by using its resources to operate activities that engage your audiences' and supporters' time, money, and effort in exchange for their *perceived benefits* and your *desired impacts*. KPIs use annual counts of these exchanges, tallies of resources used, numbers of activities, evaluation findings, market demographics, and other *data fields* in calculations that may indicate changes in your museum's performance in achieving your desired impacts.

Such indicators and measures are not impacts per se. Just measuring is not enough. Museums must actually have beneficial impacts, in addition to good measures. Hence, museums need to use other methodologies from time to time to test whether the desired impacts are occurring and whether the indicator is valid. This combination of large and small data, of operating data and evaluation studies, and of quantitative and qualitative data translates into the mantra: *Measure regularly; validate periodically*.

You can follow the step-by-step processes in this chapter to determine your KPIs, collect their data, and analyze the results. Table 6.1 shows a framework for nesting KPIs within the desired impacts for IP #1, along with periodic evaluations. This can be cloned for IP #2 . . . n. Worksheet 6.1 "KPI Framework" in Appendix E shows examples of these for the Sample Museum in MidCity. Additionally, each KPI has two or more *data fields*.

While this KPI process is done logically after the intentional purposes process in the previous chapter, both can be done together (internally staggered) and involve largely the same people. The processes can also be scaled: at a small museum with only one or two purposes, the director and board chair might be able to do all of this during one or two meetings.

Examples of KPIs, formulas, and worksheet templates are illustrated in Appendix D. These are based on Stephen E. Weil's foundational theory—a museum's value lies in what it accomplishes—and on the definitions and concepts developed in this book and collected in Appendix A.

Table 6.1. Framework for Key Performance Indicators (KPIs). Note: For clarity, only the central column is showing.

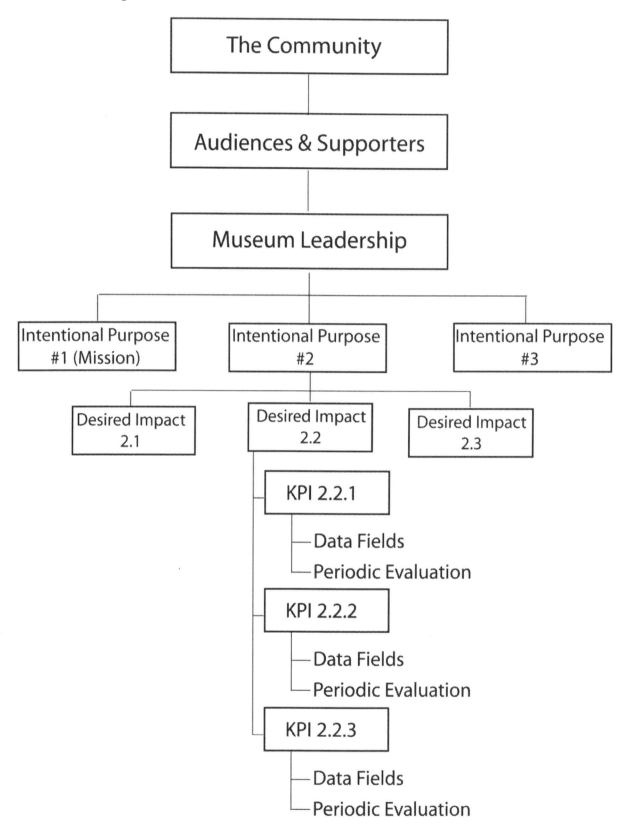

DETERMINE YOUR KPIs

You will notice that these steps are similar to those you used in chapter 5 when you selected impact indicators, but with important distinctions:

- KPIs involve numbers and math, while purposes and impacts are mostly qualitative words and groupings of ideas.
- This chapter focuses on indicators in the middle steps of the Theory of Action: Resources; Activities; Output and evaluation data; and KPIs (Steps 3–6). The first three of these are data fields (e.g., number of square feet of gallery space, number of programs offered, and number of renewing memberships); the last step uses these and other data fields to calculate KPIs.
- While chapter 5 starts with your museum's planning and research and later adds missing pieces from MIIP 1.0, this chapter starts with MIIP 1.0, because the indicators in MIIP 1.0 include the most standardized, available, and road-tested data definitions. Later, you will invent or add data fields to fill in the gaps.
- Discussion and innovation are needed to lock down KPI definitions that are both meaningful and workable. Deciding on your museum's KPIs is deciding on how you want your museum's performance to be evaluated. As a great deal is at stake, all stakeholders should be involved in forming and understanding the selection rationale and the potential data sources for the museum's KPIs.

To select your KPIs, work through a process that first identifies a large list of potential KPIs and then fine-tune a selection, through a series of cuts. Involve governance in the final round. Follow your own version of the following steps for each of your museum's intentional purposes (IPs) and desired impacts:

1. Brief governance on the need for your museum to establish and measure prioritized Key Performance Indicators, based on the prioritized intentional purposes previously approved by governance. Describe your proposed process to return to them with Recommended Key Performance Indicators. Invite suggestions, discussion, and participation in the Core Team that will guide the process. Obtain any necessary approvals to proceed, including resource approvals. During the process, provide governance with status updates.
   a. This and its parallel governance step at the end are optional. You may want to grow the use of KPIs quietly over time, and wait until a robust number of KPIs are successfully in use before codifying them formally.
2. Filter the MIIP 1.0 database and paste the First Cut into an Excel spreadsheet modeled on Worksheet 6.2, "Potential KPI Master List."
   a. Use the drop-down filter menus in MIIP 1.0 to select potential KPIs (Steps 6a and 6b). Use the filters you developed in Worksheet 4.1 for those impact categories most relevant to your Intentional Purpose #1. Additionally, you will find Steps 1, 6b, and 7 helpful.
   b. If "art," "science," "Scotland" or "STEM" appear but are not relevant to your museum, try searching for and replacing with your disciplines and context.
   c. If the list is too large to absorb, do some gross editing of obvious non-contenders.
   d. Add at least the following columns inside the database for your use: "Desired Impact" and "Selection."
      i. For each candidate KPI, enter the names of your museum's desired impacts that relate to this KPI.
      ii. Delete KPIs with no matches.
      iii. Add blank rows for any desired impact that is unmatched with at least one MIIP KPI.

iv. Enter "First Cut" in the Selection column for all remaining rows.

e. Circulate the Potential KPI Master List First Cut to your Core Team.

f. Do this for Intentional Purpose # 2 . . . #n.

3. Convene the Core Team to discuss how to measure changes in the impact and performance of the desired impacts for each Intentional Purposes #1 . . . #n, informed by the suggestions in the Potential KPI Master List.

a. Brainstorm the ways you might observe the impacts you desire from your Intentional Purposes: If we are successful at achieving Purpose #1, who or what will be different? Revisit the theories of action for achieving the desired impacts that you developed in chapter 5.

b. For each of those changes that you agree are desirable outcomes or impacts, ask, "How will we know a difference has happened?" "What might indicate that the change has occurred?" and, "Are we are the cause of that difference?" If one of your purposes is to contribute to your neighborhood's quality of life, and one of your desired impacts is that the neighborhood is connected to and uses its public resources, then a KPI that divides the number of neighbor memberships by the total number of memberships might track increasing or decreasing neighborhood connections and use. Combine that output data with evaluation findings to understand why, using surveys and focus groups to understand changes in satisfaction levels and reasons for attending.

c. Discuss how you might be able to observe and possibly measure indicators of each desired impact over time. Some measurements may only explore correlations, but a few might be caused by the museum's activities.

d. Review the MIIP KPIs (Selection = First Cut) to see if the group agrees on cutting more to make the list more manageable.

e. Add ideal indicators of the changes you desire that the Core Team suggests and insert them as new rows in the Potential KPI Master List, noting "Core Team: Suggested Ideal" in the Source column. Code those that remain plus the new ones as "Second Cut." Delete or archive the rest.

f. You should end the workshop with a more focused list of potential indicators from broadly two sources: Suggestions from MIIP 1.0 and ideal indicators suggested by the Core Team. This is the Potential KPI Master List Second Cut.

4. Analyze the Potential KPI Master List Second Cut for operational and data collection logistics: What data fields are needed to calculate each of the KPIs? Can we get this data?

a. Add a column to categorize (tag) each of the KPIs by the availability of its data using these tags or your equivalents: (1) existing data fields, (2) provisional data fields, (3) aspirational data fields, and (4) a mix of data fields.

- *Existing data fields* are data fields that you collect already. Ideally, your peers are also using them and have been for years. The most stable and historic of these are likely to be the museum's attendance records and audited financial data.

- *Provisional data fields* are trial or experimental data collection fields. The museum may be able to collect this data, and the results may be meaningful, but you will have to try it and evolve it over time. Some of these may be data fields collected by other museums, but not yet by your museum. Others may not have been counted, collected, or factored in this way before. Others will be regarded as interim data fields, pending the development of more meaningful measurements.

    For instance, on-site attendance is only one component of the museum's annual physical engagements, which also include outreach, program participants, volunteer shifts, and even meeting attendance. Many of these other forms of engagement often are not counted systematically or reported in association databases. Some museums add these forms of engagement to attendance, but typically categories will be missing. The museum also needs to think about how it wants to count its virtual, social media, and other digital engagements. For now, museums might first focus on physical engagements, then add digital or virtual engagements. On-site visitor attendance is well documented and reported by many museums, so it is a useful data field. However, it is not equal to the museum's total engagements, just a component of that figure. Hence, annual attendance should be regarded as a provisional and partial indicator of annual engagements, until full engagement counts are routinely reported.

- *Aspirational data fields* are those no one yet knows how to measure, such as a museum's more intangible benefits or its game-changing singular outcomes, such as inspiring a Nobel Prize winner. In one way, they are challenges to evaluation professionals, and, over time, aspirational data fields should move toward becoming first provisional data fields, and eventually, existing data fields. Yet some impacts will continue to elude quantification, and this is an important reminder that a museum's total contributions can never be measured.

b. Go back into MIIP 1.0 to review Resources, Activities, and Operating and evaluation data (Steps 3–5) to find data fields that may be useful to invent new KPIs for desired impacts not yet sufficiently covered by candidate KPIs. Import and tag these into the database.

c. Sort the Second Cut for IP#1 by availability of data, so that the most easily available and widely used are at the top of the list and the most challenging to measure are at the bottom.

d. Think about the possible connections between your Core Team's ideal indicators and the filtered suggestions from MIIP 1.0. What are their ideal indicators trying to get at? What kinds of measurements might fit the bill or might do part of the job, even as provisional or aspirational indicators? See if the most available and widely used indicators might shed some light on whether you are achieving your intentional purposes.

e. Thin the candidates as much as possible on your own, and tag the remainder "Third Cut."

f. Inevitably, there will be gaps–desired impacts as yet unmatched with enough strong KPIs. Start a Gap List.

5. Convene the Core Team to review and edit the Third Cut and brainstorm possible solutions to the Gap List. Encourage the invention of KPIs that are meaningful ratios of existing resource, activity, and output data (Steps 3, 4, and 5 of the Museum Theory of Action). For instance, year-over-year comparisons of the ratio of participants to capacity for your teacher professional development workshops could be a KPI indicating an aspect of an intentional purpose like Serving the K–12 system, with higher capacity ratios being one indicator of a potential increase in impact. This KPI uses these data fields: number of teachers served in the Base Year, number of teachers served the Current Year, and the maximum capacity (number of program spaces x their average seating capacity x the maximum number of time slots). End the meeting having added new rows for the Core Team's possible solutions. Reduce the Gap List to reflect those covered by possible solutions.

6. Study the Third Cut, which should be familiar by now. What makes sense at this point? Which indicators are both measurable and meaningful? Which are shared by your peers? Return to the start: How do you measure your performance in achieving your Intentional Purpose #1? Which of these in the Third Cut might work, and what is still lacking? Synthesize the best of these into four or so candidate KPI's per desired impact. Label these "Fourth Cut."

7. Conform and align to existing research and data collection standards. Once your prioritized intentional purposes and their KPIs are in rough draft, look among existing and potential data sources for reliable data definitions, such as those from data collection surveys (see MIIP 1.0 indicators #1–#209 and other sources listed in Appendix B). This process of wordsmithing your purpose statements and defining the data fields that go into your KPIs will require some

compromise from your ideals, but will result in more practical choices that can be implemented in line with peers and community practice.

   a. Go back to the original source (see Appendix B) of any MIIP 1.0 indicator in the Fourth Cut to get the full text and most recent language in order to standardize with others.

8. Draft a briefing document called "Candidate Key Performance Indicators (Fourth Cut)" with the following sections:

   a. Summary of all Proposed Key Performance Indicators: Listed by Intentional Purpose and desired impact; listed by availability of data, and listed by implementation phases.

   b. Relationships among the Proposed Key Performance Indicators: Do they offer multiple perspectives? Do they align or suggest opposite conclusions? Are some either more comprehensive or meaningful than others?

   c. Implementation: How will the data collection and reporting procedures be organized and managed? What is the implementation plan—the schedule, scopes, and responsibilities? Are there phases, perhaps starting with a few indicators and adding more as they become operational?

   d. Risk Mitigation: Might an institutional focus on these measures have other consequences? Might some desired impacts be compromised because they are not being counted? How do we monitor and mitigate these risks?

   e. Next steps for governance and the Core Team.

9. Review the draft with the Core Team. Incorporate their edits and suggestions, and review more drafts as needed.

   a Double check that data can be collected per the desired definitions (Note: the Core Team should include managers familiar with the museum's evaluation and operating data).

10. Present the revised "Candidate Key Performance Indicators" to governance (Note: the Core Team could be an ad hoc governance committee). Facilitate a governance workshop for them to prioritize the candidate KPIs, resulting in a final selection. End the workshop with a recommendation to adopt the selected and prioritized KPIs that result.

    a. Summarize the KPIs and their priorities in a table modeled on Worksheet 6.4, "Prioritized KPIs."

    b. Set up a new Excel worksheet modeled on Worksheet 6.5, "Data Fields," to keep track of the data field inputs for your KPIs.

11. Once governance has approved, circulate the updated version of the policy document as the "Museum's Key Performance Indicators" and start its implementation.

COLLECT AND ANALYZE YEAR-OVER-YEAR KPIs

Once you have determined your KPIs, you can collect the data, populate the KPIs with that data, and analyze the results using the steps and the data collection logistics listed in this section.

12. Establish a "Data Input Log" modeled on Worksheet 6.6 (or add columns to Worksheet 6.5) with a separate record/row for each data collection field needed by the KPIs. For each data field, list the following columns: (a) Source (of data), (b) Base Year, (c) Current Year, (d) Change Index.

13. Enter the data for your Base Year.

14. Enter the data for your Current Year (or Year 1) into the Data Input Log in a column beside the Base Year; calculate the change index by dividing the Current Year by the Base Year.

15. In a new worksheet called "KPI Calculations" modeled on Worksheet 6.7, list the KPIs by IP and desired impact with a row per KPI.

16. Write the KPIs as mathematical formulas that link to the data fields in the Data Input Log. See table D.2 in Appendix D for examples of KPI formulas.

17. Test and correct the KPI formulas: Do the results make intuitive sense? Is the original data strong enough to report this KPI? Is the math right?
18. Document the readings for all KPIs, noting anomalies and interim measures.
19. Look at the results: Do they make sense? Are there explanations or mitigating circumstances? Are the results somehow misleading? Do you need to factor inflation and population growth? What will it take to improve results? Are those actions real improvements or just gaming the numbers? Do you need to commission an evaluation study?
20. Provide these year-over-year KPI figures to the museum's leadership to inform planning and objective setting.
21. Propose changes to the KPIs that emerge from the process of recording and calculating data. Over time, the museum's set of KPIs should evolve to address new desired impacts and priorities and to improve the meaningfulness and accuracy of the selected indicators.

At this point, you have selected KPIs for each of your desired impacts for each of your intentional purposes. Then, you collected the data for your Base Year and Current Year, calculated your KPIs for both years, and analyzed your year-over-year performance. Collectively, changes to these KPIs may measure changes in your impact and performance.

In the next chapter, you will form a network of your peer museums, and, using a shared database of operating data, you will use a similar process to this chapter to compare your KPIs to your peers.

CHAPTER 7

COMPARE YOUR MUSEUM TO YOUR PEERS'

How does a museum compare its performance to peer museums in similar contexts?

Museums with similar missions, business models, resources, and contexts can compare their relative performance. Sectors of the U.S. museum field have been doing this for years through their associations; AAM, AAMD, ACM, ASTC, and other museum associations collect operating data shared with members for planning and advocacy.

Comparing a museum's KPIs with those of peer museums is an informative exercise that helps museum leadership see where your museum excels and where there may be growth or efficiency potentials. Comparing a museum's metrics to the average and mean of a sample of peer museums becomes more meaningful as the definition of *peer* gets closer to the museum's unique definition, and as the sample size gets larger. Large outdoor living history museums like Plimoth Plantation, Connor Prairie, and Old Salem Village have enough in common to learn from each other's practices, but such large, U.S. outdoor living history museums are too few and diverse for the average of their aggregated operating data to be statistically meaningful.

Children's museums, however, are a more coherent and numerous sample. In 2012, members of the Association of Children's Museums (ACM) included 270 open museums plus almost seventy emerging museums. Enough members responded to past annual data surveys that an ACM member can filter for smaller samples that are even closer to the museum's definition. Perhaps a 75,000 square foot children's museum in a 450,000 market population defines its peers by bracketing its own market and size: Other children's museums located in a population of 350,000 to 550,000 and having a museum size of 65,000 to 85,000 square feet. The ACM Benchmarking Calculator lets museum leadership filter for a defined number of main qualities that they think will make a fair sample of comparables, or *peer museums*.

PEER MUSEUMS

Peer museums are:

- The same type, discipline, or sector of the museum field, such as other collection-based art museums, or other historic house museums, or municipal zoos.
- Funded by similar business models: Peer museums will have similar revenue sources, which can be approximated by looking at their share of earned-to-support revenue, and, within support, to the relative share of public or private funding. A government or university museum with free admission is not a peer to a museum dependent on admissions revenues.
- Operators of similar resources: A museum's operating data is shaped by its physical resources (site, facility, collections, and exhibits), human resources, and endowment. Ideally, meaningful

comparables should have roughly the same components, building size, staff size, annual budget, and/or capital assets.

- Located in contexts as similar as possible: Comparable museums should be in similarly sized cities, communities, or markets, ideally in the same climate and with similar disposable household incomes and similar education levels (two key indicators of museum attendance). Similar governance and control are needed; university, government, and nonprofit mandates are different. Location is also a factor: urban or suburban, unique building or tenant in a complex, coastal or central.

When enough museums share these filters, they form a peer group that can start to make meaningful comparisons and assess relative performance for specific KPIs. Such data comparisons have been useful to several sectors of the museum field to guide management, evaluation, and advocacy.

We can compare performance among peer museums once we make some basic assumptions or rules about the sample of peers:

- The sample will contain peer museums of the same type and with similar business models, resources, and contexts, with anomalies noted. Your museum is included in the sample of peer museums, appearing near the middle of the sample when sorted by population, budget, or size.
- You and your peers use identical data definitions for all compared data fields and ideally share data for the same year or, at most, one year apart.
- The museum participates in relevant data-sharing systems, particularly those run by the museum associations, the government (IMLS and IRS in the United States), and DataArts (in some U.S. states).
- Enough of your peers have reported these data fields to create a meaningful sample.

COMPARE KPIs TO THOSE OF YOUR PEERS

This process is about comparing your performance in your selected areas of impact and performance to that of your peers. Find out what you do better than the norm, and what you could improve. Your museum is likely to have lessons to teach, and some to learn. A corollary idea is to establish a positive and collaborative relationship among your peers. If you are in separate markets, you are not competing, but helping each other. You have a lot to share with your peers, ideally with collective gain over the years, expanding and shifting the membership of the peer group as each museum evolves in purposes and resources.

The management approach called *appreciative inquiry* starts such comparisons on a positive note, asking more about what is going well and how to maximize it than the alternative *deficit inquiry* model that investigates what is going poorly and focuses on fixing it.

1. Select an existing or create a new museum database with consistent sources for peer museum operating data. Look at the existing databases maintained by museum associations. In the United States, several of these are organized by museum sector (art, science, children's, etc.), while others are field-wide (IMLS, DataArts, AAM). Be careful about mixing data from various associations, as the reporting periods, data definitions, and interpretations vary. Regional museum associations and government cultural agencies have also collected museum data.
   a. You want this Selected Database to: (a) give you access to enough other peer museum data to make comparisons useful; (b) establish and enforce a consistent set of data definitions for all participating museums (including yours); (c) take advantage of centralized data collection and

tabulation (and reduce the burden on groups of museums trying to do it themselves); and (d) allow you to filter the database (or import it into an Excel worksheet) to identify your most comparable museums.

b. Your museum should participate in this database, submitting your data periodically by their definitions. You should use your museum's data as it appears in the selected database unless you note corrections. Do not, for instance, replace the attendance number with your current figure, as all the peers might have changed as well.

c. Some association surveys have limited data, and you will need to ask your peers to share additional data in return for sharing your compilation and analysis.

d. Or, create your own peer network if there is no existing database of similar museums. If you already know your peers, create a data-sharing network among your colleagues in similar circumstances in other cities. Many ad hoc data-sharing networks like this have been formed, but they are hard to enforce and difficult to maintain. If you have an active association database to work with, you are well ahead. If some of your colleagues are not included, ask them to join and submit their data.

e. You may need to follow up on some data points with individual museums to make sure they use the same definitions or to clarify data that does not look right.

2. Identify standard sources of high-quality community and other external data, such as metro population, community diversity, and household income.

3. Establish numeric parameters that bracket your museum's data. Filter the database for peer museums by using bracketed filters for this first cut: Type of museum; business model (similar share of earned-to-support revenue); market population (the context); and the museum's scale and resources (size or annual expense budget).

a. Bracket your business model, population, and scale figures by ±20 percent. See how large a sample of similar museums this produces; adjust the bracket up and down until you find a satisfactory balance between sample size and similarity.

b. This step identifies your first-cut list of similar museums. As some will be deleted in the next step, it should have at least ten to fifteen museums including yours, which should appear in the middle of the group when sorted by the bracketed filters.

4. Look at the museums on the list, if they are named. Do you think of them as peers? If the data is anonymized, look for the outliers by finding data points removed from the rest of the cluster. View their websites, visitor maps, and annual reports. Are your cities similar? Does each museum in the sample feel like you?

a. Look for anomalies. Two museums may look similar at first glance, but if one has collections and the other none, they will have many other differences; they are trying to serve different purposes for different audiences and supporters.

b. Anomalies should not disqualify, however. No other museum is exactly like yours, and the objective is to form a [mostly] peer network of four to eight "close enough" peers, and then to understand the differences and how they might show up in the data. Is one of your peers a green building with unit energy costs lower than yours? Does another museum have utility costs paid by a government entity?

5. Create other kinds of museum groups for other kinds of comparisons: If your museum is contemplating a significant change, then you may want a second set of museums that are like what you want to become. Perhaps you are contemplating an expansion—what do museums of that size look like, and what do they earn and cost to run?

a. Broader samples can be useful, as museums of the same facility size and similar components can compare operating expenses, even if their types and context are different.

b. Local museum networks are also useful for some kinds of comparisons, even though they involve different types of museums. All museums in a city have the same climate and economy to deal with.

c. Seeing your museum in the larger context of all museums of your type (unfiltered) is useful for board members and others to calibrate expectations and explore potential growth.

d. Certain KPIs may want their own peer groups. For instance, museums with giant screen theaters (e.g., IMAX®) tend to have higher average ticket prices (ATPs) than those that do not; two science centers may be similar in size and market, but if one has an IMAX® and the other does not, then their ATPs will not be comparable.

6. Circulate a draft list of Peer Museums to the Core Team and others knowledgeable about other similar museums. After revisions, additions, and adoption, document the list of Peer Museums.

7. Import peer museum data already in your Selected Database into an Excel worksheet for analysis modeled on Worksheet 7.1, "Peer Museum Data" in Appendix E. Determine which data collection fields you use that your peers also share and report. How many of your KPIs can you compare? Can you adjust your KPIs to make them more compatible? Make a list of desired but missing data fields from your peers.

a. Import external data for the peer museum locations as needed. These data fields might include their market population, household income, education levels, school enrollment, etc.

8. Engage your Peer Museums: Establish liaisons and let them know you are analyzing their data as it appears in your Selected Database. Ask them to review and proof their data. Ask for any missing data points for the same term as the database. Agree to send them your comparison tables. The result should be a sharing of data and a social contact for stories and helpful practices. Your museum's peer data-sharing network, however you end up defining it, should also become your staff's peer professional network.

9. Calculate the KPIs for each Peer Museum: Calculate their versions of your selected KPIs, then calculate both the median and the average of the sample, discarding any museums with empty data for a particular KPI. Use Worksheet 7.2, "Peer Museum KPI Analysis" as a model. For instance, if service to the pre-K–12 system is a priority purpose and one of your KPIs is the ratio of schoolchildren served to metro population, calculate that same KPI for the peers, but discard any for whom "metro population" is not applicable, like a rural museum in a sample of mostly center-city museums.

10. Calculate the individual KPIs, and then average the KPIs. Do not average the data point total of the whole sample and then calculate a KPI using the totals. You want to compare your museum's performance to other individual museums, not to an imaginary combined museum.

11. Determine the median and average of the sample: The median and the average are suited for different applications, but for now, use them as a range.

a. The median is the figure where there are an equal number of museums above and below the figure, whereas the average is the total of the sample divided by the number in the sample. Depending on the KPI, each has different uses. In looking at household income, for instance, the median is usually a better indicator of consumer spending power; a few very wealthy households may inflate the average.

b. For the purposes of comparing your KPIs mathematically to your peers' KPIs, the sample SHOULD NOT include your museum.

c. For the purposes of showing your museum graphically or in charts, the sample SHOULD include your museum, typically in a distinct color or pattern.

d. You may also want to compare your collected data to that of the average and median for your larger museum field group, such as all natural history museums.

12. Note the degree of clustering versus divergence and understand the statistical meaningfulness of the sample size: The rule of thumb is that larger samples are more statistically representative, but smaller samples can still be meaningful if the data points cluster closely around the average and median. This step is about understanding the reliability and meaningfulness of your aggregated data.

13. Compare your Key Performance Indicators: Use the bottom of Worksheet 7.2, "Peer Museum KPI Analysis" as a model to compare the average and mean of the peer KPIs to your current KPIs to see if yours fall inside or outside the sample's range—inside the range is "normal" and outside suggests further investigation. The mathematical relationship between your KPI and the average or median of your peers' KPIs is your museum's *peer performance index* (PPI). For each of your indicators, the performance index will be near 1.0 if the museum's performance on that KPI is close to the average or median, above 1.0 if above average or median, and below 1.0 if under.

    a. Do not expect this process to result in fine statistical distinctions. The sample sizes are small, or as they grow larger, the differences among the samples become greater. Some of the data sources are imperfect, and definitions and methodologies may vary. The process might let you make statements like "It looks like we are better than average among our peers in service to K–12," but it is not likely to let you be so exact to say, "We are 22.3 percent ahead of our average peers in service to K–12," even though that may be the calculation. The purpose of making the calculation is only to see the rough scale of the difference.

14. Research and analyze why your museum might be performing outside peer norms. You may have successes that merit investing in growth and other areas where you have work to do. Peer performance indexes inform institutional strategic planning.

15. Study peers' best practices and incorporate lessons learned into planning and implementation: Talk with and visit the best practice museums in the sample. Find out why they are performing better than you are and find out how they do it. Adapt those lessons to your museum's context, and keep your new friends at the best practice museum in the learning loop as you implement changes. See if the changes result in improved KPIs.

16. Share your experiences with the museum field so that your sector and all museums can improve: The museum field is wonderfully collaborative and open to sharing information that will help the whole sector. Just as we can learn from others, so should we teach. This step is about self-improvement modeled and coached by your best practice peers in specific areas, while you offer them your best practices in return.

The processes in this chapter enable you to compare yourself to your peers in order to see where you are performing on par, or above, or below your peers' normal ranges. In the process, you will form a network of your peers, which can lead to many other benefits and kinds of sharing. From this network you will learn their best practices, and use that information to improve your impact and performance, raising the bar for your network and for the museum field as a whole. The next chapter integrates your results from these last three chapters into a dashboard to inform your museum's planning and decisions.

CHAPTER 8

REPORT CHANGES IN YOUR IMPACT AND PERFORMANCE

How does a museum develop a data-informed culture?

In the last three chapters, your museum determined and prioritized its intentional purposes (IPs) and their desired impacts; selected and prioritized your key performance indicators (KPIs), and compared those KPIs to earlier years and to your peers. This chapter considers how you can disseminate your findings routinely to inform leadership and become part of the operating culture, leading to greater impact and performance.

By its nature, this chapter is less prescriptive; you will know best how to run a communications campaign in your museum. The objective is to get the findings in front of decision makers and stakeholders on a sufficiently reliable and frequent basis that monitoring KPIs becomes routine and trusted. There are many ways to achieve this objective, and you should design an ongoing communication plan that suits your museum, using the suggestions in this chapter as you want.

To achieve that goal, the reporting of impact and performance indicators needs to be:

1. Reported clearly, accurately, and regularly
2. Analyzed to point out exceptional readings and possible issues and opportunities
3. Studied by every leader and manager as a routine part of their work and job description
4. Considered in any planning and decision-making meeting or process
5. Used as the basis for setting quantified objectives
6. Evaluated periodically for the KPI's validity as a measure of the museum's desired impacts, and for the usefulness of the reporting process toward advancing the museum's goals

REPORTING YOUR MUSEUM'S KPIs

Circulating KPI numbers from time to time meets transparency needs for sharing data, but such numbers in isolation are but points in time and place, and do not tell a story over time and across walls. KPIs begin to tell a story when they can be compared—the same KPI at different times; the same KPI at different museums.

Given the need to show KPIs in comparison, the following reports can be generated visually as graphs and bar charts in Excel using the KPI data, then these visuals can be imported into reports, slide decks, and screens for internal circulation.

Target Comparisons

The most frequently requested report is likely to be your running tally of KPIs against the target figures set for the year during the budget season. How are we doing compared to budget? The most closely watched KPIs tend to involve attendance and revenue targets both because they are the museum's lifeblood and because they are open to course corrections.

Year-over-Year Comparisons

Year-over-year (YOY) comparisons focus readers on the degree of change from the previous year, which can relate to target objectives set the previous year. Did we meet or exceed our objectives? Presented raw, on its own, a YOY comparison of all KPIs can be read by stakeholders as a report card, with praise and concern attributed to the associated managers. A better report is introduced with a narrative overview of the year and its impacts on operations, and then each significant plus and minus change number has a story, an explanation. Ideally, the report ends with a summary of what deserves praise and what needs attention. See Worksheet 8.1, "Summary Report."

Historical comparisons reveal the big-picture trends, particularly if you can go back enough years to see the historical trend as a continuum or a range in a line graph, with years along the bottom and the KPI readings along the vertical. Is school attendance to population index in a long-term decline, or just in another one of its cycles? Might school groups return to former levels, or should we adapt to a new normal?

Peer Comparisons

Peer comparisons put your museum in the context of other museums like yours. Are you spending too much or not enough on marketing, compared with museums that are attracting the attendance you seek? How do your peers fare in membership retention rates? Comparisons with your peer museums are often shown as bar graphs, with your museum standing out in a distinctive color. Again, narratives can explain some of the anomalies. It is also worth reporting the best practices, both yours as identified by a high KPI and those of your peers, identified by their high KPIs.

The most thorough peer comparison report is a "Performance Assessment and Recommendations Study," which looks at your KPIs and other operating numbers in comparison with your peers'. Such reports will certainly highlight the same pluses and minuses, but with the added benefit of educating board members, media, and other stakeholders about setting realistic expectations and appreciating that your museum is running within normal ranges of similar museums.

Alignment and Validity Analysis

This narrative analysis is a meta-study that looks at the findings as a group, at the alignment between intent and results, at the validity of the KPIs as indicators of impact and performance, and at the process as a whole. The objective of the analysis is to improve the meaningfulness and utility of your evolving set of desired impacts and the KPIs used to measure them.

What are all these measurements telling us as a whole about your museum? Do the KPI findings reinforce each other, or seem at odds? Are the narratives balanced, or is every success attributed to staff brilliance and every failure to outside forces? Do the KPIs work operationally? Is the data collection process accurate? Is the indicator actually relevant to the desired impacts you are trying to measure? Answers to such questions will respond to critics and propose changes that will improve KPI meaningfulness and data collection accuracy.

Summary Report (Worksheet 8.1)

An executive summary highlights the key findings from the more detailed reports, sets the context, and provides commentary and summary recommendations.

Future Adjustments and Target Objectives

A follow-up report will remind leadership of the findings and recommendations as they get under way with the next cycle of planning.

Periodically share your reports with governance. Decide how transparent you want to be with public access to the museum's impact and performance results. Look at the Dallas Museum of Art for examples of public transparency.

DEVELOPING A DASHBOARD OF FACTORED KPIs

At this stage, you have determined KPIs for each of your museum's prioritized intentional purposes. You have also set up data collection and reporting processes that feed the KPI calculations for both year-over-year and peer museum comparisons.

Dashboards are arrays of information that help leaders and managers see how the museum is operating. To extend the automobile metaphor, they are arrays of dials and gauges, often with danger zones, that help those driving the museum see how it is running. The metaphor implies real time, which would certainly be ideal: How many visitors are in the galleries right now? Has the dwell time in Gallery E increased since last night's news? Are volunteer hours back up since school started? Did our Net Promoter Score go down with last weekend's crowds?

Dashboards are also digests, snapshots, and summaries of the KPIs important to the museum and its leaders, managers, and staff. They are part of the reporting process outlined above, but are more current and visible. Dashboards should be important enough to the operating culture that they are desktop icons.

There will be other KPIs not officially linked to the museum's intentional purposes that are important operationally, and these *operational KPIs* might show up in their own area of the dashboard. Operational KPIs like cash liquidity, actual to budget comparisons, expenses per building square foot, and current payroll account balances are examples of other kinds of operational KPIs managers may need to track in addition to the museum's impact and performance KPIs.

1. Determine how you can get a clear KPI dashboard readout to managers' attention. This is a local resource and culture question; the dashboard could be as simple as a printout pinned to a bulletin board or an e-mail notice, or as complicated as a screen full of readouts, updated in real time from the museum's sensors, accounting, and ticketing systems. Best to start simple.
2. Design a prototype Dashboard 0.1 for managers that tracks the selected Key Performance Indicators, flagging changes that deserve attention. Each IP should show its target and summary KPIs, with the source KPIs and data fields available.
3. Try the prototype with managers. Collect comments and suggestions, and revise as needed.
4. Circulate Dashboard 1.0 and set up the process for continued updates to the Dashboard.
5. Start a file for improvements to the museum's IPs, KPIs, and Dashboards.

PERIODICALLY TESTING THE
MEANINGFULNESS AND ACCURACY OF EACH INDICATOR

Indicators of impact and performance are only indicators of the larger picture, and it is important to test their validity as indicators from time to time using other methodologies, such as surveys, interviews, and focus groups, to see if the results support or question the selected indicators of impact and performance.

For instance, teacher repeat use may be a good indicator that those teachers find enough benefit to return. Because they are teachers, and therefore qualified educators, we might assume that the impact they receive is educational, but this assumption is worth evaluating qualitatively: "Why do the teachers return?" Is it because of the museum's educational value to their students? Or because they are rewarding their students and themselves with a fun day off in a safe environment? What is the relative share of these and other perceived benefits, and how does that affect the validity or interpretation of the indicator?

As noted earlier, the museum also has intangible values that are hard to count in units of time, effort, or money. A museum's symbolic value to its community, for instance, is hard to quantify. So are the museum's potentials or capacities to inspire a genius, soothe a grieving soul, or spark a romance. If the museum's intangible benefits and resources remain roughly constant, then changes in the tangible value may indicate changes in the museum's total perceived value. However, you should consider whether the museum's intangible benefits or resources may have changed in the same period, and this may be particularly true in a year when a significant capital addition opens. For instance, a museum may add new and better collection storage space, which means its capital value in heritage preservation increases, but few operating revenue numbers may change in the early years to indicate this increase in annual impact and benefit.

Revise your theories of action, intentional purposes, desired impacts, and KPIs periodically to incorporate lessons learned. If qualitative evaluation invalidates an indicator, then try another indicator; if it validates an indicator, but with qualifications, such as finding that the museum's impact is only part of the reason, then incorporate that correction factor into a revised KPI. Talk with the staff: What are they doing that achieves the results? How do their answers align with the narrative in the theory of action? Make the necessary changes to either their practice or your theory.

PRIORITIZING YOUR PERFORMANCE MEASURES

John Falk and Beverly Sheppard in *Thriving in the Knowledge Age: New Business Models for Museums and Other Cultural Institutions* suggest that museums should decide among levels of performance in five different categories, which they adopted from Crawford and Matthews: Access, Experience, Price, Service, and Product. They observed that a museum should try to dominate (best in class) in only one area, to be distinguished in one other, and to be acceptable in all the rest (Falk and Sheppard 2006).

Falk and Sheppard's work suggests that you will also want to prioritize where you want to perform best in class. MIIP 1.0 has many suggestions for performance indicators, and you are likely to select more than five and want to be best in class in more than one of those. The objective is to prioritize your KPIs into desired levels of performance. What do you want to be known for? What impacts do you want to be so good at that other museums come to see how you do it? Adequate performance in your other areas can have its own benefits in resource conservation, innovation, and growth.

A strong word of caution before proceeding with mathematical calculations using priorities, especially as they are aggregated into overall performance scores. Ranking a group of options by percentage is a useful way for leadership to express their opinion about the relative importance among the choices, but it is less useful as those numbers are imported into algorithms where some of the other numbers are also opinions, especially if some of the base data is shaky. This section outlines how to calculate an overall performance number, but does not recommend doing so until at least several years after your selection of KPIs is running smoothly.

1. Review the priority assignments you made earlier to each of your intentional purposes and their desired impacts. Each IP should have a percentage; the total of the IPs should equal 100 percent. Under each IP are one or more desired impacts, again assigned priority percentages totaling 100 percent within the IP. Multiply these two percentages to get each desired impact's percentage of the whole, which should again total 100 percent.
   a. If you have three IPs, each with three desired impacts, each of which is monitored by three KPIs, you would have 27 KPIs, each of which would have an average 3.7 percent of the whole.
   b. This is too many KPIs: The few that are really important will minimize the rest to rounding errors, and 27 are too many to keep track of.
   c. One solution is to nest related KPIs into a smaller number of summary KPI numbers. A manager can zoom in to the components if needed.
   d. Another solution is to limit the number of KPIs the museum can support.
2. Invent a unified scoring system that converts your different kinds of KPI results into a shared kind of number. Perhaps you set every Base Year number at a 100 index, and translate your current year KPIs into a ±100 index. Or you give every KPI a grade, where C is average or the same as last year, A is better and F is much worse; then you can calculate a grade point average. Use a method that you and your stakeholders respect, and keep it as mathematically pure as possible, avoiding judgment calls.
   a. Factor these individual KPI scores by their percentage of the total and add them up to calculate the museum's overall score.
   b. Use this figure with the greatest of caution and many caveats—it is way out on a limb of calculations.

CONCLUSION

KPI findings are designed to prompt and inform, not dictate, leadership policy setting and management decisions, with the objective of constant evolution and improvement.

No one should expect, or fear, that your selection of KPIs will henceforth rule all decisions. We are museums, not factories or service agencies, and the innovation and passion of museum professionals will buffer excessive "metricitis." Though many staff members complain about being chained to attendance and associated revenues, the number of museum-selected KPIs envisioned in this book goes beyond that single attendance metric that oversimplifies a museum's value.

Some might argue that museums should be free of formulaic evaluations because museums provide the kinds of impacts that elude the bean counters. An argument can be made that *museum quality* cannot be measured in dollars or popularity, but is some form of absolute truth and beauty achievable by only a few talents working with no resource limits. Perhaps the Getty, with its huge endowment, can operate without worrying about external revenue judgments, but most other museums are answerable to their communities, particularly to the audiences and supporters who give life to their operation.

Increasingly, we need to account for our museum's impact and performance, as detailed in the introduction and chapter 1. Museum professionals may want job security, resources, and freedom to do what they want on a museum's prestigious stage, but that is neither the long-term trend nor the likely future.

It is also not a community service perspective, nor is it responsive to our audiences and supporters. In the fiercely competitive market for time, effort, and money, they will pass judgment with their choices, and go elsewhere. A better route is to collaborate with them: some of what they want, and some of what the museum wants. KPIs keep track of this collaboration by monitoring the actual behaviors and exchanges made in return for their museum engagements.

Museums are also in a roiling river of change, hazard, and opportunity. Government cuts, sudden bequests, demands from the governor, loss of a director, picketing by activists—whenever unpredictable black swans come your way, there may be an impact on your KPIs, and maybe on your ability to collect meaningful data. However, a system of KPIs is also a way to ride the river of change, once you can read where it is going. As Susan Raymond says:

> The most successful nonprofits in serving the societal commons will be those whose leaders, boards, and programs are (1) sufficiently courageous to focus on the horizon and (2) sufficiently disciplined to put in place navigational strategies that take advantage of the winds of change to build stable revenue strategies, anticipate upcoming storms, weather them when they blow, and move ever forward to better society. (Raymond 2010)

REFERENCES

Falk, John H., and Beverly K. Sheppard. *Thriving in the Knowledge Age: New Business Models for Museums and Other Cultural Institutions.* Lanham, MD: AltaMira, 2006.
Raymond, Susan U. *Nonprofit Finance for Hard Times: Setting the Larger Stage.* Hoboken: Wiley, 2010.

CHAPTER 9

SUMMARY AND FUTURE POTENTIALS

What has been accomplished? How do you further advance the museum field, your museum, and your profession? What lies ahead?

The rich work to date by museum professionals and associations around the globe grounds the rationale, theory, and analysis developed in the first three chapters of this book and applied in the following five.

The previous chapters overlaid established evaluation frameworks to reveal an underlying Museum Theory of Action that fits the way museums actually operate today—how museums do what they do. The journey also uncovered many museum impacts, which can be organized into categories of why museums do what they do, and went on to apply these findings to the practice of measuring museum impact and performance.

This final chapter summarizes the theory and practice of measuring changes in impact and performance; gives you latitude and a set of opening KPIs to short-cut these processes if you need; looks to the potential future benefits of using the right metrics; and discusses the heresies or innovations that underlie this approach.

Museums are complex; an evaluation framework has to accommodate this complexity, yet be useful to a single museum. The Museum Theory of Action and its definitions are proposed as a synthesis of prior work and as a potential way to help museums align purposes to results in order to improve impact and performance. The Museum Indicators of Impact and Performance (MIIP 1.0) reveals a wealth of valuable impacts benefiting public, private, and personal needs and aspirations.

The Theory of Action evaluation framework can help individual museums account for how and what they are currently doing, plan actions that will improve their impact, and select indicators that monitor whether they are succeeding. MIIP 1.0 can help individual museums understand their potential impacts and their full range of possible public, private, and personal benefits. The evaluation and planning framework can help museums make the hard choices about what to focus on, yet not be as limiting as single-mission evaluations.

A *museum engagement* involves time, effort, and often money on the part of a museum's audiences and supporters. Typically, people have to travel to your museum to engage in your on-site visitor experiences, scheduled programs, evening functions, grant progress reviews, and exhibit advisory meetings. Physical museum engagements can also happen off-site, as part of a museum's outreach programs. The goal of outreach is to reduce audience effort, specifically, travel distances and hassles, but it still takes some effort to show up at a science festival or for an after-school art workshop. Virtual museum engagements happen online and require even less effort and no money—just time.

Time is likely to become our audiences' and supporters' scarcest commodity. There are so many things out there clamoring for attention, so many inspiring and effective social programs seeking funds, and so many entertainments and learning experiences vying for time. There are, in fact, so many other museums out there competing for a museum's audiences and supporters.

Museums need to compete, and it helps to select which public, private, and personal benefits a museum wants to deliver, and to understand how it can keep improving its impact and performance metrics.

MEASURING MUSEUM IMPACT AND PERFORMANCE

This book follows a logical development from research to theory and findings, and then onto applying the theory to practice, with respect to measuring museum impact and performance.

Chapter 1 starts with a literature review of eleven evaluation frameworks to reveal an underlying Museum Theory of Action with seven steps.

The narrative version of this action sequence is: The museum, in service to its community, decides on its intentional purposes and desired impacts. Then, guided by its principles, the museum uses its resources to operate activities for its community and its audiences and supporters that result in valued impacts and benefits. Engagements with these activities generate operating and evaluation data that can be incorporated into KPIs that monitor the museum's effectiveness and efficiency. This Theory of Action is diagrammed in table 9.1 as a two-way loop, and in table 1.3 as a logic model.

Chapter 2 also starts with a literature review, this time drawing on fifty-one respected museum sources (see Appendix B) to create a representative database of potential museum indicators of impact and performance (MIIP 1.0). Analysis of these 1,025 indicators reveals fourteen Categories of Potential Museum Impacts with sixty data content topics. The fourteen Categories of Potential Museum Impacts include seven categories of public impacts (broadening participation, preserving heritage, strengthening social capital, enhancing public knowledge, serving education, advancing social change, and communicating public identity and image); two private impacts (contributing to the economy and delivering corporate community services); three personal impacts (enabling personal growth, offering personal respite, and welcoming personal leisure); and two institutional impacts (helping museum operations and building museum capital). The 1,025 indicators also populate all seven steps of the Theory of Action, with none that do not fit.

Chapter 3 builds on both the Theory of Action and the Categories of Potential Museum Impacts to establish the theoretical basis for measuring changes in museum impact and performance. The chapter considers evidence of value; distinguishes between value and worth and between impact and benefit, the supporters, and the community at large; explores free-choice exchanges of time, effort, and money as measures of impact; describes the benefits of tracking measurements; and introduces quantitative key performance indicators to evaluate qualitative impacts.

STEPS IN THE MUSEUM THEORY OF ACTION

Step 1: Intentional purposes—What the museum wants to deliver.
Step 2: Guiding principles—The museum's character, brand identity, and standards.
Step 3: Resources—The museum's collections, facilities, reputation, and people.
Step 4: Activities—The museum's exhibitions, programs, and other services.
Step 5: Operating and evaluation data—The annual activity counts and survey findings.
Step 6: Key performance indicators—Selected formulas using changes in activity data to measure changes in impact and performance.
Step 7: Perceived benefits—What the audiences and supporters think they receive from the activities.

Table 9.1. Museum Theory of Action: Two-Way Version

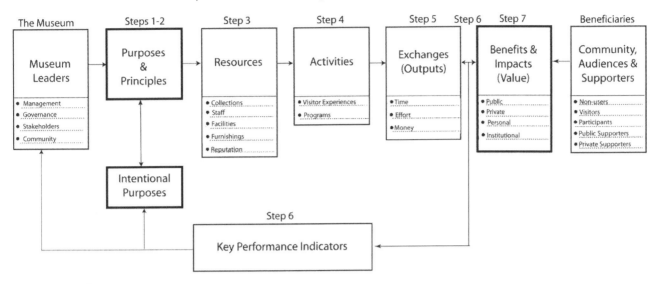

Source: The White Oak Institute

Table 9.2. Categories of Potential Museum Impacts

		# of MIIP indicators
Public Impacts		
A	Broadening participation	85
B	Preserving heritage	47
C	Strengthening social capital	76
D	Enhancing public knowledge	43
E	Serving education	56
F	Advancing social change	40
G	Communicating public identity & image	27
Private Impacts		
H	Contributing to the economy	85
I	Delivering corporate community services	9
Personal Impacts		
J	Enabling personal growth	147
K	Offering personal respite	4
L	Welcoming personal leisure	11
Institutional Impacts		
M	Helping museum operations	308
N	Building museum capital	87
Total indicators in the MIIP 1.0 database		1,025

Source: The White Oak Institute

Part 2: Practice applies the concepts developed in the first three chapters to museum practice so that your museum can measure its selected impacts and performance. The tone shifts from academic to practical and is addressed to "you," as the museum professional responsible for developing "your museum's" prioritized selection of KPIs. Chapter 4 sets up the processes and ground rules, with some suggestions for getting started.

In chapter 5, you collect many perspectives about what your museum should or could deliver from your audiences and supporters, community leaders and spokespeople, regional planning documents, existing partners, internal SWOT exercises, suggestions from MIIP 1.0, and the museum's most recent strategic plan. All these ideas about why your museum should exist go into a database to analyze and prioritize. Through research and rounds of discussion, you prioritize your museum's intentional purposes and desired impacts—giving each selected purpose and its desired impacts a ranking that totals 100 percent. You express a theory of action describing how your museum intends to achieve each impact.

Given this clarity about what impacts the museum desires to achieve and how, chapter 6 links each of your desired impacts to Key Performance Indicators (KPIs) that you select to measure changes in representative aspects of each desired impact.

For instance, as developed in the worksheets, the second of the Sample Museum's three intentional purposes is to "Contribute value to the community." The Sample Museum decided that one of the ways they would contribute value to the community is to help "Strengthen civic connections." They then decided that they might see evidence of that desired impact by observing four KPIs: (a) the degree that staff and leadership reflect the diversity of the community; (b) changes in their number of partnerships; (c) whether the museum's managers spend 5–10 percent of their time in community projects; and (d) the ratio of their regional corporate support to that of their peers—each with a rationale connecting these indicators to the desired impact.

These KPIs may indicate the desired impacts, but this assumption needs to be tested periodically using evaluation methods; the numbers may be responding to other forces: Does team diversity actually result in programing and audience diversity? Does the number of partnerships indicate civic connections? Do community leaders see our managers strengthening civic connections? Do our corporate supporters see us as strengthening civic connections?

Chapter 7 relates your museum to your peers. The comparison helps you and your governance see where you fit among similar museums in similar contexts, where you have potential to grow and where you are establishing best practices. The chapter walks you through the process of forming a peer museum network and using existing data collection sites to compare your KPIs with those of your peers.

Chapter 8 outlines ways to get your findings out to your colleagues and stakeholders by developing dashboards that track performance of your museum's selected desired impacts and its operating status, thereby building a culture of data-informed decisions.

LEAPFROGGING OVER HURDLES AND COMPLICATIONS TO GET STARTED

The processes in the second half of this book are complicated and involve many stakeholders over time. Of course, there are simpler ways to measure impact and performance, but my goal has been a systematic approach that could work for the most complicated museum and for any museum anywhere. While I recommend the full processes described in chapters 4–8, I sympathize with those museum leaders who cannot afford the time and want to get started immediately with metrics, perhaps due to board pressure. You can and should tailor the process to suit your needs and resources.

If you need, you might skip ahead and just intuitively select a handful of prototype indicators, while planning to double back later to do a proper job. Recognize and anticipate the risks of such shortcuts: lack of buy-in, skewing the museum toward simplistic number goals, lack of data, negative first impressions, and poorly informed choices.

While I have avoided recommending indicators thus far, in this final chapter, I share the following indicators that a museum could adapt directly, if you have access to the data:

- The ratio of external operating revenue from the museum's key service markets compared to the priority ratio of its intentional purposes. This indicator explores the relative alignment between a museum's intentional purposes and the benefits it actually delivers. Full alignment may not be desirable, but significant misalignment suggests investigation.
- The diversity profile of the museum's audiences and supporters compared to its community's diversity profile. This is an indicator of access and appeal to different constituencies.
- The market ratio of a museum's total annual museum engagements (exclude virtual visits) divided by the community population. This indicates the amount of effort spent by the community on the museum.
- The Net Promoter Score (NPS) (#641) from a single question asked periodically of audiences exiting a museum's main public venues. The NPS has a long track record as a simple and predictive indicator of customer perceived value.
- Support revenues from continuing supporters compared to previous years. Repeating supporters indicate their belief that the museum is achieving its intentional purposes.
- Total revenue and total engagement counts minus the budget forecasts. These indicate desired operating value, with negative numbers signaling shortfalls.

Most museums will want to add at least one indicator directly relevant to their mission, or as this book calls it, their top-priority Intentional Purpose #1.

Some museums, fearing that KPIs may force a straightjacket, might want some KPIs that directly encourage creativity, innovation, and outside-the-KPI ideas.

FUTURE POTENTIALS FOR INDIVIDUAL MUSEUMS, MUSEUM PROFESSIONALS, AND THE MUSEUM FIELD

The Theory of Action is usable in at least three ways: for assessing and measuring current impacts; for planning next year's operations, as well as new museums or expansions; and for researching for correlations and causality between activities and results.

Each unique museum can adapt the Theory of Action evaluation framework to prove and improve its unique impact and performance. Given the museum's intentional purposes and its desired impacts, it can measure changes in how effectively and efficiently its activities serve those purposes: How well does it use its resources, and do the activities conform to its guiding principles? The museum can select indicators of each purpose at each step, and use that data to inform, but not dictate, leadership decisions.

The museum, of course, is run by individuals, and is not itself a rational unity. Just as the museum field is a collection of widely diverse museums going in different directions for different purposes, so the mid- to large-size museum is also the result of diverse individual interests—staff, finance officers, curators, marketers, registrars, educators, trustees, exhibit developers, directors, etc.

Museum professionals can use the Theory of Action to ask themselves: What are my intentions? What impacts do I want to have, and on whom? Do others agree that these impacts are also the benefits I bring and that they need? How do my priorities align with those of my colleagues and of the museums I work with? How can I improve alignment?

The theory and practice developed in this book can help the museum field advocate for its many values with evidence of impact and performance, communicate the wide diversity of its members, and identify and share best practices and innovations. The Museum Theory of Action can help the museum field professionalize through adoption of shared evaluation frameworks, definitions, and research agendas with the broader impact of improving our value and raising the bar for all museums.

These potential sample uses are diagramed in table 9.3:

Table 9.3. Sample Uses of the Museum Theory of Action Evaluation Framework

Type of Use	The Museum Field	An Individual Museum	A Museum Professional
Measuring Current Status (Documentation)	Museum Advocacy	Annual Impact and Performance Statement	Resume
Setting Future Objectives (Planning)	Strategic Professional Development	Strategic Plan	Goal-setting
Research Framework (Research & Evaluation)	Standardized Indicator Definitions	Organizational Learning Agenda	Self-assessment Diary

Source: The White Oak Institute

Two examples illustrate the potential advantages of these approaches: Once a museum's measurement systems have matured, the museum can calculate returns on social investments (ROSI); and, museums and the museum field can study how closely their intentions align with their actual results.

Potential to Calculate Your Museum's Annual Return on Social Investment (ROSI)

As discussed in chapter 1, *return on social investment* (ROSI) is a common nonprofit KPI that divides the value of the impact by the cost. In the future, once your museum's KPIs are operating, you might be able to test ROSI when planning a capital campaign: If we add to our capital assets, will we see enough of a rise in our impacts and their revenues at least to match our current ROSI? In other words, will the contemplated capital campaign make the museum a more effective and efficient institution?

Alignment of Purposes to Impacts

An initial analysis of the relationship between internal purposes and external perceived benefits suggests that future research might explore the hypothesis that museums' intentional purposes are not fully aligned with what their audiences and supporters value, and that closer alignment will benefit all parties and the community as a whole: How do our intentional purposes align with our perceived benefits? Is a closer alignment more effective and efficient?

The initial analysis looked at the relative pervasiveness (i.e., relative share of the total) for each of the impacts in MIIP 1.0 between intentional purposes (Step 1) compared to perceived benefits (Step 7). Different levels of pervasiveness/attention may indicate the degree of alignment between the museum field's intentions and its results as shown in table 9.4.

For instance, using the boxed percentages in table 9.4, strengthening social capital is more pervasive as a perceived benefit (15 percent of all perceived benefit indicators) than it is among intentional purposes (9 percent of all intentional purposes). Perhaps museums can increase this impact by being more intentional about serving as a community gathering place, cultural bridge, and/or honest trusted

Table 9.4. Relative Pervasiveness of Impacts in MIIP 1.0

Potential Museum Impacts	Total Indicators by Impact	STEP 1 # of Indicators of Intentional Purposes		STEP 7 # of Indicators of Perceived Benefits		Step 1 vs. 7 '+/-	'% chng	Beneficiary
A. Broadening participation	85	11	12%	23	6%	-5.2%	-45%	Public
B. Preserving heritage	47	13	14%	10	3%	-10.9%	-80%	
C. Strengthening social capital	76	9	9%	53	15%	5.2%	55%	
D. Enhancing public knowledge	43	5	5%	18	5%	-0.3%	-5%	
E. Serving education	56	9	9%	18	5%	-4.5%	-47%	
F. Advancing social change	40	11	12%	25	7%	-4.6%	-40%	
G. Communicating public identity & image	27	2	2%	24	7%	4.6%	217%	
H. Contributing to the economy	85	5	5%	60	17%	11.4%	217%	Private
I. Delivering corporate community services	9	0	0%	4	1%	1.1%		
J. Enabling personal growth	147	18	19%	95	26%	7.4%	39%	Personal
K. Offering personal respite	4	1	1%	3	1%	-0.2%	-21%	
L. Welcoming personal leisure	11	0	0%	10	3%	2.8%		
M. Helping museum operations	308	5	5%	5	1%	-3.9%	-74%	Institutional
N. Building museum capital	87	6	6%	12	3%	-3.0%	-47%	
	1025	95	9%	360	35%	0%		

broker. Contributing to the economy accounts for 17 percent of the perceived benefit indicators as opposed to only 5 percent of the intentional purposes. Cities lure businesses and governments provide stimulus funds to create jobs; museums also create jobs, but many museums pride themselves, whether by choice or necessity, on running lean and mean—perhaps one of our purposes should be to create jobs. There are also impacts that may be more highly valued by the museum than by its community and its audiences and supporters. Preserving heritage accounts for 14 percent of museum intentions, but only 3 percent of the result indicators.

While these calculations are not evidence, they suggest further inquiry: Are museums not sufficiently intentional about strengthening social capital and contributing to the economy? And, does the public not sufficiently value museums' intentions to preserve heritage? If intentions are out of alignment with results, then adjustments made to the steps in the Theory of Action may increase effectiveness and efficiency and, therefore, impact and performance.

HERESIES OR INNOVATIONS?

Both the Theory of Action and the Categories of Potential Museum Impacts are based on the field's literature and fit with decades of observations about what museums do and why they do it. However, both assume ways of looking at museums that are different from the last century.

We have known we need measurements for years. Yet no standardized ways of measuring have emerged. No organizing paradigm. During four decades of museum analysis and strategic planning for over a hundred museums internationally,[1] I find that three twentieth-century dogmas guard the gates to the possible answers: the Mission-Focused Dogma, the Public Value Dogma, and the Output versus Outcome Dogma. Fortunately, the dogmas are tired and are no longer really able to explain how today's most vibrant museums operate and what they contribute. I suggest new approaches. Some may see these as heresies and others, I hope, as innovations.

The Mission-Focused Dogma: The assumption that the museum's mission is the museum's singular end, with everything else just a means to achieve the museum's mission. As I developed in "The Community Service Museum: Owning up to Our Multiple Missions," most mid to large museums accomplish far more than just their mission impact (Jacobsen 2014); hence, evaluating a museum on just its mission accomplishments short-changes that museum's full social value. This book pluralizes mission and calls them intentional purposes to avoid the accurate but awkward Mission 1, Mission 2, Mission 3, etc.

The Public Value Dogma: The belief that a museum's public value is the only value that really counts. Instead, treating public, private, and personal values as conceptual equals provides a more complete picture of a museum's external values, and reflects the reality of contemporary museum operating budgets, which contain support, sponsorship, and earned revenues. In the United States, museums have been losing public funding as a share of their total revenues for decades (Merritt and Katz 2009). Because museum costs for operating public buildings and conserving collections cannot get smaller, lost taxpayer revenues have resulted in increases in private and personal revenues. Given this long-term shift away from public funding, museums will need to become more intentional about delivering private and personal benefits, without feeling either guilty or nostalgic for shifting some emphasis away from delivering public impacts.

Output versus Outcome Dogma: The belief that a museum's operating data—its output counts—do not qualify as evidence of outcomes. This denial does not respect the expertise of our community and its audiences and supporters, nor does it recognize the competitive marketplace where they make their choices. Parents, teachers, grant officers, volunteers, tourists, and donors all have expertise and make conscious choices based on that expertise. In a free-choice, competitive marketplace, their votes of money, time, and effort are indicators of value in the eyes of experts. Of course, these exchanges may be affected by other factors, and periodically such behavioral indicators need to be tested and perhaps revised or refined: Do teachers return because they trust the museum's educational impact or because it is easy?

Once on the other side of these three dogmas, we can see museums more clearly, and new evaluation strategies and principles open up. These assumptions are among the foundations for this evaluation framework:

- In a multiple-mission museum, the totality of the museum and its yearly activities can be valued, rather than just evaluating the mission-related impacts and dismissing the rest as ancillary means to the mission ends.
- Multiple missions and unique resources mean complicated differences among museums; hence, there is no one standard by which all museums can be judged, but rather each museum must intentionally determine its missions (called *intentional purposes* in this book) and how it intends to measure its *desired impacts*.
- Once we treat public, private, and personal impacts as conceptual equals, then we can also respect all of our community and its audiences and supporters and pay more attention to the changes they want the museum to make; hence we can use audience and supporter behavior and opinion data to continually improve and evolve all of our community services.
- Today, all museum revenues, engagements, and dwell time are won in a competitive market, and all museum engagements are marketplace exchanges of time, effort, and sometimes money; hence, we can track these exchanges as indicators of the value of the impacts and benefits perceived by our community and its audiences and supporters.
- Once we respect that some operating data tally yearly choices by experts such as teachers and grant officers, then we can add a new class of impact evaluation metrics combining operating and evaluation data: carefully selected key performance indicators (KPIs) explored periodically by qualitative evaluation that can measure changes in impact and performance.

NEXT STEPS AND CONCLUSIONS

Museums and others in the cultural sector have a transition period before the field shifts to a culture of data-informed decisions. Data quality and consistency need to improve in the museum field, but so does the demand from leaders for more and better data. As the UK publication "Counting What Counts: What Big Data Can Do for the Cultural Sector" by Anthony Lilley OBE with Professor Paul Moore says:

> The current approach to the use of data in the cultural sector is out-of-date and inadequate . . . failing to make the most of the considerable financial and operational benefits which could arise from better use of data. In addition, a significant opportunity to better understand and possibly increase the cultural and social impact of public expenditure is going begging.
>
> It is high time for a step-change in the approach of arts and cultural bodies to data and for them to take up and build on the management of so-called "big data" in other sectors. (Lilley and Moore 2013)

As suggested in the introduction, museums need to integrate evaluation data with museum operating data in order to see a fuller picture of impact and performance. This combination of quantitative big data and qualitative small data requires rather than replaces leadership, vision, and expertise, a view supported by data scientists Peysakhovich & Stephens-Davidowitz:

> Big data can tell us whether certain teachers are helping their students; small data gives us the best hope to answer a crucial question: How are they doing it? . . . No one data set, no matter how big, is going to tell us exactly what we need. The new mountains of blunt data sets make human creativity, judgement, intuition and expertise more valuable, not less. (Peysakhovich and Stephens-Davidowitz 2015)

The good news is that museums start with substantial capital resources, both tangible and intangible. Collections, buildings, sites, staff expertise, networks, existing revenue lines, public trust, and cultural value are resources we can harness to offer our communities the activities and services they want and that meet our mutual desire to build a better and more democratic society (Hein 2006).

The evaluation framework developed in this book addresses the *why* of museums by listing fourteen categories of potential impacts and benefits, and it addresses the *how* of museums in the seven steps of a theory of action that combines the work of other museum professionals. By using this framework and selecting appropriate KPIs, museums can measure their impacts and performance to make more effective and efficient use of their resources.

In conclusion, after Stephen Weil's introductory warning about the complexity of the task, I return to Weil for more good news:

> What remains most remarkable to me is how broad a range of purposes the good museum has available to choose from in shaping its public-service efforts. . . . As most good museums ultimately arrive not at just one purpose but at some mixture of purposes . . . a museum can be a good one in an almost infinite number of ways. In everything museums do, they must remember the cornerstone on which the whole enterprise rests: to make a positive difference in the quality of people's lives. Museums that do that matter—they matter a great deal. (Weil 2002, 74)

NOTE

1. This work has been done by White Oak Associates, Inc., a museum planning and analysis firm owned and run by Jeanie Stahl and the author.

REFERENCES

Hein, George E. "Museum Education." In *A Companion to Museum Studies*, by S. MacDonald. Oxford: Blackwell, 2006.

Jacobsen, John W. "The Community Service Museum: Owning up to Our Multiple Missions." *Museum Management and Curatorship* 29, no. 1 (2014): 1–18.

Lilley, Anthony, and Paul Moore. "Counting What Counts: What Big Data Can Do for the Cultural Sector." Magic Lantern Productions Ltd. February 2013.

Merritt, Elizabeth E., and Philip M. Katz. *Museum Financial Information 2009.* American Association of Museums. August 1, 2009.

Peysakhovich, Alex, and Seth Stephens-Davidowitz. "How Not to Drown in Numbers." *New York Times*, May 3, 2015, SR 7.

Weil, Stephen. *Making Museums Matter.* Washington, D.C.: Smithsonian Institution, 2002.

APPENDIXES

APPENDIX A

Definitions and Assumptions

Differences in definitions bedevil shared data and understanding. This book consistently uses the definitions listed in this Appendix A. Most definitions are based on existing survey instruments and evaluation frameworks and are synthesized from definitions adopted by museum associations and professional interest groups.

The terms appear in *italics*, and they are described not alphabetically but in groups of terms related to six topics: Museum; Theory of action; Impact and performance; Museum engagements; Community, audiences, and supporters; and Value exchanges.

Table A.1 shows all the terms alphabetically, listing the paragraph numbers for their main appearances.

MUSEUM

1. The framework builds on the International Council of Museums' (ICOM's) definition of *museum*: "A museum is a nonprofit, permanent institution in the service of society and its development, open to the public, which acquires, conserves, researches, communicates and exhibits the tangible and intangible heritage of humanity and its environment for the purposes of education, study and enjoyment" (ICOM Statutes 2007). ICOM defines these terms broadly enough to include science centers, children's museums, zoos, and planetariums, and this book adopts the AAM's categories, as listed in table A.2.

2. Additionally, the definition of *museum* in this book includes four concepts that museums in North America, the United Kingdom, and the Eurozone might agree with, though the implications may not be clear:

   a. Stephen Weil's introduction to John Cotton Dana's selected writings from the 1920s quoted Dana's maxim that museums should find what the *community needs* and fit the museum to those needs (Peniston 1999, 16).

   b. Weil's own Theory of Museums bases a museum's worth on the good it has accomplished, and the museum's resources are the means to that end. The *performance* evaluation is then of the museum's *effectiveness* at achieving its purposes and of the *efficiency* of its resource use (Weil 2002; 2005).

   c. John Falk and Lynn Dierking in describing their Contextual Model of Learning place emphasis on museums' unique business model of free-choice learning that meets personal and sociocultural needs in physical contexts (Falk and Dierking 2000, xii; Falk and Sheppard 2006; Falk and Dierking 2012, 33). *Free choice* means museums are in a competitive marketplace dependent on voluntary engagements. No one has to visit. No one has to give museums money. This is a fundamental difference in museum business models from schools, where attendance is enforced by truancy laws. While private schools and higher education are consumer choices,

Table A.1. Alphabetical List of Definitions and Assumptions

Term	#	Term	#	Term	#
activities	12	human resources	10	programs	29
admissions, gallery	31	impact and performance KPIs	23	public impacts	44
aligned	42	impacts	13, 15, 16, 19	purposes	2.b
annual totals	56	impacts on others	18	purposes, intentional	9
attendance	31	indicators	20	resident market	36
audiences	32	institutional impacts	44	resource indicators	11
authorizing environment	34	intangible assets	10	resources	3.b, 10
beneficiaries, direct	32	intentional purposes	9	results	15
beneficiaries, indirect	32.a	key performance indicators (KPIs)	22	Return on Social Investment (ROSI)	57
benefits	13, 15, 19, 32	key service markets	45	revenue, earned	53
benefits to others	18	KPIs	23	revenue, support	53
business model	52	market ratios	39	ROSI	57
capital asset net income	53	means	2.b	school student market	36
capital assets	58	MIIP 1.0	21	secondary market	36
capital projects	55	money	43, 51	services	14
capital resources	10	museum	1, 4	site visit	28
CBSA	38	museum economic theory	5	society	34
community[ies]	2.a, 32	museum engagement[s]	25, 26	support revenue	53
community needs	34	Museum Theory of Action	8	supporters	32
constituents	34	non-users	32.a	supporters, private	35
Core Based Statistical Area (CBSA)	38	off-site	27, 29	supporters, public	35
core market	36	on-site	27, 29	Theory of Action	7
day trippers	36, 37	on-site attendance	31	Theory of Action, Museum	8
Designated Market Area (DMA)	38	operating revenues, external	51	time	43
desired impacts	6, 9	operating revenues, total	54	tourists	36, 37
DMA	38	operational KPIs	23	unaligned	42
dwell time	50	outcomes	6, 15, 16	unintended impacts	9
earned revenue	53	perceived benefits	6	users	33
effectiveness	2.b	perceived value	45	value	40, 41, 42
efficiency	2.b	performance	2.b, 3.b, 24	value, exchanged	45
effort	43, 49	personal impacts	44	value, perceived	45
endowment income	54	person-trip	49	venue visits	28, 31
ends	2.b, 15, 16	physical museum engagement	27, 49.a	virtual	27, 29
exchanged value	45	primary market	36	visit	28
fiscal year	56	private impacts	44	visit, site	28
free-choice	2.c	products	14	visitor venues	28
gallery admissions	31	program participation/participant	30, 33.a	visitors	33.a

Table A.2. Types of U.S. Museums. Source: American Alliance of Museums, 2012

- Anthropology Museum
- Aquarium
- Arboretum/Botanical Garden/Public Garden
- Art Museum/Center/Sculpture Garden
- Children's or Youth Museum
- General or Multidisciplinary Museum
- Hall of Fame (e.g., sports, entertainment, media)
- Historic House
- Historic Site/Landscape
- Historical Society
- History Museum
- Military Museum/Battlefield
- Natural History Museum
- Nature Center
- Planetarium
- Presidential Library
- Science/Technology Center/Museum
- Specialized Museum (single topic/individual)
- Transportation Museum
- Visitor Center/Interpretive Center
- Zoo/Animal Park

once a student is enrolled, attendance is expected and ritualized. This is not so in museums. Museums have to attract and benefit our audiences and supporters for each engagement.

    d. George Hein builds a wide mission on John Dewey's progressive education that is sharable by all museums: the mission of building a better and more democratic society (Hein 2006, 349).

3. These conceptual foundations have implications for today's museum leaders:

    a. Dana's Implication: Museums are responsible for offering their communities services that address their needs and aspirations.

    b. Weil's Implication: Museums should use their *resources* (*means*) to achieve their *purposes* (*ends*), and be evaluated on how effectively and efficiently they do that (*performance*).

    c. Dierking and Falk's Implication: Museums operate in a competitive, *free-choice* marketplace by offering physical and social services valued by their audiences and supporters.

    d. Hein's Implication: Museums aspire to make the world better and more democratic, such as advancing community development and social good.

4. This book does not define or limit *museum* any further than these broad generalities.

5. Synthesized, these concepts underlie *museum economic theory*: The community funds the museum to use its resources to provide effective services back to the community. The museum provides these services efficiently and, instead of privatizing its net revenues, contributes to community development and social good.

6. The *outcomes* from a museum's activities may have the museum's *desired impacts* on their community, audiences, and supporters. The museum's community, audiences, and supporters choose to engage with the museum in return for their *perceived benefits*. The alignment between the museum's desired impacts and the markets' perceived benefits may be an indicator of efficiency. A wide gap may suggest closer alignments between intents and results that will reduce friction and focus resources. Conversely, too close an alignment may indicate not enough visionary and leadership thinking.

THEORY OF ACTION

7. *Theory of action*: "Theory-Based Evaluation in Practice (TBE) is an approach to evaluation that requires stating the assumptions on which the program is based in considerable detail: what activities are conducted, what effect from each activity, what the program does next, what the expected response is, what happens next, and so on, to the expected outcomes" (Birckmayer and Weiss 2000).[1]

8. The *Museum Theory of Action* hypothesizes that a museum, in service to its community, decides on its intentional purposes. Then, guided by its principles, the museum uses its resources to operate activities for its community, audiences, and supporters that result in benefits and other impacts. Engagements with these activities generate operating and evaluation data that can be incorporated into key performance indicators (KPIs) that monitor the museum's effectiveness and efficiency.

9. A museum's *intentional purposes* (aka, mission, vision, goals, strategies, objectives) aspire to lead to its *desired impacts* (aka, outcomes, impacts, benefits, ends). There are also other unacknowledged and *unintended impacts* from a museum's operation, some of which may be beneficial.

10. A museum uses its long-term *resources* to pursue its purposes. Resources include a museum's *capital resources*, such as its endowment, land, buildings, collections, equipment, and exhibits; *human resources*, such as staff, leadership, contractors, and suppliers; and *intangible assets*, such as its reputation, location, community relationships, brand identity, and historic legacy. Resources are long-term and capital considerations.

11. *Resource indicators*, such as the number of staff and the square feet of a gallery space, report status at the end of the fiscal year, with an explanation of any significant changes in status.

12. A museum uses its resources to produce and deliver its operational *activities*, such as its visitor experiences, conservation work, exhibitions, research, theater presentations, marketing campaigns, projects, and programs. Activities aspire to have effective impacts and benefits and to achieve these with efficient resource-to-output ratios. Activities are operational considerations.

13. Activities are the vehicles or instruments for the delivery of the museum's *impacts* and *benefits*. An activity such as curating an artist's retrospective exhibition is not an impact or benefit per se, but the process of producing it and the eventual public engagement with the exhibition can have outcomes including preserving heritage, enhancing public knowledge, developing economic impact, and enabling personal growth. To what degree the activity actually generates such impacts and benefits is an evaluation question, parallel to the larger question of whether the museum actually achieves its purposes.

14. With a few exceptions like catalog publications and educational kits, a museum's activities deliver *services*, not *products*. Museums are in the service sector as well as in the cultural and educational sectors. Weil flips the emphasis from mission to services: "The emerging public-service-oriented museum must see itself not as a cause but as an instrument . . . [and] to be of profound service, to use their competencies to enrich the quality of individual lives and to enhance their community's well-being" (Weil 2002, 49).

IMPACT AND PERFORMANCE

15. There is overlap among the terms describing the results of a museum's activities. While there are distinctions, the following terms share the far right of the Theory of Action logic model (tables 0.1 and 1.3), where the *results* of all this effort finally appear: *Outcomes, ends, impacts,* and *benefits*.

16. *Outcomes, ends,* and *impacts* are words for the changes that the museum is making (or wants to make) to individuals and to society, with the underlying hypothesis that the museum is the active agent implementing these changes. Prepositions matter in their distinction: Outcomes result *from* the museum's activities, and impacts are *on* the museum's community, audiences, and supporters.

17. In some cases, an accumulation of sufficient individual outcomes can become an impact on the greater social group, but this is neither a given nor a prerequisite of a societal impact.

18. The activities the museum operates may result in *impacts on others* and *benefits to others*. Most impacts, we hope, will be beneficial, but others, such as a museum's carbon footprint, may not be.

19. A museum aspires to have *impacts* on its community, audiences, and supporters. The community, audiences and supporters receive *benefits* from the museum. The benefits can be different from the impact: A family visiting an aquarium receives the benefit of a quality family experience, while the aquarium's desired impact on the family is to heighten their awareness of conserving biodiversity. Or, the benefits and impacts can be aligned: New parents bring their toddler to a children's museum to see her develop and learn with new kinds of challenges; the children's museum's mission is child development. Studying the alignment between a museum's benefits and impacts may illuminate potentials and inefficiencies. It is useful to remember the distinction, which hinges on their prepositions: Society, individuals, and organizations receive benefits *from* the museum. The museum has impacts *on* society, individuals, and organizations. Benefits are in the eyes of the receiver; impacts are in the desires of the museum.

20. Potential *indicators* of a museum's impacts and benefits on others and its performance in achieving those impacts include evaluation criteria, institutional success measures, foundation objectives, management resources, proposed indicators, research findings, and data collection fields from

routinely asked surveys. Indicators are either quantitative or qualitative, and may indicate to some expert audience potentially meaningful data related to measuring museum impact and performance. *Indicator* is the generic, encompassing term. A mission statement is an indicator of the museum's primary purpose; its annual budget is an indicator of the scale of operations; and its visitor satisfaction levels and supporter repeat levels are indicators of its impacts on visitors and supporters, respectively.

21. The *Museum Indicators of Impact and Performance (MIIP 1.0)* is a database of 1,025 indicators drawn from fifty-one sources (see Appendix B) compiled by the White Oak Institute and available to all for free (see the link on the copyright page). Every indicator is tagged by its category of potential impact and its step along the theory of action and the content of its data.

22. *Key performance indicators (KPIs)* are quantitative formulas such as ratios, averages, and comparable benchmarks that measure the effectiveness and efficiency of the activities. KPIs typically use evaluation and/or operating data in formulas that are meaningful to managers.

23. Key performance indicators (KPIs) are a subset of all indicators in MIIP 1.0. They are tagged Step 6a and 6b. Step 6a KPIs tend to be *operational KPIs*, while Step 6b KPIs may be *impact and performance KPIs*, depending on each museum's context. Most KPIs are mathematical formulas that incorporate two or more *data fields*. A data field can have *data entries* for different terms, such as this year and last year, and come from different sources, such as peer museums and market data.

24. *Performance* is a measure of efficiency and/or effectiveness. While a performance metric might be measurable at a moment in time, performance measures are useful mostly in comparison, such as to a museum's year-over-year (YOY) measures, and to the measures of peer museums. Performance is measured using key performance indicators (KPIs).

MUSEUM ENGAGEMENTS

25. A *museum engagement* is defined as one physical person-trip to a museum or to a museum-sponsored program off site by a person not employed or contracted by the museum to be there. The person-trip is a measure of effort spent by the person (time and often money are also spent).

26. The umbrella definition of *museum engagements* collects a museum's many potential kinds of activities—gallery attendance, lecture series attendance, volunteer shifts, board meetings, interactions with partners, outreach participants, etc.—into one number across all the museum's activities. Annual engagements are an indicator of the effort the museum's beneficiaries are willing to make in return for the personal, private, and public benefits they receive. To date, no association is counting total engagements, just total attendance.

27. Engagements can be *physical* face to face, both *on site* at a museum facility and *off site*, or *virtual*. Virtual engagements are not yet included in most reporting of attendance.

28. The most common and counted engagement is a museum *site visit*. A site visit is one individual who comes on site intending to visit the museum's galleries or to participate in a program. Each person-trip is counted as one museum engagement or site visit, even if the trip involves more than one activity or venue. For instance, an admissions ticket that combines two *visitor venues* (e.g., galleries + garden tour) during a single site visit is counted as one *site visit* but two *venue visits*. A *visit* has a narrower meaning than site visit as it assumes just exhibit and theater attendance, whereas site visits include those visits plus all the other reasons to come to the museum site.

29. People also come to museums to participate in *programs*. A museum can hold its programs *on site*, *off site*, and *virtually*—the last two are also called *outreach*. While one of the goals of outreach is to reduce audience effort, there is still some effort to attend an off site program, so each *program participation* is counted as one per person-trip, even if it is off site. If a ceramics workshop has six sessions and a *program participant* attends all of them, that counts as six museum engagements.

30. Any museum engagement that is not a *visit* is a *program participation.* By this definition, board meetings, volunteer shifts, meetings with grant officers, and event rentals are programs and the individuals attending them are *program participants.*

31. *On-site attendance* includes both visitors and program participants counted by person-trips to the museum's site. The motivation to make the trip is the distinction between visitors and program participants—did they come primarily for a visit or a program?—and usually shows up in the museum's transaction records—did they buy an admission ticket or pay for a program or get a pass to attend a meeting? Many exhibit *gallery admissions* get programs included free, some school groups add fee-based programs to their base admission, and some patrons buy combo tickets. These multiple *venue visits* do not increase on-site attendance; they do not increase the number of person-trips.

COMMUNITY, AUDIENCES, AND SUPPORTERS

32. A museum's *community, audiences, and supporters* are the *direct beneficiaries* of its activities, receiving *benefits* of value to them from their engagements with the museum's activities.
    a. *Non-users* and future generations can also benefit from a museum's activities as *indirect beneficiaries.*

33. The intended individual recipients of our impacts and benefits are a museum's *audiences* or, less frequently, its *users.* The core idea is that engaging with a museum activity will impact and/or benefit an audience member for the better—Weil's "How has somebody's life been made a little better?" (Weil 2000, 10).
    a. Audiences are segmented by their primary admission/registration transaction type into *visitors* and *program participants.*

34. The intended collected recipients of our broader societal impacts, or those groups of stakeholders the museum is trying to impact or serve, are a museum's *communities* or, less frequently, its *society,* *constituents,* and *authorizing environment.* This book defines *community* as broadly as possible: the external world. However, each museum must get specific about what communities it serves. The National Museum of the Marine Corps (Triangle, Virginia) serves at least two communities: The nearby residents and the community of people around the globe affiliated with the U.S. Marine Corps.
    a. When using such terms as *contributing to social good* and *adding public value* to talk about a museum's potential impact on its community, the term *community* refers to the general public and society at large.
    b. When an urban museum thinks of its city and region as its community, it can use population and market data to quantify their resident community.
    c. If a museum receives substantial annual support from a government entity, such as History San Jose from the city of San Jose and the State Historical Museum of Iowa from the state of Iowa, then the museum is wise to think of its community as equal to the city or state, thereby serving the constituencies who support them with tax dollars.
    d. Community is also used with modifiers to reference specific affinity groups, such as the Hmong community, the science and technology community, the donor community, the abutting neighbors, underserved communities, the Churchillians, the home-schoolers, etc.

35. The organizations and people who support the museum financially are the museum's *private* and *public supporters.* Ideally and often, these supporters share the museum's intentional purposes and aspire to kindred impacts on the same audiences. Social investing reflects a recent trend to equate support funds to quantifiable social outcomes (Raymond 2010), and support funds can be tied to

outcomes, such as a foundation grant for a program with learning outcomes expected to have a desired impact on its audiences.

    a. Supporters benefit from the museum by advancing their philanthropic goals, along with other benefits from their museum partnerships and engagements, such as visibility and network building.

36. Many regional- and city-based museums count on their geographic *resident market* and organizations for their principal audiences and supporters. The resident market can be usefully segmented into *core* (optional), *primary*, *secondary*, *day-trippers*, *tourists*, and *school students*.

    a. *Core market* is useful when the museum's immediate neighborhood or center city location is distinct from the rest of its primary market. The core market might be the city's population.

    b. *Primary market* refers to residents of the museum city's greater surrounding region, typically within commuting distance of downtown.

    c. *Secondary market* refers to residents who live outside the primary or core markets but still within the larger media market reached by television stations.

    d. *Day-trippers* are those who live outside the media market but not so far that they cannot drive roundtrip the same day.

    e. *Tourists* live far enough outside the market to spend the night before traveling home.

    f. *School students* are those who come as part of organized school and youth groups. This market is counted separately because children come to museums both with school groups and with their caregivers.

37. *Day-trippers* and *tourists* are counted differently in different markets, and often by chambers of commerce and tourist and economic development agencies. Some tourist destinations can do an excellent job of counting tourists, such as Honolulu, and for others it is not worth the effort. Definitions are not standardized as rigorously as resident populations.

38. *Core Based Statistical Area (CBSA)* and *Designated Market Area (DMA)* are both useful standards in the United States for market data such as population, including by age and ethnicity, income, household buying power, psychographic profiles, and attitudes. Both are typically based on county lines, with the CBSA covering a city's greater metropolitan area and the DMA adding the larger region around the CBSA.

    a. The official U.S. government definition for CBSA is "metropolitan and micropolitan statistical areas (metro and micro areas) are geographic entities delineated by the Office of Management and Budget (OMB) for use by Federal statistical agencies in collecting, tabulating, and publishing Federal statistics. The term 'Core Based Statistical Area' (CBSA) is a collective term for both metro and micro areas. A metro area contains a core urban area of 50,000 or more population, and a micro area contains an urban core of at least 10,000 (but less than 50,000) population. Each metro or micro area consists of one or more counties and includes the counties containing the core urban area, as well as any adjacent counties that have a high degree of social and economic integration (as measured by commuting to work) with the urban core."

    b. CBSAs are sometimes referred to as MSAs (Metro/Micro Statistical Areas).

    c. Designated Market Area (DMA) refers to the larger region surrounding the CBSA that is reached by that city's media, often aligning with the reach of the television stations. Like CBSAs, DMAs are designated along county lines; typically, the DMA has more counties than the CBSA, and the population difference between the two is the secondary market. Nielsen Media Research defines the DMA as "an exclusive geographic area of counties in which the home market televisions hold a dominance of total hours viewed." With the rise of cable stations and digital devices, this market is not as meaningful as it was; however, the county lines of the DMA may still be a useful way to define the outer limits of a city's sphere of influence and gravitational pull.

39. *Market ratios*, which divide a museum's operating number by a resident market number, do not account for tourists and day-trippers. Changes in market ratios may be suspect indicators if there has been a major change in regional tourism, or a peer museum is in a different tourist market.

VALUE EXCHANGES

40. The question of *value* starts with "of value to whom?" For instance, a visitor's experience in a museum exhibition has a value to that visitor, and exposing that visitor to the content of that exhibition has a value to some supporters and possibly to the greater community. Museum activities result in impacts and benefits that have value to others.

41. *Value* is in the eye of the beholder, not in the mind of the owner. A museum cannot set its own value, but it can measure indicators of its value to its community, audiences, and supporters.

42. A museum's *value* lies in its impacts, says Weil (2005). However, the museum's value is actually expressed in terms of the value of the benefits. Since value is in the eye of the beholder, any valuation must first track the value the community and its audiences and supporters place on their perceived benefits, and then see if those findings relate to measuring the museum's desired impacts. When the desired impact is the same as the perceived benefit, such as the children's museum example where both the museum and the visitor want child development, the impact and the benefit are *aligned*. When they are different, such as the aquarium example, they are *unaligned*. Some degree of unalignment may be desirable for strategic or advocacy reasons.

43. Museums are free-choice marketplace organizations. No one has to go to, pay admissions, or fund a museum. People and organizations choose to spend *time*, *effort*, and *money* on their museum engagements in exchange for perceived benefits.

44. The analysis of MIIP 1.0 found four main categories of impacts: *Public impacts* benefit the community and society as a whole; *private impacts* benefit businesses, donors, and private foundations, who are often also pursuing public impacts; and *personal impacts* benefit individuals, families, and households. A museum's activities can also benefit the museum institutionally, such as increasing its resources or improving its performance, resulting in *institutional impacts*.

45. A museum's *perceived value* is a judgment of the value of the benefits and impacts from engaging with the museum's activities by its community, audiences, and supporters and is usually a qualitative expression of what they received. *Exchanged value* is a quantification of the amount of time, effort, and/or money the community, audiences, and supporters actually exchanged for the benefits they received. Exchanged value can be an indicator of perceived value.

EFFORT, TIME, AND MONEY

46. Changes in the amounts of time, effort, and money a museum's community and its audiences and supporters exchange for their museum benefits are indicators of changes in their perceived value of the benefits.

47. The museum's *key service markets* are its main sources of engagements and external operating revenue. There are three umbrella external service markets: (1) the community as a whole, (2) audiences, and (3) supporters. These do not have to align with the museum's key community, audience, and supporter segments, but they could, and significant misalignments may be difficult to sustain. The museum itself is an internal market.

48. When the benefits to a key service market are the same as the desired impacts, then the value of the impact might be indicated by the exchanged value of the benefit. To the degree they are unaligned, the value of the impact would have to be discounted.

49. *Effort* is measured by the number of person-trips to a museum-sponsored location to engage one or more museum activities. Like a physical museum engagement, a *person-trip* is defined one physical (non-virtual) trip to a museum or to a museum-sponsored program off site by a person not employed or contracted by the museum to be there.

    a. The number of *person-trips* is equal to the number of *physical museum engagements*.

50. *Dwell time* can be measured by recording the length in minutes for each museum engagement from site arrival to site departure. Dwell time is not yet routinely measured or reported.

51. *Money* paid to the museum for its operational activities is measured as *external operating revenues*. The amounts are the monetary value of the museum's engagements to its direct beneficiaries, according to the subjective theory of economics (Menger 1871). Revenues are indicators of the money the museum's community, audiences, and supporters are willing to pay in return for the personal, private, and public benefits they receive.

52. A museum's *business model* is the mixture of activities and benefits provided to its community, audiences, and supporters in return for their money.

53. Revenue sectors are classified as *earned revenue*, *support revenue*, and *capital asset net income* (e.g., endowment, intellectual property, or lease income).

    a. Accounting practices distinguish between government and nongovernment support as public and private support revenues. Revenues for personal benefits tend to be categorized as earned revenues.

54. *Endowment income* and other capital asset net income can be added to the museum's external operating revenues to result in *total operating revenues*. Museums with substantial endowments can cover a higher percentage of their operating costs internally, making them less dependent on external, competitive marketplace funding from the community, audiences, and supporters. Conversely, museums with no endowment must be very responsive to their community, audiences, and supporters.

55. Money paid to the museum for *capital projects* is investing in the museum's resources and is not considered operating revenues related to the museum's operating activities.

56. For evaluation consistency and sample size, *annual totals*, typically aligned with the museum's *fiscal year*, are preferred. Some museum associations report annual totals as submitted by some of their museum members.

57. *Return on Social Investment (ROSI)* is a common nonprofit KPI that divides the value of the impact by the cost. In many cases, this is a conceptual rather than mathematical fraction, as the value and cost can be intangible (e.g., treating Ebola at the risk of lives), but some ROSI calculations can be quantitative, such as the potential annual increase in museum engagements and revenue divided by the capital cost of a larger temporary exhibition gallery.

58. The dollar amount or tangible value of a museum's *capital assets* is drawn most consistently from the financial statements. However, these figures are mostly tallies of depreciated capital investments (e.g., the last expansion or gallery overhaul less its assumed wear and tear), the endowment and, if the museum is fortunate, additional capitalization in the form of reserve funds, working capital, capital for facility replacement needs, and risk capital. The original building, if fully depreciated, is often no longer on the books, nor is the real estate value of the land or the value of the collection and the museum's nonprofit tax status. There are valid arguments for using a higher capital evaluation than just the balance sheet listing; however, objectivity and consistency are important in how your museum calculates the denominator when comparing ROSI from one year to another, and balance sheet numbers may be your most stable indicators of your museum's total assets.

NOTE

1. The original cited Suchman 1967; Weiss 1972, 1995, 1997, 1998; Bickman 1990; Chen 1990; Chen and Rossi 1987; Costner 1989; Finney and Moos 1989 at this point.

REFERENCES

Birckmayer, Johanna D., and Carol Hirschon Weiss. "Theory-Based Evaluation in Practice: What Do We Learn?" *Evaluation Review* 24, no. 4 (August 2000): 407–31.

Falk, John H., and Lynn D. Dierking. *Learning from Museums: Visitor Experiences and the Making of Meaning.* Walnut Creek: AltaMira, 2000.

———. *Museum Experience Revisited.* Walnut Creek: Left Coast Press, 2012.

Falk, John H., and Beverly Sheppard. *Thriving in the Knowledge Age: New Business Models for Museums and Other Cultural Institutions.* Lanham, MD: AltaMira, 2006.

Hein, George E. "Museum Education." In *A Companion to Museum Studies*, by S. MacDonald. Oxford: Blackwell, 2006.

ICOM Statutes. *Development of the Museum Definition according to ICOM Statutes (2007–1946).* August 24, 2007. Accessed November 11, 2014. http://archives.icom.museum/hist_def_eng.html.

Menger, C. *Principles of Economics.* New York: New York University Press, 1871.

Peniston, William A. *The New Museum: Selected Writings by John Cotton Dana.* American Alliance of Museums Press, 1999.

Raymond, Susan U. *Nonprofit Finance for Hard Times: Setting the Larger Stage.* Hoboken: Wiley, 2010.

Weil, Stephen. *Making Museums Matter.* Washington, D.C.: Smithsonian Institution, 2002.

———. "A Success/Failure Matrix for Museums." *Museum News* (January/February 2005): 36–40.

———. "Transformed from a Cemetery of Bric-a-Brac." In *Perspectives on Outcome Based Evaluation for Libraries and Museums*, 4–15. Washington, D.C.: Institute of Museum and Library Services, 2000.

APPENDIX B

Source Documents for MIIP 1.0

MIIP 1.0 has 1,025 indicators from fifty-one sources. The sources and the indicator numbering system are listed this Appendix B, which starts by describing the categories of sources, and then lists the fifty-one sources each with its numbered indicators.

CATEGORY OF SOURCE DOCUMENT

Data Collection Fields (2 sources with 209 indicators total = "2/209"): These two sources are themselves distillations of other surveys, peer refinement, and/or years of evolution. The AAM survey (2012) has evolved over decades with considerable input from participating museums and from the AAM's statisticians. The fifty-nine Museum Operating Data Standards White Oak Institute and the American Association of Museums (Jacobsen et al. 2011) were synthesized and peer-reviewed from another aggregation of ten international museum association surveys with over a thousand data collection fields among them.

Evaluation Criteria (9/113) come from foundations and agencies (NSF, UNESCO, Kellogg, the National Research Council) and from advice to nonprofits and private companies, such as the S.M.A.R.T. ways of writing goals and objectives. Many of these establish evaluation language shared by their program officers and peer reviewers and understood by professional evaluators.

Institutional Evaluations (4/153) come from four comprehensive museum success measures, each set developed over time by very experienced museum directors, and each containing a menu of indicators used by leadership and stakeholders to evaluate the museum year by year: The Indianapolis Children's Museum (Sterling 1999); Metrics of Success in Art Museums (Anderson 2004); Heureka's Key Performance Indicators (Persson 2011); Wisconsin Historical Society (2013).

Foundation Objectives (4/20) are statements of potential funders' goals and objectives, which supplicant museums heed carefully in order to initiate or continue support and grant funding: They come from the Welsh (UK) government, the NSF (U.S.), the National Research Council (U.S.), and the Institute of Museum and Library Services (U.S., IMLS, Semmel).

Management Resources (2/56) include a toolkit of indicators from the Museum, Libraries and Archives Council (UK) and the online Benchmark Calculator from the Association of Children's Museums (U.S., 2011), with a field-reviewed and tested menu of standardized KPIs and comparable reports developed by the White Oak Institute.

Proposed Indicators (16/136) come from the museum field's formal literature (journal articles and books) by and for museum leaders and thinkers. Because the field is evolving and troubled by uncertain economics, the best minds have been at work developing theories and suggesting ways to improve impact and performance. Influential museum writers like John Falk, Robert Janes, Beverly Sheppard, Emlyn Koster, Mary Ellen Munley, Beverly Serrell, and Carol Scott have distilled their experience into these suggested indicators, and analysts from the larger business and nonprofit fields ave developed sophisticated and well-tested systems, such as Fredrick Reichheld's Net Promoter Score and Jason Saul's benchmarks for nonprofits.

Research Findings (14/339) come from comprehensive surveys commissioned by government agencies, museum associations, and individual museums. The findings are typically from the general public and museum audiences and supporters. Perspectives on museums and the values they bring come from New Zealand, the Netherlands, Britain, Scotland, the United States, and two global studies of economic impact. Additionally, the PISEC family learning indicators and the Pekarik, Doering, and Karns (1999) synthesis of visitor satisfaction findings are in this section.

Fifteen of these fifty-one sources cover wider territories than just the museum sector, such as nonprofits or the K–12 system. Some of these indicators may need to be adapted for museum use, and some might not even apply, such as "Presence of URS [under-represented students] in STEM majors at undergraduate and graduate levels" (#238). These non-museum-specific indicators have been retained to preserve the source integrity, to remind future museum users of indicators found meaningful in other fields, and to embrace the larger themes from other sectors of America's cultural and nonprofit landscape, just as indicator #238 reminds us that the intentional purpose of broadening participation needs indicators that measure participation at all levels of engagement.

There are a small number of duplicate indicators due to researchers including crosswalk questions to other researchers (e.g., Stevenson and Yocco), researchers updating their previous work (Scott and Travers), or surveys adopting standard data definitions (AAM and MODS). If a duplicate indicator fits more than one tag, the duplicate got the other tag. The finding that most indicators are unique is a reflection of the lack of standardization in the museum field, and actually is an issue to be addressed.

I. DATA COLLECTION FIELDS (209)

1. American Alliance of Museums. Museum Benchmarking Online 2.0. Contains indicators numbered 1–130.
2. The White Oak Institute and the American Association of Museums: Recommended Data Collection Fields for Museums Count: The IMLS National Museum Census, also called the Museum Operating Data Standards (MODS 1.0). Contains indicators numbered 131–209.

II. EVALUATION CRITERIA (113)

3. Berger, K., Penna, R., & Goldberg, S. (2010). The Battle for the Soul of the Nonprofit Sector. Philadelphia Social Innovations Journal. Contains indicators numbered 210–15.
4. Clewell, B., & Fortenberry, N. (Eds.). (June 30, 2009). Framework for Evaluating Impacts of Broadening Participation Projects. Contains indicators numbered 216–51.
5. Doran, G. T. (1981). There's a S.M.A.R.T. Way to Write Management's Goals and Objectives. Management Review 70(11) (AMA FORUM):35–36. Contains indicators numbered 252–56.
6. McCallie, E., Bell, L., Lohwater, T., Falk, J. H., Lehr, J. L., Lewenstein, B. V., Needham, C., & Wiehe, B. (2009). Many Experts, Many Audiences: Public Engagement with Science and Informal Science Education. A CAISE Inquiry Group Report. Washington, D.C.: Center for Advancement of Informal Science Education (CAISE), 12–13. Contains indicators numbered 257–60.
7. Mulgan, G. (2010). Measuring Social Value. Stanford Social Innovation Review. Contains indicators numbered 261–67.
8. National Research Council. (2013). Monitoring Progress Toward Successful K–12 STEM Education: A Nation Advancing? Washington, D.C.: The National Academies Press. Contains indicators numbered 268–81.

9. The National Science Foundation. (2012, 2013). Grant Criteria from Grant Solicitation Advancing Informal STEM Learning (AISL) Solicitation NSF 13-608 and NSF 12-560. Contains indicators numbered 282–93.
10. United Nations Educational, Scientific and Cultural Organization (UNESCO). (July 11–14, 2012). Expert Meeting on the Protection and Promotion of Museums and Collections. Contains indicators numbered 294–310.
11. W. K. Kellogg Foundation. (2004). Logic Model Development Guide. Contains indicators numbered 311–22.

III. INSTITUTIONAL EVALUATION (153)

12. Anderson, M. (2004). Metrics of Success in Art Museums. Paper commissioned by the Getty Leadership Institute, J. Paul Getty Trust. Copyright © 2004 Maxwell L. Anderson. Contains indicators numbered 323–424.
13. Children's Museum of Indianapolis. (1999). 25 Indicators of Success. Sterling, P., in personal correspondence with the author. Contains indicators numbered 425–53.
14. Persson, P. E. (2011). Rethinking the Science Center Model? The Informal Learning Review 111 (November–December 2011). Contains indicators numbered 454–65.
15. Wisconsin Historical Society. Division of Executive Budget and Finance Department of Administration. (2013). State of Wisconsin Executive Budget for the Wisconsin Historical Society, 245. Contains indicators numbered 466–75.

IV. FOUNDATION OBJECTIVES (20)

16. CyMAL—Museums Archives and Libraries Wales, UK. (2010). A Museums Strategy for Wales. Contains indicators numbered 476–81.
17. Duschl, R. A., Schweingruber, H. A., & Shouse, A. W. (Eds.). (2007). Taking Science to School: Learning and Teaching Science in Grades K–8. Committee on Science Learning, Kindergarten through Eighth Grade. National Research Council, Board on Science Education, Center for Education. Division of Behavioral and Social Sciences and Education. Washington, D.C.: The National Academies Press. Contains indicators numbered 482–87.
18. NSF EHR Core Research (ECR) NSF EHR Program Announcement 13-555. Contains indicators numbered 488–91.
19. Semmel, M. L., & Bittner, M. (2009). Demonstrating Museum Value: The Role of the Institute of Museum and Library Services. Museum Management and Curatorship. Contains indicators numbered 492–95.

V. MANAGEMENT RESOURCES (56)

20. Association of Children's Museums, White Oak Institute and Advisory Committee Leaders. (2011). Key Indicators and Benchmark Calculator. Developed under an Institute of Museum and Library Services grant under the 21st Century Museum Professionals program. Contains indicators numbered 496–522.
21. Museums, Libraries and Archives Council. Inspiring Learning: An Improvement Framework for Museums, Libraries and Archives Toolkit. Contains indicators numbered 523–51.

VI. PROPOSED INDICATORS (136)

22. Browne, C. (2007). The Educational Value of Museums. New England Museum Association Annual Conference. Contains indicators numbered 552–57.

23. Coble, C. (2013). North Carolina Science, Mathematics, and Technology Education Center. Strategies That Engage Minds: Empowering North Carolina's Economic Future. Contains indicators numbered 558–62.

24. Davies, S., Paton, R., & O'Sullivan, T. (2013). The Museum Values Framework: A Framework for Understanding Organizational Culture in Museums. Museum Management and Curatorship 28(4): 345–61. Contains indicators numbered 563–70.

25. Falk, J. H., & Sheppard, Beverly K. (2006). Thriving in the Knowledge Age: New Business Models for Museums and Other Cultural Institutions. Lanham, MD: AltaMira Press. Contains indicators numbered 571–74.

26. Jacobsen, J., Stahl, J., & Katz, P. (2011). Purposes Framework from the Museum Census Roadmap including MODS 1.0. White Oak Institute and the American Association of Museums for the Institute of Museum and Library Services for Museums Count: The IMLS Museum Census. Contains indicators numbered 575–98.

27. Janes, R. (Fall 2011). Museums and the New Reality. Museums & Social Issues 6(2): 137–46. Left Coast Press. Contains indicators numbered 599–604.

28. Koster, E., & Falk, J. (2007). Maximizing the External Value of Museums. Curator 50: 191–96. Contains indicators numbered 605–9.

29. Moore, M. (1995). Creating Public Value: Strategic Management in Government. Cambridge, MA: Harvard University Press. Contains indicators numbered 610–12.

30. Munley, M. E. The Human Origins Initiative (HOI). What Does It Mean to Be Human? MEM & Associates for National Museum of Natural History. Contains indicators numbered 613–16.

31. Noyce Leadership Institute. (April 18, 2011). Cohorts 1 and 2 on Community Impact. Contains indicators numbered 617–40.

32. Reichheld, Frederick F. (December 2003). One Number You Need to Grow. Harvard Business Review. Contains indicators numbered 641.

33. Saul, J. (2004). Benchmarking for Nonprofits: How to Measure, Manage, and Improve Performance. St. Paul, MN: Fieldstone Alliance Publishing Center. Contains indicators numbered 642–45.

34. Scott, C. A. (2009). Exploring the Evidence Base for Museum Value. Museum Management and Curatorship. Contains indicators numbered 646–73.

35. Serrell, B. (May 15, 2006). Judging Exhibitions: A Framework for Assessing Excellence. Left Coast Press. Contains indicators numbered 674–77.

36. Serrell, B. (March 15, 2010). Paying More Attention to Paying Attention blog. Posted on informalscience.org: Learning Sciences. Contains indicators numbered 678–86.

37. Sheppard, S., Oehler, K., Benjamin, B., & Kessler, A. (2006). Culture and Revitalization: The Economic Effects of MASS MoCA on Its Community. Center for Creative Community Development. Contains indicators numbered 687.

VII. RESEARCH FINDINGS (338)

38. Borun, M., Dritsas, J., Johnson, J., Peter, N., Wagner, K., Fadigan, K., Jangaard, A., Stroup, E., & Wenger, A. (1998). Family Learning in Museums: The PISEC Perspective. Philadelphia: PISEC c/o The Franklin Institute. Contains indicators numbered 688–97.

39. BritainThinks. (March 2013). Public Perceptions of—and Attitudes to—the Purposes of Museums in Society. Report prepared by BritainThinks for Museums Association. Contains indicators numbered 698–706.

40. Groves, I. (2005). Assessing the Economic Impact of Science Centers on Their Local Communities. Questacon—The National Science and Technology Centre. Contains indicators numbered 707–33.

41. Ministry for Culture and Heritage. (2009). Cultural Indicators for New Zealand. Contains indicators numbered 734–53.

42. Museums Association. (2013). Museums Change Lives—The MA's Vision for the Impact of Museums. Contains indicators numbered 754–86.

43. Netherlands Museums Association. (April 2011). The Social Significance of Museums. Contains indicators numbered 787–811.

44. Nonprofit Finance Fund (NFF) and GuideStar. 2.0 of Financial SCAN. Contains indicators numbered 812–37.

45. Pekarik, Andrew J., Doering, Z. D., & Karns, D. (1999). Exploring Satisfying Experiences in Museums. Curator: The Museum Journal 42(2): 152–73. Contains indicators numbered 838–51.

46. Persson, P. E. (2000). Community Impact of Science Centers: Is There Any? Curator: The Museum Journal, 43: 9–17. Contains indicators numbered 852–71.

47. Scott, C. (August 2007). Advocating the Value of Museums. Paper presented at INTERCOM/ICOM, Vienna, August 20, 2007. Contains indicators numbered 872–962.

48. Stevenson, D. (2013). Reaching a "Legitimate" Value? A Contingent Valuation Study of the National Galleries of Scotland. Museum Management and Curatorship, 28(4): 377–93. Contains indicators numbered 963–81.

49. Travers, T., and Brown, R. (2010). Treasurehouse & Powerhouse: A Report for the Natural History Museum. Contains indicators numbered 982–89.

50. Travers, T., Glaister, S., & Wakefield, J. (2003). Treasurehouse & Powerhouse: An Assessment of the Scientific, Cultural and Economic Value of the Natural History Museum. Contains indicators numbered 990–1006.

51. Yocco, V., Heimlich, J., Meyer, E., & Edwards, P. (2009). Measuring Public Value: An Instrument and an Art Museum Case Study. Visitor Studies 12(2): 152–63. Contains indicators numbered 1007–25.

NOTE

1. The fifty-one sources for MIIP 1.0 are also referenced earlier in this Appendix B.

REFERENCES

Anderson, Maxwell L. *Metrics of Success in Art Museums.* Los Angeles: The Getty Leadership Institute, J. Paul Getty Trust, 2004.

Persson, Per-Edvin. "Rethinking the Science Center Model." *Informal Learning Review* no. 111 (November–December 2011): 14–15.

Sterling, P., in personal correspondence with the author. *25 Indicators of Success.* Children's Museum of Indianapolis, 1999.

Wisconsin Historical Society—Division of Executive Budget and Finance Department of Administration. *State of Wisconsin Executive Budget for the Wisconsin Historical Society.* 2013.

APPENDIX C

Potential Museum Impacts: Selected Examples

Analysis of the MIIP 1.0 indicators reveals twelve broad areas of external service and two of internal service. The external services have beneficiaries and funders. The direct beneficiaries are not always the funders. A foundation might pay for a teen workshop, benefiting teens directly while benefiting the foundation indirectly by serving its purposes. The service areas are divided into Public Impacts (seven), Private Impacts (two), Personal Impacts (three), and Institutional Impacts (two). Public impacts benefit the public as a whole, and tend to be funded by government and private foundations; private impacts tend to benefit businesses and corporations and tend to be funded by economic development agencies and corporate sponsors; personal impacts benefit individuals, families, and groups and tend to be funded by combinations of earned and support revenue; and institutional impacts benefit the museum.

The 1,025 indicators in MIIP 1.0 collect quantitative and qualitative data on at least sixty different data content topics, many with sub-topics. Within the fourteen service areas there are sixty data content topics—What data is this indicator measuring? What information is it collecting? Some topics appear in more than one area. The topics are listed in table C.2 in order of frequency in MIIP 1.0.

Table C.1. Categories of Potential Museum Impacts. Source: The White Oak Institute

		# of MIIP indicators
Public Impacts		
A	Broadening participation	85
B	Preserving heritage	47
C	Strengthening social capital	76
D	Enhancing public knowledge	43
E	Serving education	56
F	Advancing social change	40
G	Communicating public identity & image	27
Private Impacts		
H	Contributing to the economy	85
I	Delivering corporate community services	9
Personal Impacts		
J	Enabling personal growth	147
K	Offering personal respite	4
L	Welcoming personal leisure	11
Institutional Impacts		
M	Helping museum operations	308
N	Building museum capital	87
Total indicators in the MIIP 1.0 database		1,025

Table C.2. Data Content Topics (60). Source: The White Oak Institute

Data Content Topic	# of indicators	Data Content Topic	# of indicators
1. Revenue	72	31. Innovation	11
2. Learning	69	32. Diversity	9
3. Economic Impact	60	33. Capital fund-raising	8
4. Resources	53	34. Societal progress	8
5. Value judgment	53	35. Advocacy for a cause	7
6. Attendance	45	36. Endowment	7
7. Intrinsic value	45	37. Broader audiences	6
8. Management culture	41	38. Marketing	6
9. Collection objects	40	39. STEM participation	6
10. Community connections	39	40. Asset	5
11. Partnerships	29	41. Facilitator	5
12. Performance	27	42. Involvement in a worthy purpose	5
13. Expenses	25	43. Missions and purposes	5
14. Knowledge	25	44. Outputs	5
15. Museum identifier	22	45. Quality of life	5
16. Balance sheet	23	46. Authorizing environment	4
17. Facility	21	47. Environmental stewardship	4
18. Cultural identity	19	48. Exhibitions	4
19. HR	19	49. Identity description	4
20. Value indicator	19	50. Preservation of memory	4
21. Access	17	51. Symbolic value	4
22. Programs	17	52. Collection properties	3
23. STEM in schools	16	53. Neighborhood redevelopment	3
24. Infrastructure	15	54. Mission alignment	2
25. Members	14	55. Special needs support	2
26. Pride	13	56. Sponsor visibility	2
27. Public value	13	57. Broader resources	1
28. Addressing problems	12	58. Capital spending	1
29. Behavior and attitude changes	12	59. Mourning	1
30. Governance	12	60. Outcomes	1
TOTAL			**1,025**

Frequency may be an indicator of the relative amount of attention paid to each topic by the fifty-one sources for MIIP, but it is not an indicator of importance or usefulness as an indicator of museum impact and performance. Revenue, economic impact, and resources are in the top five, reflecting the frequency of quantitative financial data in MIIP 1.0; however, learning and value judgments are also in the top five, reflecting the museum field's qualitative commitments to education and to listening to their audiences and supporters.

The following sections have only a few samplings of the 1,205 indicators in MIIP 1.0, and the indicators have been edited for brevity. The full MIIP 1.0 is available by following the link on the copyright page. Please refer to MIIP 1.0 and then to the original texts for the exact language/definition. The indicator numbers are referenced in Appendix B.

PUBLIC IMPACTS—BENEFITS TO SOCIETY AND THE PUBLIC AT LARGE

A. Broadening participation (85): The public benefit of increasing social justice and inclusion is addressed by these indicators about audience diversity, access policy, inclusivity, community connections, management culture, and approach to learning. Broadening participation is particularly important to free-choice learning institutions for broadening services as well as audience development and new revenues. Representative indicators include: How many free days? (#148); Number of trustees from minority groups (#414); Extent of alignment of visitor demographics with demographics of local population (#382); and Percentage of employees from minority groups managing two or more staff members (#327).

B. Preserving heritage (47): The public benefit of caring for and interpreting our past, both physically and culturally through stewardship of collections, historic sites, and cultural neighborhoods. Heritage preservation contributes to a sense of belonging and where we come from; a place for communal archives, lessons of history, display of property and collections; and the preservation of memory. Representative indicators include: Total number of accessioned works in the collection (#410); Preserving and displaying collections that are touchstones to emotional events (#598); Number of full-time staff with PhDs in art history (#325); and Celebrating achievement (#596).

C. Strengthening social capital (76): Positive social capital is defined as the "networks, norms and trust that enable cooperation for mutual benefit" (Fukuyama 2002 as referenced in Scott 2007) and "build a sense of trust between people" (Ministry for Culture and Heritage 2009, 41). Strengthening social capital indicators monitor the potential contributions a museum makes to the health and structure of its community through its community connections and partnerships; serving as a place for different groups, generations, and cultures to come to learn from each other—each bringing diverse perspectives to a trusted, neutral environment; providing the means for communication and debate; serving as an honest broker through its partnerships with funders, companies, libraries, public agencies, educational organizations, etc.; facilitation of events in cooperation with other organizations resulting in expanded learning opportunities and trust in the museum's brand. Museums are part of a community's capital assets, adding to its cultural, educational, and economic infrastructure. Museums and other cultural facilities add public value and build public trust (Holden 2004) by creating museum-quality brand relationships. As capital-intensive, physical structures open to the public, they add to a city's balance sheet. As collectors and stewards of a community's material culture, they maintain its valuable objects. Representative indicators include: Connecting generations and cultures (#790); Serving as a community gathering place (#593); Allow public mingling, discussion, and education within a safe and easy environment (#996); Number of organizational partners (#461); Potential for proposed activity to benefit society or advance desired societal outcomes (#293); and Development of positive social capital, defined as the networks, norms, and trust that enable cooperation for mutual benefit (#874).

D. Enhancing public knowledge (43) indicators monitor the research and reference contributions a museum makes to the body of public and professional information and scholarship, and its access by individuals, the community, and the economy. Fifteen of the indicators refer specifically to a museum's contributions to scholarship. Reputation refers to the museum's trusted expertise and the quality of museum staff, exhibitions, and collections. Representative indicators include: Number of articles published by full-time museum staff in panel-edited scholarly journals" (#328); Facilitate professional exchange within academic and museum institutions" (#295); Providing new models of learning and research" (#487), and Scientific and humanities research (#604).

E. Serving the educational system (56) indicators monitor potential museum services to both formal education (schools) and museum professionals through student programs, educational initiatives and campaigns, STEM learning, school partnerships, and resources for educators. Representative indicators include: On-site attendance by K–12 students in school groups (#127); Modeling civil behavior (#880); Improving science literacy (#484); Number of full-time educators (#324); and Ranking by schoolteachers as important to them (a) in the classroom (#393); and Teacher professional development offered by the center is in demand (#640). Note: Learning outcomes are handled mostly under Enhancing personal growth.

F. Advancing social change (40) indicators monitor a museum's potential services in leading people and communities to make changes deemed beneficial by society, such as addressing social problems, health initiatives, global environmental conservation, education, social justice, human rights, tolerance, fairness and equality, and anti-discrimination, poverty, and reflecting on lessons from the past to envision new ways of living in the future (Museums Association 2013). Representative indicators include: Using institutional resources to address community issues (#594); influence on government policies and priorities (#862); Potential health outcomes (including likely impact on quality-adjusted life years and patient satisfaction) (#265); Total dollar amount of support from foundations for non-capital expenses (#366); and Social transformation and community engagement (#303).

G. Communicating public identity and image (27) indicators monitor potential museum services that help a region, a community, or individuals think about, discuss, develop, and communicate their desired identity and image. At the city level, a museum can serve as a symbol, a statement of pride, an affirmation of a culture, and a reflection of local priorities. At the individual level, a museum can become an important personal relationship, a symbol of who we are, a part of our identity, and a brand we trust. Representative indicators include: Museums give the "Holland" brand an identity (#800); Celebrating local identity and community pride (#591); Reflects local, regional, and national developments in plans and priorities (#545); Expression of communal meanings (#946); and Celebrating local identity and community pride (#591).

PRIVATE IMPACTS—BENEFITS TO BUSINESSES AND THE ECONOMY

H. Contributing to the economy (85) indicators monitor the museum's contributions to the regional and local economy by motivating tourism, increasing land and tax values, direct spending, neighborhood development, providing jobs, and developing the workforce and the quality of life. Generally, a museum's economic impact supports businesses, and, in a ripple effect, generates incremental taxes. Representative indicators include: Value of local services purchased (#655); Visitors from outside Helsinki metropolitan region (#465); Full-time paid positions (#109); and Increased prosperity due to the option to use museums (#796); A community asset for economic development, signaling that the community values science and mathematics (#719); A supporter of teams of scientists involved in cutting-edge research; and a facilitator of interactions between the scientists and members of the public (#724).

I. Delivering corporate community services (9) indicators monitor potential museum services to businesses that are fulfilling their community service responsibilities (CRS), associating their brand with the museum through sponsorships, and providing value to their employees by giving them museum access privileges. Representative indicators include: Major exhibitions from which many businesses can benefit (#967); How many corporate memberships did your institution have at the end of the fiscal year end indicated above? (#95); A source of opportunities for local businesses to promote their products and services through association with the science center (#718); and What is the retention rate for corporate members? (#97).

PERSONAL IMPACTS—BENEFITS TO INDIVIDUALS, FAMILIES, AND SOCIAL GROUPS

J. Enabling personal growth (147) indicators monitor the benefits individuals, groups, and families get from their museum engagements that help them grow in abilities, awareness, and understanding. Enabling personal growth has the most indicators of the twelve external potential museum services, reflecting the museum field's focus on providing benefit to its free-choice audiences. Personal growth in museums can happen in many ways, and the most pervasive is learning, again reflecting the field's commitment as places of informal learning and to AAM's priorities for education (Hirzy 2008). Education refers to what the teachers want to impart, while learning is what the individual aspires to receive. Museums can help people learn and develop their capacities, knowledge, perspectives, sense of relevance, and social and family insights. This area also includes the intrinsic benefits a museum can provide its visitors and program participants, such as affirmation, belonging, enlightenment, excitement and awe, insight, joy, perspective, reflection, satisfaction, and meaning. Museums can engage individuals in worthy purposes through volunteer opportunities. Representative indicators include: Use the services and facilities to develop their knowledge and understanding (#541); Being moved by beauty (#845); Discovery of "personal beliefs" among universal truths (#944); How many youth volunteers does your institution engage, for how many hours each year? (#556); Career directions formed (#856); Seeing rare/uncommon/valuable things (#848); Imagining other times or places (#842); Providing opportunities for intergenerational learning (#585); Providing exhibits, theaters, and programs for adult and family audiences (#584); Average length of time spent by visitors in front of ten significant works in the collection (#380); and Percentage of visitors who would rank visit as exceeding expectations (#390).

K. Offering personal respite (4) indicators monitor the benefits individuals, groups, and families get from museum engagements that help them find comfort, spend time alone safely and quietly, or get away from their daily pressures. Representative indicators include: Feeling a spiritual connection (#841); Preserving a memorial or shrine and providing a respite for those seeking solace (#597); An intangible sense of elation—a feeling that a weight was lifted off their shoulders (#377); and Feeling a spiritual connection (#841).

L. Welcoming personal leisure (11) indicators monitor the benefits individuals, groups, and families get from their museum engagements that help them relax, have fun, and be entertained. These services are also offered by theme parks, movie theaters, and other entertainment centers. Representative indicators include: Visiting museums is fun (#811); Museums offer adventure and entertainment (#809); and Comfortable—opening the door to other positive experiences (#674).

INSTITUTIONAL IMPACTS—BENEFITS TO THE MUSEUM ITSELF

M. Helping museum operations (308) indicators monitor the museum's yearly operating activities. Some are used for accounting and for assessing performance and efficiency. The data in these indicators tend to change periodically, and are reported on at least yearly; some are reflected in a museum's statement of activities for a fiscal year. There are more indicators monitoring museum operations than any other area, reflecting a natural preoccupation with how the museum and its staff, collections, facilities, and budgets are running. Revenues, expenses, HR data, attendance, activity listings, management culture, marketing, performance, and value judgments characterize this area of indicators. Representative indicators include: Total on-site attendance for the fiscal year end indicated above (#128); Principal audiences (checklist) (#153); Analysis of programs (#1); Number of participants (#430); Percentage of all collections cataloged online (#471); Who pays the majority of the operating and maintenance expenses for your building? (#7); A Strategic Plan that is approved annually by a formal board vote (#425); Demonstrates that the museum, archive, or library is a learning organization through staff development and evaluation (#542); Total staff (FT & PT) who leave during a year as a percentage of total number employed (453); Ratio of attendance to facility square footage and to exhibit square footage (#496); Which of the following online/virtual platforms does your institution regularly use to engage with the public? (#126); Revenue by category: earned, private support, public support, endowment/interest income (#519); and Total dollar amount of support from peer-panel-awarded government grants (#367).

N. Building museum capital (87) indicators monitor the museum's long-term resources and assets, both tangible (facilities, endowment) and intangible (brand reputation, type of museum, e-mail address); these categories list what the museum is and has. Some of these indicators are reflected in balance statements. These indicators tally capital assets, listings of community resources, and public benefit components; track capital campaigns, governance, and parent organizations, institutional data (address, formal name, DUNS #), long-term community trust, in-house expertise, and management culture; and provide counts of collections, square feet of space, acres of land, and dollars in reserve. Representative indicators include: National legislation and policies to implement them (#299); Value of endowment at beginning of the fiscal year end indicated above (#83); Gross building square footage (range and #) (#159); Percentage of trustees who believe in a clear division of responsibilities between the board and the director and staff and can articulate those boundaries in relation to decisions made over the last year (#422); Which of the following best describes your institution? (#93); Ranking of museum as a significant asset among local community members (#394); and Is your institution accredited by AAM? (#90).

REFERENCES

Hirzy, E. C. (2008). *Excellence and Equity: Education and the Public Dimension of Museums*. American Alliance of Museums.

Holden, John. "Capturing Cultural Value." Demos (2004). Accessed November 4, 2014. http://www.demos.co.uk/files/CapturingCulturalValue.pdf.

Ministry for Culture and Heritage. 2009. Cultural Indicators for New Zealand.

Museums Association. "Museums Change Lives." July 2013. Accessed November 4, 2014. http://www.museumsassociation.org/download?id=1001738.

Scott, Carol. "Advocating the Value of Museums." *INTERCOM*. August 2007. Accessed November 4, 2014. http://www.intercom.museum/documents/CarolScott.pdf.

APPENDIX D

Example Measurement Formulas

This attachment contains example KPI formulas and worksheets that help guide the step-by-step processes described in Part 2: Practice.

EXAMPLES OF DATA FORMULAS

Table D.1. Indicators of the Value to Beneficiaries of the Perceived Benefits

Dwell time	=	Value in time spent (person-minutes at location)
Engagements	=	Value in effort spent (person-trips to location)
Revenues	=	Value in money spent (dollars)

Table D.2. Example KPI Formulas

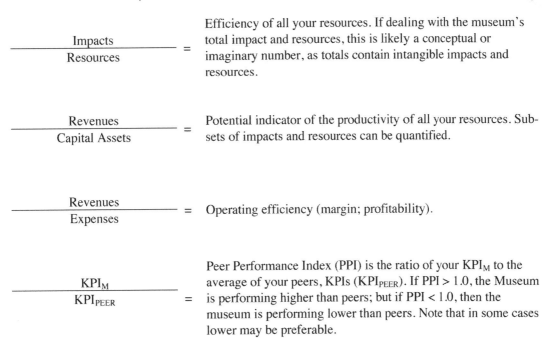

$$\frac{\text{Impacts}}{\text{Resources}} =$$ Efficiency of all your resources. If dealing with the museum's total impact and resources, this is likely a conceptual or imaginary number, as totals contain intangible impacts and resources.

$$\frac{\text{Revenues}}{\text{Capital Assets}} =$$ Potential indicator of the productivity of all your resources. Subsets of impacts and resources can be quantified.

$$\frac{\text{Revenues}}{\text{Expenses}} =$$ Operating efficiency (margin; profitability).

$$\frac{\text{KPI}_{M}}{\text{KPI}_{PEER}} =$$ Peer Performance Index (PPI) is the ratio of your KPI_M to the average of your peers, KPIs (KPI_{PEER}). If PPI > 1.0, the Museum is performing higher than peers; but if PPI < 1.0, then the museum is performing lower than peers. Note that in some cases lower may be preferable.

Table D.2. Example KPI Formulas

$$\frac{\text{Total Museum Engagements}}{\text{Metro CBSA Population}} = \text{Potential indicator of effort by residents of the greater region.}$$

$$\frac{\text{Change in Annual}}{\text{Exchanges by Experts}} = \text{Potential indicator of a change in impact and effectiveness by the cumulative choices of individuals who are expert in making such choices (grant officers, teachers, etc.).}$$

$$\frac{\text{Expenses}}{\text{\# of Engagements}} = \text{Cost of an average engagement, and an indicator of efficiency and/or quality.}$$

$$\frac{\text{Museum Engagements}}{\substack{\text{Full-Time Equivalent (FTE)} \\ \text{Employees}}} = \text{Number of engagements per staff can indicate degree of service, overworked staff, and/or poor or high service.}$$

$$\frac{\text{Earned Revenue}}{\text{Marketing Investment}} = \text{Potential indicator of marketing efficiency in dollars earned per marketing dollar spent.}$$

$$\frac{\text{Change in Earned Revenue}}{\substack{\text{Change in Marketing} \\ \text{Investment}}} = \text{Potential indicator of marketing effectiveness.}$$

$$\frac{\text{Support Revenue}}{\text{Development Cost}} = \text{Potential indicator of development efficiency in dollars raised per development dollar. A common KPI comparison.}$$

$$\frac{\text{School Group Attendance}}{\substack{\text{CBSA or DMA School} \\ \text{Population} \\ \text{Grades [ ] to [ ]}}} = \text{Market ratio of school population served, assuming most school groups are within the DMA. Changes may indicate value fluctuations. When comparing to peers the CBSA population may be easier to obtain.}$$

$$\frac{\text{Earned Revenue Per Cap}}{\substack{\text{Metro Household Disposable} \\ \text{Income}}} = \text{This ratio relates a museum KPI to a relevant market indicator, to put the KPI in context – changes in metro disposable income may affect earned revenue like other consumer products.}$$

$$\frac{\text{School Districts Served}}{\text{Total Regional Districts}} = \text{The Museum's degree of service to a political zone's schools. Important for advocacy of public funding and access to K-12.}$$

Table D.2. *(continued)*

$$\frac{\text{Public Funding Share Of Revenue}}{\text{National Average For Museum Sector}} =$$ Are your peer museums getting more or less support from their governments?

$$\frac{\text{Total Admission Revenue}}{\text{Total Visits, Including Free}} =$$ Average Ticket Price (ATP) is a common KPI. Higher Expenses/Visit can quantify the additional benefit.

$$\frac{\text{Gift Store Revenues}}{\text{On-site Attendance}} =$$ Spending per capita in the museum store.

$$\frac{\text{Total Expenses}}{\text{Gross Square Feet (GSF)}} =$$ Operating expenses per square foot of facility. Common comparison among peers for rough order of magnitude budgeting.

$$\frac{\text{Cost of Utilities(Energy)}}{\text{GSF}} =$$ An indicator of carbon footprint, and a common KPI used to monitor green initiatives, using \$/GSF reduction goals.

$$\frac{\text{Gallery Visits}}{\text{Net Square Feet (NSF) Of Galleries}} =$$ A measure of the degree of gallery utilization: higher numbers than peers may indicate crowdedness and need for expansion; lower numbers may indicate empty and inefficient galleries.

$$\frac{\text{Metro Population}}{\text{GSF}} =$$ Is the museum too large or too small for our population? This ratio is informative only in comparison to peers in other metros.

$$\frac{\text{Square Feet of Free and Subsidized Public Space}}{\text{CBSA Population}} =$$ An advocacy argument for the museum as common ground, in comparison to peers in other CBSAs.

$$\frac{\text{HR Dept. Expenses}}{\text{Full Time Equivalent Employees (FTEs)}} =$$ HR costs per employee.

$$\frac{\text{Payroll \& Benefits}}{\text{FTEs}} =$$ Average salary and benefits.

$$\frac{\text{CEO Salary \& Benefits}}{\text{Lowest Salary and Benefits}} =$$ An indicator of the museum's salary spread monitored by others for possible income gap and inequality issues.

Table D.2. (continued)

$$\frac{\text{Number of Volunteer Shifts}}{\text{Number of Volunteers}} = \text{Measure of commitment from and benefit to the volunteers.}$$

$$\frac{\text{Current Year Partnerships}}{\text{Last Year Partnerships}} = \text{May indicate changes in the degree of the museum's community connections. At the same time a growing number of connections may indicate being spread too thin.}$$

APPENDIX E

Worksheets: Blanks and Versions by the Sample Museum

To illustrate the use of the worksheets in this appendix, there are two versions for each worksheet: a blank for you to adapt, and a completed worksheet filled in by the "Sample Museum" as it followed the processes described in Part 2.

ASSUMPTIONS ABOUT THE SAMPLE MUSEUM IN MIDCITY, USA

The Sample Museum (a fictional amalgam of peer museum data) is located in downtown MidCity. The history and science museum has collections related to regional history and technology, and was founded as a municipal museum until privatized as a 501(c)(3) nonprofit thirty years ago. The Sample Museum (SM) has grown to 165,000 GSF indoors, of which 50,000 NSF is dedicated to exhibits. Admission is charged at a variety of rates and memberships, resulting in an ATP of $4.82 based on 253,013 visitors and $1,754,170 in admission and membership revenues in the Current Year. Additionally, the Sample Museum has five program spaces, a flexible theater, an entrance plaza, lobby, and outdoor terrace, as well as a café and retail store. Collection storage, offices, and modest work-room support spaces are also within the total GSF. Total operating income for the Current Year was $6,457,536 as shown in table D.3. Total full time equivalents (FTEs) were eighty-six people on staff, who received an average of $48,339 based on total salaries and benefits of $4,157,154.

Table E.1. Sample Museum: Financial Snapshot

Sample Museum	Base Year	Current Year	Change
Earned Revenue	$3,256,233	$3,313,605	2%
Support Revenue	$2,856,867	$3,143,931	10%
Endowment/Trust Income for Operations	$660,448	$623,860	-6%
Total Revenue	**$6,773,549**	**$7,081,396**	**5%**
Salaries and Related Expenses	$4,083,679	$4,157,154	2%
Other Costs (excludes depr./amort./financing)	$2,452,198	$2,878,691	17%
Total Expenses	**$6,535,878**	**$7,035,845**	**8%**
Net Surplus/Deficit	**$237,671**	**$45,551**	**-81%**

MidCity's city limits are identical with the county line, and the core market population is 332,565 in the Current Year. The greater region surrounding MidCity, also called its CBSA, has a population of 1,445,920, including MidCity. During the Current Year, MidCity lost jobs and had a higher than average unemployment level. Overnight tourism declined slightly, although tourism is not one of MidCity's main economic drivers.

MISSION AND PURPOSES

The Sample Museum's mission is to spark interest and engagement in creativity and innovation and their impact—past, present, future—on MidCity and our lives.

Given the community needs and the context, museum leadership expressed the following three intentional purposes:

IP#1: Spark interest and engagement
IP#2: Contribute public value to the community
IP#3: Help build economic value

BLANK AND SAMPLE WORKSHEETS

The results of the Sample Museum going through the process in this book are shown on the left pages. These filled-in worksheets illustrate one way of using the blank worksheets on the right pages of this section. Your museum will doubtless end up with very different ways; do not try to follow the examples exactly. Only one of the Sample Museum's three purposes is illustrated (IP#2). The choice of a generic secondary purpose for the sample is intentional; primary proposes will be more specific to each unique museum.

You may well disagree with the choices made by the fictional Sample Museum. As you will see, the Sample Museum has issues, unmet data needs, and ups and downs—just as many real museums will as they get started.

Table E.2 presents all the worksheets that follow this introduction, listed by the chapters that describe their use.

Table E.2. List of Worksheets: Each worksheet has two facing versions: The left page is filled out for the fictional Sample Museum, and the right page is a blank form for you to adapt and fill in.

Chapter 4 Worksheet: Organization	
4.1	Matrix of Intentional Purposes (IPs) & MIIP Categories
Chapter 5 Worksheets: Purposes and Impacts	
5.1	Operating Revenue Comparisons
5.2	Key Audience and Supporter Segments
5.3	Potential Purposes & Impacts Database: 3rd Cut
5.4	Potential Purposes & Impacts Shortlist: 4th Cut
5.5	Theories of Action Rationale
Chapter 6 Worksheets: KPIs	
6.1	KPI Framework
6.2	Potential KPI Master List
6.3	Performance Evaluation Rationale
6.4	Prioritized KPIs
6.5	Data Fields for KPI Calculations
6.6	Data Input Log
6.7	KPI Calculations
Chapter 7 Worksheets: Peer Comparisons	
7.1	Peer Museum Data
7.2	Peer Museum KPI Calculations
Chapter 8	
8.1	Summary Report

Our Prioritized Intentional Purposes	Our Desired Impacts	Share	A. Broadening participation	B. Preserving heritage	C. Strengthening social capital	D. Enhancing public knowledge	E. Serving education	F. Advancing social change	G. Communicating public identity & image	H. Contributing to the economy	I. Delivering corporate community services	J. Enabling personal growth	K. Offering personal respite	L. Welcoming personal leisure
IP #1: Spark interest and engagement (50%)	[Not developed for this sample]													
IP #2: Contribute social value to the community (30%)	2.1 Build regional identity	30%	✓	✓	✓				✓			✓		
	2.2 Strengthen civic connections	40%	✓		✓						✓			
	2.3 Enrich quality of life	30%	✓		✓				✓	✓	✓	✓	✓	✓
IP #3: Help build regional economic value (20%)	[Not developed for this sample]													

Worksheet Status: ☑ Discussion Draft   ☐ Proposed   ☐ Recommended   ☐ Adopted

Worksheet 4.1.   Matrix of Impacts and MIIP Categories: Sample Museum

Our Museum's Intentional Purposes	Our Desired Impacts	Share	A. Broadening participation	B. Preserving heritage	C. Strengthening social capital	D. Enhancing public knowledge	E. Serving education	F. Advancing social change	G. Communicating public identity & image	H. Contributing to the economy	I. Delivering corporate community services	J. Enabling personal growth	K. Offering personal respite	L. Welcoming personal leisure
IP #1:														
IP #2:														
IP #3:														

Worksheet Status: ☐ Discussion Draft ☐ Proposed ☐ Recommended ☐ Adopted

Worksheet 4.1. Matrix of Impacts and MIIP Categories

Key Service Markets	Financial Statements	Base Year	% of Op. Rev.	Current Year	% of Op. Rev.	Current vs Base
	Earned Revenues					
Visitor	Admissions Revenue	$1,150,391	19%	$1,223,262	19%	1.06
Visitor	Shops and Merchandise Sales	$171,978	3%	$153,945	2%	0.90
Visitor	Membership	$484,949	8%	$530,908	8%	1.09
Program	Facility Rental Income	$399,614	7%	$402,618	6%	1.01
Program	Program Revenue	$941,846	15%	$914,700	14%	0.97
Program	Enterprises	$82,462	1%	$68,980	1%	0.84
Program	Other Income	$24,993	0%	$19,191	0%	0.77
	Total Earned	**$3,256,233**	53%	**$3,313,605**	51%	1.02
	Support Revenues					
Public	County	$1,062,377	17%	$1,087,677	17%	1.02
Public	State	$247,074	4%	$242,037	4%	0.98
Public	Federal	$61,112	1%	$121,332	2%	1.99
Public	Municipal	$92,889	2%	$75,226	1%	0.81
Private	Contributions	$384,983	6%	$470,483	7%	1.22
Private	Major Gifts	$163,855	3%	$253,953	4%	1.55
Private	Bequests	$108,487	2%	$70,415	1%	0.65
Priv: Corp.	Corporate Support	$736,091	12%	$822,809	13%	1.12
	Total Support	**$2,856,867**	47%	**$3,143,931**	49%	1.10
	TOTAL REVENUE FROM OPERATIONS	**$6,113,101**	100%	**$6,457,536**	100%	1.06
Asset Inc.	Endowment + Investment Income	$627,547		$603,016		0.96
Asset Inc.	Lease Income	$32,901		$20,844		0.63
	TOTAL REVENUE	**$6,773,549**		**$7,081,396**		1.05
HR	Number of Full Time Equivalents (FTEs)	83.5		86		1.03
HR	Management FTEs	14		15		1.07
HR	Assumed Full Time hours/yr	2000		2000		1.00
HR	Avg self-reported hrs in community work	120		170		1.42
HR	Share of hrs in community work	6%		9%		1.42
HR	Total Managerial Hrs in Community Work	1680		2550		1.52
Exp: HR	Salaries and related expenses	$4,083,679	62%	$4,157,154	59%	1.02
Exp: Other	Other costs (excluding depr costs)	$2,452,198	38%	$2,878,691	41%	1.17
	TOTAL EXPENSES (pre Depr/Amort)	**$6,535,878**		**$7,035,845**		1.08
HR	Avg salary & benefits cost per FTE	$48,906		$48,339		0.99
	SURPLUS/DEFICIT (pre (Depr/Amort)	**$237,671**	4%	**$45,551**	1%	0.19

Museum Engagements		Base Year	% of Op. Rev.	Current Year	% of Op. Rev.	Current vs Base
Visitor	Admissions:					
Visitor	Adult	62,725	20%	58,643	18%	0.93
Visitor	Student	76,130	24%	77,694	24%	1.02
Visitor	Senior	13,004	4%	8,437	3%	0.65
Visitor	Guest (Free)	41,882	13%	35,943	11%	0.86
Visitor	Member	76,245	24%	72,296	22%	0.95
Visitor	Subtotal Visitor Admissions	269,986	85%	253,013	79%	0.94
Program	Other On-Site	46,060	15%	68,962	21%	1.50
	Total On-site Attendance	316,046		321,975		1.02

Worksheet 5.1. Operating Revenue Comparisons: Sample Museum

Key Service Markets	Financial Statements	Base Year	% of Op. Rev.	Current Year	% of Op. Rev.	Current vs Base Change
Visitor Program	Earned Revenues					
Public Private	**Total Earned** Support Revenues					
	Total Support					
	TOTAL REVENUE FROM OPERATIONS					
Asset Inc.	Capital asset income allocated to ops.					
	TOTAL REVENUE					
HR Exp:HR Exp:Other	Full time equivalents (FTEs) Salaries and related expenses Other costs (excluding depr.)					
HR	**TOTAL EXPENSES (pre Depr/Amort)** Avg. salaries and related costs per FTE					
	SURPLUS/DEFICIT (pre (Depr/Amort)					

Museum Engagements		Base Year	% of Op. Rev.	Current Year	% of Op. Rev.	Current vs Base Change
Visitor	Admissions:					
	Subtotal Visitors					
Program	On-site Programs Off-site Programs					
	Subtotal Programs					
	Total Attendance (Physical Engagements)					

Worksheet 5.1. Operating Revenue Comparisons

Key Service Markets	Engagements	Dwell Time	Revenue
Key Audience Segments			**51%**
Visitors: On-Site	**79%**		**30%**
Visitors	32%	POS	22%
Members	23%	POS	8%
Groups (incl. student)	24%	POS	Incl.
Program Participants: On-Site	**21%**		**21%**
Participants	21%	POS	14%
Rentals	Incl.	POS	6%
Enterprises	DNA	—	1%
Program Participants: Off-Site	—	—	—
School Outreach	—	—	—
Program Participants: Virtual			
Key Support Segments	**Meetings**	**Time Spent**	**49%**
Public Supporters			**34%**
County (=MidCity)	POS	POS	17%
State	POS	POS	4%
Federal	POS	POS	2%
Municipal	POS	POS	1%
Private Supporters			**25%**
Major Gifts & Bequests	POS	POS	5%
Contributions	POS	POS	7%
Corporate Support	POS	POS	13%
Income from Capital Assets			Not incl.
Endowments & Trusts	—	—	—
Totals			**100%**

Legend

DNA	Data not available or not meaningful
POS	Data might possibly be obtained, but is not currently available
—	Does not apply or count
Incl.	Included in a larger sub-total

Worksheet 5.2. Key Audience and Supporter Segments: Sample Museum

Key Service Markets	Engagements	Dwell Time	Revenue
Key Audience Segments			
Visitors: On-Site			
Visitors			
Members			
Groups			
Program Participants: On-Site			
Participants			
Rentals			
Groups			
Program Participants: Off-Site			
School Outreach			
Program Participants: Virtual			
Key Support Segments	**Meetings**	**Time Spent**	
Public Supporters			
County			
State			
Federal			
Municipal			
Private Supporters			
Major Gifts & Bequests			
Contributions			
Corporate Support			
Income from Capital Assets			
Endowments & Trusts	—	—	—
Totals			100%

Legend

DNA	Data not available or not meaningful
POS	Data might possibly be obtained, but is not currently available
—	Does not apply or count
Incl.	Included in a larger sub-total

Worksheet 5.2.   Key Audience and Supporter Segments

	Paste Mission Statement Here: Spark interest and engagement in creativity and innovation and their impact—past, present, future—on Mid City and our lives.	Mus. Plan.	202	Final IP #1	IP #1
Personal growth					
Our identity	Type of Museum: History and science	MIIP 1.0	207	3rd Cut	IP #1.
Our identity	"Well known and respected in the community"	Comm. Needs		3rd Cut	IP #1.
Personal growth	Decide to do something different in their lives	MIIP 1.0	534	3rd Cut	IP #1a
Personal growth	New expereinces	Audiences		3rd Cut	IP #1a
Personal growth	Creating inspiring and accessible learning environments	MIIP 1.0	528	3rd Cut	IP #1a
Personal growth	Spark interest and engagement	Core Team		3rd Cut	IP #1a
Personal growth	Provide lifelong learning opportunities	MIIP 1.0	479	3rd Cut	IP #1b
Personal growth	Access to the learning opportunities that they want	MIIP 1.0	531	3rd Cut	IP #1b
Personal growth	Become more self-confident, questioning, motivated and open to others' perspectives	MIIP 1.0	532	3rd Cut	IP #1b
Personal growth	Develop skills as a result of using museums, archives and libraries	MIIP 1.0	535	3rd Cut	IP #1b
Personal growth	Use the services and facilities to develop their knowledge and understanding	MIIP 1.0	541	3rd Cut	IP #1b
Personal growth	Identity development	Audiences		3rd Cut	IP #1b
Personal growth	Family services	Supporters		3rd Cut	IP #1c
Personal growth	"Work with very young parents to break the cycle of poverty"	Comm. Needs		3rd Cut	IP #1c
Formal school support	Pre- K12 support	Supporters		3rd Cut	IP #1d
Formal school support	Developing programs for K-12 students	MIIP 1.0	580	3rd Cut	IP #1d
Contribute public value to the community	**Contribute public value to the community**	Core Team		Final IP #2	IP #2
Contribute public value to the community	Leverage our strength in programs and rich catalog of in-house programs with additional campus and on-line programs developed in partnership with others	Mus. Plan.		3rd Cut	IP #2a
Gathering place	Develop the Campus as an indoor/outdoor community event, activity and gathering place, build new gateway connections, and strengthen and renew the existing structures to meet 21st century museum standards	Mus. Plan.		3rd Cut	IP #2a
Identity	Hold, care for and continue to develop collections for the nation which represent our rich and diverse culture.	MIIP 1.0	476	3rd Cut	IP #2a
Identity	Celebrating local identity and community pride	MIIP 1.0	591	3rd Cut	IP #2a
Identity	Building on history/experiences as a source for understanding and tolerance	MIIP 1.0	595	3rd Cut	IP #2a
Identity	Preserving and displaying collections that are touchstones to emotional events.	MIIP 1.0	598	3rd Cut	IP #2a
Personal growth	Providing exhibits, theaters and programs for adult and family audiences	MIIP 1.0	584	3rd Cut	IP #2a
Broadening praticipation	Audience parallels community diversity	MIIP 1.0	621	3rd Cut	IP #2b
Broadening praticipation	New learning opportunities are created as a result of partnerships	MIIP 1.0	538	3rd Cut	IP #2b
Contribute public value to the community	Quality of life enhancement	Supporters		3rd Cut	IP #2b
Contribute public value to the community	Using institutional resources to address community issues	MIIP 1.0	594	3rd Cut	IP #2b
Gathering place	"Diversity issues - different social classes want to avoid contact with one another"	Comm. Needs		3rd Cut	IP #2b
Partnerships	Identifies suitable partners and evaluates the benefits of working in partnership to support learning	MIIP 1.0	524	3rd Cut	IP #2b
Partnerships	Become an essential partner and player in MidCity's network of other quality organizations, corporations, universities and schools	Mus. Plan.		3rd Cut	IP #2b
Economic development	**Help build economic value**	Core Team		Final IP #3	IP #3
Economic development	Contributing to economic welfare of the community	MIIP 1.0	575	3rd Cut	IP #3
Broadening praticipation	Centrality of diversity and broadening participation in institutional strategic planning	MIIP 1.0	239	3rd Cut	IP #3a
Broadening praticipation	Invites people from outside the museum, archive or library to bring new perspectives and broaden the appeal and opportunities.	MIIP 1.0	525	3rd Cut	IP #3a
Broadening praticipation	"Deep economic divides between city, county and suburb – the donut."	Comm. Needs		3rd Cut	IP #3a
Personal leisure	Quality time with friends and family	Audiences		3rd Cut	IP #3a
Economic development	Participating in neighborhood development	MIIP 1.0	577	3rd Cut	IP #3b
Economic development	Stimulates discovery and research	MIIP 1.0	551	3rd Cut	IP #3c
Economic development	Economic development: Jobs	Supporters		3rd Cut	IP #3d
Economic development	"Losing population – particularly young people. Income levels have dropped."	Comm. Needs		3rd Cut	IP #3d
Workforce development	"JOBS are the biggest issue."	Comm. Needs		3rd Cut	IP #3d
Workforce development	Providing workforce development	MIIP 1.0	578	3rd Cut	IP #3d
Legend					
Audiences	=Perceived benefits from audiences				
Comm. Needs	=Ideas from community needs interviews				
Core Team	=Ideas from the project team members				
MIIP 1.0	=Ideas from the MIIP database				
Mus. Plan	=Museum planning documents				
Supporters	=Perceived benefits from supporters				
IP	=Intentional Purposes				

Worksheet 5.3. Potential Purposes and Impacts: Sample Museum

Content Goup	Potential Purpose or Impact	Source	Selection	Relates to IP#

Legend

Audiences	=Perceived benefits from audiences
Comm. Needs	=Ideas from community needs interviews
Core Team	=Ideas from the project team members
MIIP 1.0	=Ideas from the MIIP database
Mus. Plan	=Museum planning documents
Supporters	=Perceived benefits from supporters
IP	=Intentional Purposes

Worksheet 5.3. Potential Purposes and Impacts

Content Group	Indicator	Source	Selection	IP #
Personal growth	**Paste Mission Statement Here: Spark interest and engagement in creativity and innovation and their impact—past, present, future—on Mid City and our lives.**	Mus. Plan.	**Final IP #1**	IP #1
Personal growth	New experiences	Audiences	4th Cut	IP #1a
Personal growth	Spark interest and engagement	Core Team	4th Cut	IP #1a
Personal growth	Use the services and facilities to develop their knowledge and understanding	MIIP 1.0	4th Cut	IP #1b
Personal growth	"Work with very young parents to break the cycle of poverty"	Comm. Needs	4th Cut	IP #1c
Contribute public value to the community	**Contribute public value to the community**	Core Team	**Final IP #2**	IP #2
Identity & engagement	Access to the learning opportunities that they want	MIIP 1.0	4th Cut	IP #2a
Identity & engagement	Hold, care for and continue to develop collections for the nation which represent our rich and diverse culture.	MIIP 1.0	4th Cut	IP #2a
Civic connections	Centrality of diversity and broadening participation in institutional strategic planning	MIIP 1.0	4th Cut	IP #2b
Civic connections	"Deep economic divides between city, county and suburb – the donut."	Comm. Needs	4th Cut	IP #2b
Civic connections	Identifies suitable partners and evaluates the benefits of working in partnership to support learning	MIIP 1.0	4th Cut	IP #2b
Civic connections	Corporations recognize the museum's value to their communities	Core Team	4th Cut	IP #2b
Civic connections	Become an essential partner and player in MidCity's network of other quality organizations, corporations, universities and schools	Mus. Plan.	4th Cut	IP #2b
Quality of life	Providing exhibits, theaters and programs for adult and family audiences	MIIP 1.0	4th Cut	IP #2c
Quality of life	Quality of life enhancement	Supporters	4th Cut	IP #2c
Economic development	**Help build economic value**	Core Team	**Final IP #3**	IP #3
Economic development	Participating in neighborhood development	MIIP 1.0	4th Cut	IP #3a
Workforce development	"JOBS are the biggest issue."	Comm. Needs	4th Cut	IP #3b

Worksheet Status: ☐ Discussion Draft   ☑ Proposed   ☐ Recommended   ☐ Adopted

Worksheet 5.4. Potential Impacts—Short List: Sample Museum

Content Group	Indicator	Source	Selection	IP #

Worksheet Status: ☐ Discussion Draft ☑ Proposed ☐ Recommended ☐ Adopted

Worksheet 5.4. Potential Impacts—Short List

IP#	Intentional Purpose
2	The Sample Museum's second intentional purpose (IP#2) is to "Contribute public value to the community" by programming our community spaces to achieve the following desired impacts: a) stronger regional identity and engagement, b) greater civic connections, and c) quality of life enrichment.
	Desired Impacts
2.1	Regional identity and engagement are stronger
2.2	Civic connections are greater
2.3	The quality of life is enriched
	Theory of Action
2	We theorize that these outcomes can be achieved at an individual level if we bring our community's diverse people and organizations together in positive, face-to-face encounters. The deeper the participation and the greater the number of these experiences, the greater the chance that the cumulative outcomes of our annual programs will become the community impacts we desire.
	The Museum will act on this theory by programming our menu of flexible community spaces, including our five program studios, outdoor terrace, and, in the evening, our plaza, lobby and auditorium, with an active schedule of programs designed to bring people and organizations together, such as community gathering events, fairs, public programs, family and business ceremonies, and other activities that contribute public value to the community. We will develop these activities true to our guiding principles and responsible to our resources.
	Audiences and Supporters
2	To maximize our impact and performance for IP#2 (Contribute public value to the community), we will focus on serving the following audiences and supporters: <ul><li>MidCity residents of all ages</li><li>Regional families with children 2-12</li><li>Regional corporations and businesses</li><li>Community development agencies and foundations</li><li>MidCity and County infrastructures</li><li>Partnering organizations, including the Pre-K-12 system</li></ul>

Worksheet 5.5. Theory of Action Rationale: Sample Museum

IP#	Intentional Purpose
2	The _____ Museum's __ intentional purpose (IP#-) is to _____ _____ by _____ to achieve the following desired impacts: a) _____, b) _____ , and c) _____
	Desired Impacts
2.1	
2.2	
2.3	
	Theory of Action
2	We theorize that _____ _____ _____ The Museum will act on this theory by _____ _____ We will develop these activities true to our guiding principles and responsible to our resources.
	Audiences and Supporters
2	To maximize our impact and performance for IP#2 (_____ _____) we will focus on serving the following audiences and supporters: • _____ • _____ • _____ • _____ • _____ • _____

Worksheet 5.5. Theory of Action Rationale

IP # 2: Contribute value to the community	
2.1	**Build regional identity and engagement**
	KPI 2.1a: Investment in heritage collections care is on par with peers
	Periodic evaluation: Does the collection build regional identity?
	KPI 2.1b: Regional residents engage with the museum
	Periodic evaluation: Do engagements with residents build regional identity?
2.2	**Strengthen civic connections**
	KPI 2.2a: The museum's leadership and team reflect the City's diversity
	Periodic evaluation: Does team diversity result in audience diversity?
	KPI 2.2b: Our partnership network is growing
	Periodic evaluation: Does the number of partnerships indicate civic connections?
	KPI 2.2c: Our managers spend 5 – 10% of their time in community work
	Periodic evaluation: Do others see our managers strengthening civic connections?
	KPI 2.2d: Corporations support the museum as they do our peers
	Periodic evaluation: Does our corporate support strengthen civic connections?
2.3	**Enrich quality of life in MidCity**
	KPI 2.3a: City residents engage with the museum
	Periodic evaluation: Do residents believe engagements add to their quality of life?
	KPI 2.3b: City residents find our programs recommendable to others
	Periodic evaluation: Do participants perceive the programs as very beneficial?
	KPI 2.3c: City housing values are increasing faster than regional housing
	Periodic evaluation: Do city homeowners believe quality of life is improving?

Worksheet Status: ☐ Discussion Draft ☐ Proposed ☑ Recommended ☐ Adopted

Worksheet 6.1. KPI Framework: Sample Museum. KPIs based on operating data can be routinely monitored—some daily and others annually. Evaluation, on the other hand, tends to involve periodic studies, often at incremental expense and staff time. The strategy is to use KPIs routinely to measure changes in impact and performance, and to test each indicator's validity periodically using other evaluation methodologies: Do changes in the KPI actually track changes in the desired impacts?

IP # 2:		
2.1	**[Desired Impact]**	
	KPI 2.1a:	
	Periodic evaluation:	
	KPI 2.1b:	
	Periodic evaluation:	
2.2	**[Desired Impact]**	
	KPI 2.2a:	
	Periodic evaluation:	
	KPI 2.2b:	
	Periodic evaluation:	
	KPI 2.2c:	
	Periodic evaluation:	
	KPI 2.2d:	
	Periodic evaluation:	
2.3	**[Desired Impact]**	
	KPI 2.3a:	
	Periodic evaluation	
	KPI 2.3b:	
	Periodic evaluation:	
	KPI 2.3c:	
	Periodic evaluation:	

Worksheet Status: ☐ Discussion Draft   ☐ Proposed   ☐ Recommended   ☐ Adopted

Worksheet 6.1.   KPI Framework. KPIs based on operating data can be routinely monitored—some daily and others annually. Evaluation, on the other hand, tends to involve periodic studies, often at incremental expense and staff time. The strategy is to use KPIs routinely to measure changes in impact and performance, and to test each indicator's validity periodically using other evaluation methodologies: Do changes in the KPI actually track changes in the desired impacts?

Indicator #	Source: Title	Indicator	Desired Impact	Selection	Content Group	Kind (Location of indicator along the Theory of Action)	Potential Impact Category
557	The Educational Value of Museums	How much time per month does your professional staff spend on community affairs as members of service organizations, municipal boards, non-profit boards, or volunteer organizations?	Civic Connections	4th cut	Social capital	6b. KPI: May Indicate Value	C. Strenghtening Social Capital
554	The Educational Value of Museums	How many partnerships with other organizations do you manage simultaneously? Might this be an indicator of effective limited resource allocation?	Civic Connections	4th cut	Social capital	6b. KPI: May Indicate Value	C. Strenghtening Social Capital
639	Cohorts 1 and 2 on "Community Impact"	Center is seen as "legitimate," a full "partner in the educational infrastructure"	Civic Connections	4th cut	Social capital	7. Perceived Benefit	C. Strenghtening Social Capital
874	Advocating the value of museums	development of positive social capital, defined as the networks, norms and trust that enable cooperation for mutual benefit	Civic Connections	4th cut	Social capital	7. Perceived Benefit	C. Strenghtening Social Capital
714	ASTC Economic Impact Study	a conduit for corporate philanthropy; for example, by creating inner-city school programs funded by corporate giving initiatives	Civic Connections	4th cut	Social capital	7. Perceived Benefit	I. Delivering Corporate Community Services
553	The Educational Value of Museums	How many evenings per month, on average, do you sponsor special events, remain open for other organizational meetings, or simply make it possible for working families to come in?	Neighborhood Value	4th cut	Cultural Access	6b. KPI: May Indicate Value	A. Broadening Participation
627	Cohorts 1 and 2 on "Community Impact"	Staff parallels community in diversity	Neighborhood Value	4th cut	Cultural Access	6b. KPI: May Indicate Value	A. Broadening Participation
593	Purposes Framework	Serving as a community gathering place	Neighborhood Value	4th cut	Quality of life	1. Intentional Purpose	C. Strenghtening Social Capital
729	ASTC Economic Impact Study	an organiser and host of cultural and educational events for the public, often in partnership with other community organisations	Neighborhood Value	4th cut	Quality of life	7. Perceived Benefit	C. Strenghtening Social Capital
801	The Social Significance of Museums	Museums improve the quality of the living environment.	Neighborhood Value	4th cut	Quality of life	7. Perceived Benefit	C. Strenghtening Social Capital
429	25 Indicators of Success: The Children's Museum of Indianapolis	Analysis of programs: 3. Quality as measured by participant evaluation	Neighborhood Value	4th cut	Quality of life	7. Perceived Benefit	J. Enabling Personal Growth
687	Culture and Revitalization: The Economic Effects of MASS MoCA on its Community	Hedonic analysis of the effects of a cultural institutions on real estate prices (gentrification)	Neighborhood Value	4th cut	Quality of life	7. Perceived Benefit	H. Contributing to the Economy
502	ACM Benchmark Calculator	On-Site Attendance as a Ratio of the Population	Regional Identity	4th cut	Cultural Access	6b. KPI: May Indicate Value	J. Enabling Personal Growth
588	Purposes Framework	Conserving significant collections, historic property and site	Regional Identity	4th cut	Identity	1. Intentional Purpose	B. Perserving Heritage
4001 701	924, 923 Public perceptions of – and attitudes to - the purposes of museums in society	Convey a sense of place and identity Bringing the community together	Regional Identity Regional Identity	4th cut 4th cut	Identity Cultural Access	1. Intentional Purpose 7. Perceived Benefit	C. Strenghtening Social Capital
954	Advocating the value of museums	Symbolic value	Regional Identity	4th cut	Identity	7. Perceived Benefit	G. Communicating Public Identity & Image

Worksheet 6.2. Potential KPI Master List: Sample Museum

Source Title	Indicator	Desired Impact	Selection	Content Group	Kind (Location of indicator along the Theory of Action	Potential Impact Category

Worksheet 6.2. Potential KPI Master List

We believe that if we are successful to some degree at achieving our desired impacts for IP#2, then changes in those impacts might be measured by the following observable and measurable key performance indications over time:

2.1.	Build regional identity and engagement: "Convey a sense of place and identity," (MIIP indicators #924 and 923)

- If the museum is to convey identity, then how much we invest in "Conserving significant collections, historic property and site" (#588) is an indicator of our stewardship of the region's legacy and identity.

  ▶ KPI 2.1a: The ratio of the (Collections-related operating expenses to our total operating expenses) divided by the (Factored average of the same ratio at our peer museums) shall be 1.0 or greater.

- If the museum serves as "Symbolic value" (#954) and "Brings the community together," (#701), then the choice to travel to the museum (on-site attendance and participations) for a physical museum engagement is an indicator of these impacts. The region is defined as MidCity's CBSA.

  ▶ KPI 2.1b: "On-Site Attendance as a Ratio of the Population" (#502). The museum will set targets for this figure annually.

2.2.	Strengthen civic connections: "development of positive social capital, defined as the networks, norms and trust that enable cooperation for mutual benefit." (#874).

- If the museum adds value to all residents of the City (defined as MidCity's county population, then the museum's foundational indicator of that intent is that "Staff parallels the community in diversity." (#627)

  ▶ KPI 2.2a: Each level of the museum's organization chart, including the Board, should have representation from the groups living in our City's CBSA in rough proportion to their share of US Census data on race and ethnicity.

- If the museum is helping maintain and build networks, then "How many partnerships with other organizations do you manage simultaneously? This might be an indicator of effective limited resource allocation" (#554).

  ▶ KPI 2.2b: The ratio of (Number of active organizational partners at the end of Current Year) divided by the (Number of active organizational partners at the end of the Base Year) exceeds 1.0.

- If the museum is connected to our region, then "How much time per month does your professional staff spend on community affairs as members of service organizations, municipal boards, non-profit boards, or volunteer organizations? (#557) is a measurement of that impact.

  ▶ KPI 2.2c: The ratio of the (Number of managerial staff hours spent annually off-site in museum-sanctioned regional activities) divided by the (Total number of managerial staff hours) should be within 5% to 10% as a norm.

- If the museum is trusted, it is "seen as 'legitimate,' a full partner in the educational" system" (#639). An indicator of that trust is the value of the museum's services as "a conduit for corporate philanthropy; for example, by creating inner-city school programs funded by corporate giving initiatives." (#714)

  ▶ KPI 2.2d: The ratio of (Annual corporate support) divided by (total operating revenue) equals or exceeds the same ratio at peer museums.

2.3.	Enrich quality of life: "Museums improve the quality of the living environment." (#801) by "Serving as a community gathering place" (#593).

- If the museum is "an organiser and host of cultural and educational events for the public, often in partnership with other community organisations." (#729), then the number of City people engaged in those events is an indicator of serving the City.

  ▶ KPI 2.3a: The ratio of the (Annual number of physical person-trips (engagements) by residents of MidCity to the museum and its off-site programs) divided by (MidCity's county population), and expressed as XX engagements per resident per year. The museum will set targets for this figure annually.

- If the museum improves the quality of life in the City, then "Analysis of program … quality as measured by participant evaluation" (#429) as indicated by the Net Promoter Score (#641 – likelihood to recommend) should be high. Long-term, the City real estate should increase in value as indicated through a "Hedonic analysis of the effects of a cultural institution on real estate prices (gentrification)." (#687). If the museum creates jobs directly, that should show up in the HR counts.

  ▶ KPI 2.3b: Evaluation of perceived benefit from participating in the museum's programs by City residents to measure 8.0 or higher on the Net Promoter Score.

  ▶ KPI 2.3c: The ratio of (Current median house price in MidCity) divided by (Current median house in the Greater MidCity CBSA region compared to the same ratio five years ago.) Results greater than 1.0 mean City values have raised relatively higher than the regional norm due to causes that might include the museum's activities.

Given our priorities and guiding principles, our specific resources and our community context, we believe our performance in achieving our desired impacts for contributing public value to the community should be outstanding in diversity and inclusion, distinguished in community relations, and acceptable for all other KPIs because our museum is uniquely capable of serving as a model of diversity, an honest broker, and a host gathering the community in our neutral, central and trusted facility and grounds. These priorities are reflected in Worksheet 6.4.

Worksheet 6.3. Performance Evaluation Rationale: Sample Museum

We believe that if we are successful to some degree at achieving our desired impacts for IP#2, then changes in those impacts might be measured by the following observable and measurable key performance indicators over time:

Desired Impact 2.1: _____

    KPI 2.1a ....n: _____

        We will periodically evaluate this KPI's validity by asking our audiences and supporters_____

Desired Impact 2.2: _____

    KPI 2.2a ... n: _____

        We will periodically evaluate this KPI's validity by asking our audiences and supporters_____

Desired Impact 2.3: _____

    KPI 2.3a ... n: _____

        We will periodically evaluate this KPI's validity by asking our audiences and supporters_____

Given our priorities and guiding principles, our specific resources and our community context, we believe our performance in achieving our desired impacts for _____[IP#2]_____ should be outstanding in _____[top performance category]_____, distinguished in _____[secondary performance category]_____, and acceptable for all other KPIs because our museum is uniquely capable of _____[Insert rationale]_____.These priorities are reflected in Worksheet 6.4.

Worksheet 6.3. Performance Evaluation Rationale

IP # 2: Contribute social value to the community: 30% of all IPs		KPI Priority	IP Priority	Factored Priority
2.1	**Build regional identity and engagement**	**30%**		
	KPI 2.1a: Investment in heritage collections care is on par with peers	5%	30%	2%
	KPI 2.1b: Regional residents engage with the museum	25%	30%	8%
2.2	**Strengthen civic connections**	**40%**		
	KPI 2.2a: The museum's leadership and team reflect the City's diversity	20%	30%	6%
	KPI 2.2b: Our partnership network is growing	5%	30%	2%
	KPI 2.2c: Our managers spend 5 – 10% of their time in community work	10%	30%	3%
	KPI 2.2d: Corporations support the museum as they do our peers	5%	30%	2%
2.3	**Enrich quality of life in MidCity**	**30%**		
	KPI 2.3a: City residents engage with the museum	15%	30%	5%
	KPI 2.3b: City residents find our programs live up to their promise	10%	30%	3%
	KPI 2.3c: City housing values are increasing faster than regional housing	5%	30%	2%
		100%		**30%**

Worksheet 6.4.   Prioritized KPIs: Sample Museum

IP # 2:		KPI Priority	IP Priority	Factored Priority
2.1	[Desired impact]			
	KPI 2.1a:			
	KPI 2.1b:			
2.2	[Desired impact]			
	KPI 2.2a:			
	KPI 2.2b:			
	KPI 2.2c			
	KPI 2.2d:			
2.3	[Desired impact]			
	KPI 2.3a:			
	KPI 2.3b:			
	KPI 2.3c:			

Worksheet 6.4. Prioritized KPIs

Used in KPI #	Data Collection Fields	Data Source	Data Type	Data Availability	Collection Method and Comments
2.1.a	Collections Expenses	Finance	Operating	Aspirational	Need to define what costs qualify
	Total Operating Expenses	Finance	Operating	Existing	Financial statements
	Peer Collection Expenses	Peers	Peer	Aspirational	Need to agree on definitions and share data
	Peer Total Expenses	Peers	Peer	Aspirational	Need to agree on definitions and share data
2.1.b	On-site Visitor Attendance	Ticketing	Operating	Existing	Ticketing system
	On-site Program Participants	Ed. Dept.	Operating	Provisional	Ticketing system for fee-based programs, but other museum engagements not yet included
	MidCity CBSA Population	Alteryx	Market	Existing	Stable demographic data
2.2.a	Race and Ethnicity (R&E)	Alteryx	Market	Existing	Stable demographic data
	R&E Profile of the Board	HR	Operating	Provisional	HR survey needs to be updated
	R&E Profile of Managers	HR	Operating	Provisional	HR survey needs to be updated
	R&E Profile of Supervisors	HR	Operating	Provisional	HR survey needs to be updated
	R&E Profile of Other Staff	HR	Operating	Provisional	HR survey needs to be updated
2.2.b	# of Organizational Partners	Admin.	Operating	Provisional	Informal list kept by Development; need to formalize
2.2.c	# of Managerial FTEs	HR	Operating	Existing	
	Managerial Community Hours per cap	HR	Operating	Provisional	Estimate provided by managers; need to formalize
	Assumed Annual Working Hours	HR Policy	Operating	Existing	
2.2.d	Annual Corporate Support	Finance	Operating	Existing	Financial statements
	Regional Corporate Giving	Journal of Philanthropy	Market	Research	Adjust for inflation
	Peer Corporate Support	990s	Peer	Research	Adjust for inflation
2.3.a	Engagements with MidCity Residents	Marketing	Operating	Provisional	Annual totals calculated from zip code survey
	MidCity County Population	Alteryx	Market	Existing	Consistent demographic data
2.3.b	Net Promoter Score	Evaluation	Eval Study	Research	To be conducted next year
2.3.c	Median House Price in MidCity County	Alteryx	Market	Existing	Consistent demographic data
	Median House Price in MidCity CBSA	Alteryx	Market	Existing	Consistent demographic data

Worksheet 6.5. Data Fields: Sample Museum

Used in KPI #	Data Collection Fields	Data Source	Data Type	Data Availability	Collection Method and Comments

Worksheet 6.5. Data Fields

Used in KPI #	Data Collection Fields	Data Source	Base Year	Current Year	Change Index
2.1.a	Collections Expenses	Finance	na	na	
	Total Operating Expenses	Finance	$6,535,878	$7,035,845	1.08
	Peer Collection Expenses	Peers	na	na	
	Peer Total Expenses	Peers	na	na	
2.1.b	On-site Attendance	Ticketing	269,986	253,013	0.94
	On-site Program Participants	Admissions	46,060	68,962	1.50
	MidCity CBSA Population	FactFinder	1,630,780	1,654,592	1.01
2.2.a	Race and Ethnicity (R&E)	US Census			
	R&E Profile of the Board	HR			
	R&E Profile of Managers	HR		See table below	
	R&E Profile of Supervisors	HR			
	R&E Profile of Other Staff	HR			
2.2.b	# of Organizational Partners	Admin.	14	22	1.57
2.2.c	# of Full-time Managers	HR	14	15	1.07
	Managerial Community Hours per cap	HR	120	170	1.42
	Assumed Annual Working Hours	HR Policy	2,000	2,000	1.00
2.2.d	Annual Corporate Support	Finance	$736,091	$822,809	1.12
	Total Revenue	Finance	$6,773,549	$7,081,396	1.05
	Peer Corporate Support (% of total $)	Peers or 990s	na	16%	...
2.3.a	Engagements with MidCity Residents	Marketing	170,665	183,526	1.08
	MidCity (County) Population	US Census	487,241	496,832	1.02
2.3.b	Net Promoter Score	Evaluation	9.2	8.4	0.91
2.3.c	Median House Price in MidCity CBSA	FactFinder	75,800	78,800	1.04
	Median House Price in MidCity DMA	FactFinder	128,200	130,600	1.02

	MidCity Core			Board							All Staff						
	Base Year	Current Year	Change	Base Year actual	% of Total	GAP	Current Year actual	% of Total	GAP	Gap reduced by	Base Year	% of Total	GAP	Current Year	% of Total	GAP	Gap reduced by
White	50%	44%	-6%	10	59%	9%	8	47%	3%		41	49%	0%	42	49%	5%	
Black or African American	41%	42%	1%	5	29%	11%	6	35%	6%		31	37%	4%	36	42%	0%	
American Indian and Alaska Native	0%	0%	-	-	-	-	-	-	-		-	-	-	-	-	-	
Asian	2%	4%	2%	2	12%	9%	2	12%	8%		8	10%	7%	6	7%	3%	
Native Hawaiian and other Pac. Islander	0%	0%	-	-	-	-	-	-	-		-	-	-	-	-	-	
Some other race	4%	6%	2%	-	0%	4%	-	0%	6%		-	0%	4%	-	0%	6%	
Two or more races	3%	4%	2%	-	0%	3%	1	6%	1%		4	5%	2%	2	2%	2%	
	100%	100%	0%	17	100%	37%	17	100%	25%	32%	83.5	100%	17%	86.0	100%	16%	5%

Worksheet 6.6. Data Input Log: Sample Museum

Used in KPI #	Data Collection Fields	Data Source	Base Year	Current Year	Change Index

Worksheet 6.6.   Data Input Log

IP # 2: Contribute social value to the community	KPI Formula	Base Year or Peer Data	Current Year	Change Index of Current from Base
2.1	**Build regional identity and engagement**			
KPI 2.1a: Investment in heritage collections care is on par with peers	((Collections-related operating expenses/ (Total operating expenses)/(Same ratio at peer museums))	na	na	
KPI 2.1b: Regional residents engage with the museum	(On-Site Attendance)/(CBSA Population)	17%	15%	0.92
2.2	**Strengthen civic connections**			
KPI 2.2a: The museum's leadership and team reflect the City's diversity	Staff Gap = The difference between current representation % and City actual %.	17%	16%	5%
	Board Gap = The difference between current representation % and City actual %.	37%	25%	32%
KPI 2.2b: Our partnership network is growing	(Number of institutional partners this year)/(Number of institutional partners last year)	14	22	1.57
KPI 2.2c: Our managers spend 5 – 10% of their time in community work	(Number of managerial staff hours spent annually off-site in museum-sanctioned community activities)/(Total number of managerial staff hours)	1680	2550	1.52
KPI 2.2d: Corporations support the museum as they do our peers	((Annual corporate support)/(Total revenue)/(Same ratio at peer museums))	16%	12%	0.72
2.3	**Enrich quality of life in MidCity**			
KPI 2.3a: City residents engage with the museum	((((On-site attendance)*(share of MidCity residents in attendance survey sample))/ (MidCity County Population)))	35%	37%	1.05
KPI 2.3b: City residents find our programs live up to their promise	Evaluation of perceived benefit from participating in the museum's programs by City residents to measure 8.0 or higher on the Net Promoter Score (#641 – likelihood to recommend)	8.4	9.2	1.10
KPI 2.3c: City housing values are increasing faster than regional housing	(((Current City median house price)/(Current CBSA median house)/(Same ratio five years ago))	59%	60%	1.02

Worksheet 6.7. KPI Calculations: Sample Museum

KPI Calculations: Year-over-Year Comparisons
Worksheet 6.7-Right

For IP # ___ ; Desired Impacts and their KPIs	Base Year or Peer Data	Current Year	Change Index of Current from Base
__.1 [Desired Impact]			
KPI 1a:			
KPI 1b:			
KPI 1c:			
__.2 [Desired Impact]			
KPI 2a:			
KPI 2b:			
KPI 2c:			
__.3 [Desired Impact]			
KPI 3a:			
KPI 3b:			
KPI 3c:			

Worksheet 6.7. KPI Calculations

Peer Museum Name	CBSA Metro Population	City Population	Museum Building Size (GSF)	Galleries (NSF)	Base Year Attendance			Current Year Attendance			Current Year	
					Visitors	Programs	Total	Visitors	Programs	Total	Corporate Support	Total Revenue
Peer Museum A	710,741	176,542	112,500	39,035	140,000	3,100	143,100	165,000	3,500	168,500	$ 544,784	$ 3,371,708
Peer Museum B	820,574	245,983	92,000	46,783	193,804	13,245	207,049	180,054	12,777	192,831	$ 652,566	$ 3,598,555
Peer Museum C	1,378,075	375,156	130,501	42,711	328,195	26,334	354,529	215,820	34,846	250,666	$ 520,316	$ 4,332,904
Peer Museum D	1,814,319	503,780	111,000	44,000	223,542	41,034	264,576	304,391	37,794	342,185	$ 157,621	$ 4,486,973
Peer Museum E	2,902,572	768,078	150,000	44,000	409,820	15,000	424,820	364,339	15,000	379,339	$ 1,005,014	$ 5,976,681
Peer Museum F	3,894,260	1,568,906	197,500	75,127	784,268	35,034	819,302	802,141	32,183	834,324	$ 1,188,904	$ 12,067,474
Peer Museum G	2,351,974	879,346	151,038	56,804	313,136	18,743	331,879	320,000	13,341	333,341	$ 1,031,532	$ 6,768,501
Peer Museum H	951,166	378,926	143,334	65,000	339,000	31,000	370,000	401,000	31,500	432,500	$ 2,582,933	$ 7,174,780
Peer Museum I	1,216,057	504,678	230,106	55,373	361,282	42,435	403,717	377,819	42,182	420,001	$ 693,142	$ 12,254,751
Peer Museum J	1,352,986	346,854	205,000	65,000	262,885	80,847	343,732	229,040	34,890	263,930	$ 2,243,831	$ 8,318,756
Peer Museum K	2,223,219	867,389	320,000	106,820	558,858	396,266	955,124	536,359	348,219	884,578	$ 4,060,354	$ 14,878,411
Average	1,783,267	601,422	167,544	58,241	355,890	63,913	419,803	354,178	55,112	409,290	$ 1,334,636	$ 7,566,317
Median	1,378,075	503,780	150,000	55,373	328,195	31,000	354,529	320,000	32,183	342,185	$ 1,005,014	$ 6,768,501
Sample Museum	1,654,592	496,832	162,000	54,500	269,986	46,060	316,046	253,013	68,962	321,975	$ 822,809	$ 7,081,396
Peer Performance Indexes												
Compared to Peer Avg.	0.93	0.83	0.97	0.94	0.76	0.72	0.75	0.71	1.25	0.79	0.62	0.94
Compared to Peer Median	1.20	0.99	1.08	0.98	0.82	1.49	0.89	0.79	2.14	0.94	0.82	1.05

Worksheet 7.1. Peer Museum Data: Sample Museum

Museum Name	Location	Population	Total Gross Sq. Foot	Gallery Net Sq. Foot	Data Field 4	Data Field 5	Data Field 6	Data Field 7	Data Field 8	Data Field 9
						Data Entry				
Museum A										
Museum B										
Museum C										
Museum D										
Museum E										
Museum F										
Museum G										
Museum H										
Museum I										
Museum J										
Museum K										
Average Peer KPI										
Median Peer KPI										
___ Museum's Data										
Compared to Peer Average										
Compared to Peer Median										

Worksheet 7.1. Peer Museum Data

Peer Museum Name	Corporate Support % of Total $	Attd/CBSA	Attd/City	Crowd-edness (Visitors/Gallery SF)	Expense$ /GSF	CBSA/Size of Museum (GSF)	Revenue$ /Attd
Peer Museum A	16%	24%	95%	4.2	$29.97	6.3	$20.01
Peer Museum B	18%	23%	78%	3.8	$39.11	8.9	$18.66
Peer Museum C	12%	18%	67%	5.1	$33.20	10.6	$17.29
Peer Museum D	4%	19%	68%	6.9	$40.42	16.3	$13.11
Peer Museum E	17%	13%	49%	8.3	$39.84	19.4	$15.76
Peer Museum F	10%	21%	53%	10.7	$61.10	19.7	$14.46
Peer Museum G	15%	14%	38%	5.6	$44.81	15.6	$20.31
Peer Museum H	36%	45%	114%	6.2	$50.06	6.6	$16.59
Peer Museum I	6%	35%	83%	6.8	$53.26	5.3	$29.18
Peer Museum J	27%	20%	76%	3.5	$40.58	6.6	$31.52
Peer Museum K	27%	40%	102%	5.0	$46.50	6.9	$16.82
Average Peer KPI	17%	25%	75%	6	$43.53	11.1	$19.43
Median Peer KPI	16%	21%	76%	6	$40.58	8.9	$17.29
Sample Museum	**12%**	**19%**	**65%**	**4.6**	**$43.71**	**10.2**	**$21.99**
Peer Performance Indexes							
Compared to Peer Avg.	0.68	0.79	0.86	0.77	1.00	0.92	1.13
Compared to Peer Median	0.72	0.91	0.85	0.82	1.08	1.15	1.27

Worksheet 7.2. Peer Museum KPI Analysis : Sample Museum

Museum Name	Location	[KPI 1]	[KPI 2]	[KPI 3]	[KPI 3]	[KPI 4]	[KPI 5]	[KPI 6]
Museum A								
Museum B								
Museum C								
Museum D								
Museum E								
Museum F								
Museum G								
Museum H								
Museum I								
Museum J								
Museum K								
Average Peer KPI								
Median Peer KPI								
Museum's KPIs								
Compared to Peer Average								
Compared to Peer Median								

Worksheet 7.2. Peer Museum KPI Analysis

Overview

Compared to last year, the Museum increased its impact slightly, but remarkably given the regional economy. Our audiences increased their efforts to visit us by 2% and, together with our supporters, found 6% more market value in our activities. Our performance efficiency declined based on both cost per engagement and engagements per staff, due to increases in expenses and staff size greater than increases in revenue and engagements.

Context Summary

The economy remained stressed, with local employers cutting back staff. The expensive travelling exhibition did not live up to its revenue targets, yet it did have the projected expenses. However, the museum's new community service initiative, authorized by the Board, is enough ahead to offset other declines.

Increased Impact and Performance [only IP #2 impacts addressed]

Desired impact 2.2 Strengthen civic connections: The three of the four KPIs monitoring this impact indicate significant increases in impact:

    KPI 2.2a: We continue to diversify our staff and board. Staff, already close to MidCity's diversity, closed the gap by 5% and the Board by 32%. The five-year audience profile (due next year) may show if diversifying staff and Board have an impact on diversifying audience.

    KPI 2.2b: Recognized partnerships are up by about 50%, although three of the eight new partners were already partners-in-practice that we have now recognized in the new partnership program. Anecdotally we see inter-partner dialog that may indicate new civic connections.

    KPI 2.2c: Museum managers are spending about 50% more time in the community working with partners on a wide range of community projects. Aside from the time metric, this has led to new and popular on-site programs marketed and run by some of our new partners.

    KPI 2.2d: Corporate support is down by about a quarter, the one disappointment in this set. Further, we are also about a quarter below our peer museums. The regional economy and loss of jobs is the reason expressed, but we need to show off our metrics and evidence of impact to local business to enforce how we are strengthening their community, in addition to offering their employees free passes.

Desired impact 2.3 Enrich quality of life: All KPIs indicate increases in impact, one dramatically:

    KPI 2.3a: MidCity's residents made more effort to come to our site, increasing site visits from 35% of the City population to 37%

    KPI 2.3b: City residents dramatically increased their likelihood to recommend this year's programs to others. Programs in the new initiative scored their engagements 9.2 on the Net Promoter Score, compared to last year's 8.4.

    KPI 2.3c: Compared to housing rates in the greater region, MidCity's housing values are increasing at a slightly higher rate. However, this difference is still too small (2%) to claim any degree of relative gentrification, much less any Museum role in that change.

Other numbers reinforce the findings that we have strengthened civic connections and enriched the quality of life: Our community programs have increased by about 50% -- we had more new program participants than we lost in gate admissions, boosting total museum engagements. Program subscriptions and the community initiative are the likely causes of our increased memberships, as the value of our membership offerings increased in the eyes of this expert audience. We also appreciate the support and even excitement of the Board and our private supporters, as their investments in our community impacts are way up, more than offsetting the drop in corporate philanthropy.

Decreased Impact and Performance [only IP #2 impacts addressed]

Desired impact 2.1 Build regional identity and engagement:

    KPI 2.3a: We have been unable to determine whether our investment in collection care is on par with peers. We cannot agree internally on what expenses count and our peers are having the same issue. We need a better KPI. There is also concern that collection spending relates too distantly to building regional identity to be a meaningful indicator even if we could get good data.

    KPI 2.1b: The region's residents made less effort to come to our site, decreasing from 17% of the CBSA population to 15% visiting.

This decreased KPI may indicate that our impact on building regional identity is declining, as regional residents are visiting us less. Our past visitor research affirms that visiting our galleries does result in identify-building outcomes for a large share of the sample. Attendance declined because fewer people came to this year's travelling exhibition, but that also meant fewer identity outcomes. We spent more promoting the exhibition, but did not connect the topic to our region's identity, needs or aspirations.

Analysis & Research Needs [only IP #2 impacts addressed]

We need to explore the linkages among KPI 2.2a, 2.2b and 2.2c in order to present data to our corporate supporters about these new community benefits. The research question is: Do a) increased diversity internally, b) a greater number of structured partners, and c) a steady, reliable presence of museum managers involved with community projects work together to actually diversify our audience and strengthen civic connections?

Implications for the Future [only IP #2 impacts addressed]

Our expanded community initiative is a direct result of our new evaluation framework that placed Contributing value to our community as our second priority intentional purpose, after IP #1 Spark interest and engagement. The need is confirmed and appears to be growing. Sustaining this growth may require expansion of program facilities and staff. Compared to our peers our building is not that crowded, which may allow us to expand without new footprint. Our impact on building regional identity, however, is less clear, and we need to ask 1) can we do this better and, if so, do we want to? 2) Can we find more meaningful and measurable KPIs?, and most importantly, 3) is Building identity something the community really wants us to do? If so, we should explore whether the community's aspirations for a technology future are of greater value than its pride in its industrial heritage.

Worksheet 8.1. Summary Report: Sample Museum

Overview: Year-over-Year and Peers Comparisons
Context Summary
Increased Impact and Performance
Decreased Impact and Performance
Analysis and Research Needs
Implications for the Future

Worksheet 8.1. Summary Report

INDEX

Notes: Many terms not covered in this index are defined in Appendix A. See Table A.1 on pg. 106 for location of specific terms. Many individuals and organizations not covered in this index are cited in the references at the end of each chapter and in Appendix B

audiences, 7; mixture of purposes, 101; museum value, 6; museums matter, 101; outcomes, complexity, 3; performance, 55; service, 11, 29; theory, 19-20; value lies in impacts; warning, 46

worthiness, 41

White Oak Institute, 4, 8, 22, 29, 30, 60

Wing Luke Museum of the Asian Pacific American Experience (Seattle), 15

worth, compared to value, 41

Yad Vashem Holocaust History Museum (Jerusalem), 29

Yale University Art Gallery, 2

year-over-year comparisons, 88

ABOUT THE AUTHOR

John W. Jacobsen, president of White Oak Associates, Inc., and CEO of the White Oak Institute, has over four decades of international experience as a museum analyst, planner, and producer. He was also associate director of the Museum of Science in Boston. During that time, the Museum served 2.2 million visitors during a twelve-month period, an unsurpassed record. Before that management position and since then, Jacobsen and White Oak Associates, Inc., have led strategic planning and marketing initiatives for over one hundred museums through hundreds of commissions. Recent projects include eight museums representing a billion dollars of actual and anticipated investment in new and expanding museums internationally. All White Oak's museum analysis and planning integrate economic and attendance indicators with conceptual and creative planning.

Mr. Jacobsen is the founding manager of the Museum Film Network (1985), the Planetarium Show Network (1988), the Ocean Film Network (1992), the American Alliance of Museums (AAM) Professional Committee on Green Museums (PIC Green 2008) and of the Digital Immersive Giant Screen Specifications (DIGSS 1.0 2011). With Ms. Jeanie Stahl, Mr. Jacobsen formed the White Oak Institute in 2007, a nonprofit dedicated to research-based museum innovation, with completed awards and contracts with the National Science Foundation, the Institute of Museums and Library Services, the AAM, and the Association of Children's Museums (ACM) to develop field-wide standards and data collection fields. Mr. Jacobsen's extensive writings and presentations on museum topics have appeared in *Curator, Museum Management and Curatorship, Informal Learning Review* and at AAM, Association of Science-Technology Centers, ACM, and other conferences. Mr. Jacobsen's BA and MFA are from Yale University.